Men of Color
to Arms!

OTHER WORKS BY ELIZABETH D. LEONARD

Yankee Women:
Gender Battles in the Civil War

All the Daring of the Soldier:
Women of the Civil War Armies

Lincoln's Avengers:
Justice, Revenge, and Reunion after the Civil War

Men of Color to Arms!

BLACK SOLDIERS, INDIAN WARS, AND THE QUEST FOR EQUALITY

Elizabeth D. Leonard

W. W. Norton & Company

NEW YORK   LONDON

Copyright © 2010 by Elizabeth D. Leonard

For information about permission to reproduce selections from this book,
write to Permissions, W. W. Norton & Company, Inc.,
500 Fifth Avenue, New York, NY 10110

For information about special discounts for bulk purchases, please contact
W. W. Norton Special Sales at specialsales@wwnorton.com or 800-233-4830

Manufacturing by Courier Westford
Book design by Helene Berinsky
Production manager: Anna Oler

Library of Congress Cataloging-in-Publication Data

Leonard, Elizabeth D.
Men of color to arms! : Black soldiers, Indian wars, and the
quest for equality / Elizabeth D. Leonard. — 1st ed.
p. cm.
Includes bibliographical references and index.
ISBN 978-0-393-06039-3 (hardcover)
1. African American soldiers—History—19th century. 2. Indians of
North America—Wars—1866–1895—Participation, African American.
3. African American soldiers—West (U.S.)—History—19th century.
4. United States. Army—African American troops—History—19th century.
5. United States—Race relations—History—19th century.
I. Title. II. Title: Black soldiers, Indian wars, and the quest for equality.
E185.63.L46 2010
355.0089'96073—dc22

2010014337

W. W. Norton & Company, Inc.
500 Fifth Avenue, New York, N.Y. 10110
www.wwnorton.com

W. W. Norton & Company Ltd.
Castle House, 75/76 Wells Street, London W1T 3QT

1 2 3 4 5 6 7 8 9 0

To my sister, Suzanne
poet, fictioneer, and inspiration

Contents

In every age our men with crowns,
Our public men of sated grins,
Have called on the masters of cold steel
To make their dreams of glory real. . . .
—Anna Sykora, May 2007

Preface

Early one morning several years ago, my son Anthony, who was six or seven years old at the time, crawled into bed with me to snuggle and, as he loves to do, to chat. "Mom," he asked me on this particular occasion, "is it true that the Union army freed the slaves and then went out and killed the Indians?" Although I had long since steeled myself for such predictable and inevitable questions as "Where do babies come from?" I was caught off guard by this seemingly precocious and morally challenging query. I groped in vain for an answer that fit comfortably with my own desire for both honesty and happy endings, but soon realized I would have to choose between them, and I went with honesty. "Yes, honey, it's true." Anthony pressed on. "But why?" he asked. "Why would the army free one group of people and then go off and kill another group?"

Although he did not say so, I knew that what troubled Anthony most was the idea that both groups in question were people of color: having freed blacks from slavery in the American South, the U.S. army then set out to subordinate (and perhaps extinguish) the continent's Native people. Moreover, something that Anthony did not yet know was that in order to accomplish its mission against the Indians on the frontier, the army enlisted thousands of the black men it had previously been responsible for emancipating. *Men of Color to Arms!* arises directly from my clumsy efforts to provide my older son with meaningful answers on that memorable day, although years of research, contemplation, and conversation with other scholars have enabled me to reach well beyond the fundamentals that Anthony and I originally discussed.

The book's title comes from an 1863 broadside designed by leading African Americans in Philadelphia, such as Frederick Douglass, to encourage black men to enlist in the United States Colored Troops (USCT). It begins with an exploration of the connections between the USCT—whose final duties took them, in disproportionate numbers, as occupation forces to the still fiercely inhospitable South—and the creation of six black regiments in the postwar Regular army. Turning west, *Men of Color to Arms!* examines the postwar black Regulars' contributions to the success of the nation's primary agenda after Appomattox: subjugating all remaining "hostiles" among the Native American people on the frontier and clearing the way for white settlement and the spread of civilization.

As will be seen, black men hoped that their efforts to do the nation's work by serving in the army would produce substantial and irrevocable results in relation to their overall quest for the rights of full citizenship. Within the army itself, their aspirations exceeded the place that had been carved out for them in the enlisted men's ranks: *Men of Color to Arms!* also considers black men's bitterly contested efforts to desegregate what was then the nation's premier officer training school, the U.S. Military Academy at West Point. Driving the entire narrative of this book is a simple question: was Frederick Douglass right in the summer of 1863, when he assured black men that enlistment in, and faithful service to, the U.S. army was a sure path to equal citizenship with white men?[1]

Men of Color to Arms! spans roughly three decades, from the 1860s establishment of the USCT and the black Regular regiments, through the frontier wars of the 1870s and 1880s that led inexorably to the collapse of Indian resistance at the Battle of Wounded Knee (1890), to the massive commemoration of national progress signified by the World's Columbian Exposition in Chicago (1893) and the stunning blow to black equality represented by the U.S. Supreme Court's 1896 ruling in *Plessy v. Ferguson* affirming the principle of racial segregation. Against the backdrop of the larger social, political, and racial developments of the late nineteenth century, *Men of Color to Arms!* offers a complex reflection on the meaning and broad implications for their equality of black men's military service in the U.S. army.

Acknowledgments

Over the years I have spent researching, writing, revising, and, finally, seeing this book through to production, I have benefited enormously from the thoughtfulness, skills, wisdom, and support of many individuals. I am pleased to be able to offer my thanks to a number of key people in this traditional, simultaneously public and intimate way.

First, I would like to thank Mr. John V. Gibson, who many years ago, in honor of his parents, John J. and Cornelia V. Gibson, endowed the history chair I have occupied at Colby College since 2004. This endowed chair accords me an annual fund that covers a substantial proportion of the expenses associated with my ongoing scholarly research. Without this fund and living in central Maine, my ability to reach crucial archival repositories and other important research sites would be severely limited. Mr. Gibson has never asked me for a thing—not even a thank-you note—in return for his generosity. This is my unsolicited thank-you note.

I would also like to thank my colleagues, past and present, in the History Department at Colby, especially Peter Ditmanson, Ben Fallaw, Jason Opal, Raffael Scheck, Larissa Taylor, John Turner, James Webb, and Robert Weisbrot. These brilliant and accomplished historians are wonderful teachers, too, and over the past eighteen years they have made coming into the office every day a pleasure and an honor. More broadly,

I wish to express my appreciation to all of the scholars who have gone before me carving out the rich historical terrain—including Civil War, post–Civil War, African American, Native American, and U.S. military history—into which this particular study fits. I am in your debt.

The staff of a number of libraries have been immensely helpful to me in the course of my research: Colby College's Miller Library staff are always resourceful and good-natured as they try to locate items for me that can be deeply obscure, or housed in some distant location, or both. Library Director Clem Guthro and Head of Acquisitions Claire Pront-nicki deserve a special acknowledgment for having agreed to locate and purchase thirty years' worth of *Army and Navy Journal* microfilm for my use. Martin Kelly, our Visual Resources Librarian, was helpful in the end stages of the manuscript's production, digitizing some of the images I have used here.

Farther afield, I have profited greatly from the expertise and assistance of archivists and other library professionals, without whom this project could not have been completed. At the Library of Congress, I owe abundant thanks particularly to Curator Dr. John Sellers, who offered excellent advice and conversation, and to Paul Hogroian, who carefully walked me through the process of ordering images from the library, and made the entire process much more comprehensible. At the National Archives and Records Administration, I would like to express my gratitude specifically to Archivist Trevor Plante, whose guidance on navigating (not to mention ordering up for examination) the army's court-martial records was invaluable. At the U.S. Army Military History Institute, in Carlisle, Pennsylvania, Dr. Richard Sommers answered every question with courtesy and wit, and led me to a number of collections I might otherwise not have discovered. At Yale University, the Beinecke Library staff made a point of sharing with me the beautiful artwork of several students from the Carlisle Indian Industrial School, and Dr. George Miles, curator of the Beinecke's Western Americana Collection, was most gracious in his assistance when it came to trying to lay my hands on a good image of Richard Henry Pratt. From West Point, Archives Curator Alicia Mauldin-Ware provided me with beautiful pictures of the three nineteenth-century black graduates, Henry Ossian Flipper, John Hanks Alexander, and Charles Young. I would also like to thank Matt Blessing at Marquette University for his assistance in obtaining the images of Black Elk and Wovoka.

A very special bouquet of thanks goes to the National Park Service staff at Fort Davis National Historic Site in Texas, and especially to its on-site historian, Mary L. Williams. Although Fort Davis itself is beautiful and well worth visiting for its own sake, Mary made my research visit there a true delight, providing not just archival assistance in abundance but also warm friendship and hospitality. In the summer of 2006, I arrived at Fort Davis, about two hundred miles southeast of the airport in El Paso, without my suitcase, the suitcase having instead been sent on by the airline (in error) from El Paso to Sacramento. Over the next several days, while my suitcase took a long and roundabout journey, first back to Texas from California and then back and forth across the Lone Star State before it finally reached Fort Davis, Mary kept me in good humor, offered me clothes to wear, welcomed me into her home, fed and watered me, and kept me company at the local bus station to which I went night after night to await the delivery of my bag. Since leaving Fort Davis, Mary has remained available for long-distance help: most recently she generously sent me a collection of images from the fort's collections for use in this book. An excellent specimen of all that is best about humanity, Mary Williams is also a scholar of black men's postwar military service in her own right. Both I and the black Regulars are lucky to have her in our corner.

As always, I must reserve some of my most enthusiastic words of appreciation for all of the talented and good people at W. W. Norton, but especially for my editor, Amy Cherry, who has shepherded to publication what was once quite an unruly flock of words and ideas. Throughout, Amy has manifested the same wise judgment, keen intelligence, patience, and kindness that I might have come to take for granted had I not been so aware of how rare her particular combination of personal and professional traits really is. I am very grateful.

And I would like to thank my sister Suzanne ("Anna") Sykora. Suzanne's courage, steadiness, advice, humor, and love have been invaluable to me over the years, and I dedicate this book to her. As the Germans (and New Yorkers who speak Yiddish) say, "Arbeit macht das Leben süß" (work makes life sweet). My work certainly sweetens my life, but it is my children who provide its most delightful and delectable flavors. I thank my two magnificent sons, Anthony and Joseph Bellavia, simply for being who they are.

Men of Color
to Arms!

☙1❧

Wanted: Black Men for Federal Army Service

Up early breakfasted and moved. Recruit came in. Marched through Williamsburg. Threw out skirmishers & advanced. Lost & recovered gauntlets. Found copy Rich[mon]d Examiner 31ˢᵗ ult. Camped near Burn ordinary. Foraged. Pig, Butter, &c. 40 miles for Richd. Weather clear but cool.

—Sergeant Major Christian A. Fleetwood
Fourth U.S. Volunteer Infantry (Colored),
to his diary, November 9, 1863

ON JULY 7, 1863, TWENTY-THREE-YEAR-OLD CHRISTIAN ABRAHAM Fleetwood of Baltimore, Maryland, met with Colonel William Birney to discuss the possibility of enlisting in the U.S. army. Birney, a white Alabama native with strong abolitionist sentiments, was in Fleetwood's hometown organizing regiments of "colored" soldiers for federal service, and the young black man was curious. Just one day earlier and a hundred miles away in Philadelphia, the great black orator, abolitionist, and former slave Frederick Douglass had issued his famous call to arms, in which he boldly declared, "Once let the black man get upon his person the brass letters, U.S.; let him get an eagle on his button, and a musket on his shoulder, and bullets in his pocket, and there is

Frederick Douglass, ca. 1865. *Courtesy of the Library of Congress.*

no power on earth or under the earth which can deny that he has earned the right of citizenship in the United States." If Fleetwood was unaware of Douglass's momentous speech when he first spoke to Colonel Birney, he surely had the opportunity to learn of it over the weeks that followed their initial conversation, as he considered his options.[1]

Born free on July 21, 1840, Fleetwood had enjoyed an atypical upbringing. His parents, Charles and Ann (or Anna) Maria, were employed by a wealthy, white Baltimore couple—the Brunes—in whose household Charles served as head steward. Childless themselves, the Brunes took a liking to the handsome and rather fair-skinned boy, offering him privileges that were beyond the imagination of most of his peers. When he was about four or five years old, Mrs. Brune began tutoring Christian privately and providing him with expensive clothing: a longtime friend later recalled seeing Fleetwood "elegantly dressed in embroidered jacket and silken hose, the pet and pride of the household." In addition, the Brunes saw to it that Christian's time was not entirely taken up with learning his lessons and availing himself of their splendid library: they made sure he took time to play, too, with their prosperous white neighbors' children.[2]

After Mrs. Brune died when Christian was fourteen, he became a clerk for the Maryland Colonization Society, an offshoot of the American Colonization Society, which had been founded in 1816 to promote former slaves' "return" to Africa, although most of them had been born in the United States. Two years later, in a journey that must have seemed tantamount to traveling to the moon, Fleetwood sailed to Liberia, and perhaps also to Sierra Leone, African outposts the colonizationists had selected for freed American slaves. Upon his return to the United States, Fleetwood enrolled at Pennsylvania's Ashmun Institute, founded in 1854 as the first black university in America and later renamed Lincoln University. Ashmun Institute's immediate goal was to train young black men for missionary service in Africa; it also aimed to create an elite group of educated black men who could move toward social and political equality and lead other black Americans in the same direction. In 1860, just shy of his twentieth birthday, Fleetwood became one of only twenty-eight black Americans to have completed college, when he graduated as his class valedictorian.[3]

Back in Baltimore, Fleetwood went to work for an import/export firm and engaged in the city's intellectual and social life. His diaries from this period describe a constant round of attending church, going to concerts and the lyceum, reading literature, visiting friends, singing in a choir, and writing and receiving letters. Somewhat surprisingly, despite the Civil War's outbreak in April 1861 and the strong pro-Confederate sentiment evident in his area, Fleetwood did not even mention the war

Soldiers of Company E, Fourth Regiment of Infantry, United States Colored Troops, at Fort Lincoln, in the District of Columbia. *Courtesy of the Library of Congress.*

for almost a year, finally commenting in spring 1862 that he had caught a glimpse of some "secesh prisoners" in Baltimore and, while visiting Washington, some wounded soldiers. Early in the war, like many young adults, Fleetwood was focused overwhelmingly on his own personal affairs.[4]

For all his elevated social status as a free and unusually learned young black man, however, Fleetwood could not avoid confronting (and commenting on) repeated examples of race prejudice in his daily life. Early in May 1862, he noted that he had been "Stopped by Police," perhaps for being out after curfew. Also in May, Fleetwood remarked that while walking home from church he had been asked to show his "pass," by which he surely meant the official papers that usually allowed him to move unmolested around the city. Still, Fleetwood made no formal notice in his diary when President Abraham Lincoln issued the Emancipation Proclamation on January 1, 1863, almost two years after the Civil War began. But in the months that followed, his commitment to black uplift became clear. He not only cofounded a journal called the *Lyceum Observer*, thought to be among the first black newspapers—if not *the* first—in the South; he also began his careful consideration of the possibility of enlisting in the U.S. army, now inexorably engaged in the work of destroying slavery. On August 17, despite his father's resistance to the idea, Fleetwood made his decision and signed on—for "the cause of my race"—to Company G of the brand new Fourth Regiment, U.S. Volunteer Infantry (Colored). The following day, at Baltimore's Camp Belger, Fleetwood mustered in as a sergeant major, to all intents and purposes the highest rank a black soldier could achieve in the wartime army.[5]

That Fleetwood was even permitted to enlist in the federal military service in the summer of 1863 should not be taken for granted. Not surprisingly, given what was at stake in this war, black men had been offering their services as soldiers to the federal government since the Confederacy's April 1861 attack on South Carolina's Fort Sumter. In the weeks and months that followed, they had continued—individually, collectively, and in vain—to petition for the right to volunteer in the nation's army. As they waited, some men organized units and drilled on their own, sometimes to the distress and confusion of their white neighbors who feared black mob violence. In part because of northern whites' fears about putting guns and swords into the hands of social and economic subordinates, and because of their simultaneous convictions about black men's incapacity for disciplined military service, federal resistance to the notion of arming black men seemed virtually insurmountable early in the war. President Lincoln's initial determination to restore the Union quickly and with minimal disruption to its racial traditions and institutions—to fight, in other words, a "soft war"—presented an additional obstacle.[6]

Some Northern military commanders, however, were committed from the start to challenging the official policy of the Lincoln administration. In March 1862, not even a year into the war, Major General David Hunter, commanding U.S. forces in the Department of the South, issued an order freeing the slaves in the area under his purview. Theoretically encompassing all of South Carolina, Georgia, and Flor-

Major General Benjamin F. Butler. *Courtesy of the Library of Congress.*

ida, in practice Hunter's department included only those islands and small pieces of land up and down the south Atlantic coast—such as the Sea Islands, off the coast of South Carolina—that the federal army had managed to capture and occupy. Upon ordering the emancipation of the slaves in his department, Hunter immediately began to organize the men into military units, until President Lincoln countermanded Hunter's order and put a stop to his premature efforts. Not long afterward, however, Brigadier General John W. Phelps, an abolitionist stationed in New Orleans in the spring of 1862 in conjunction with the federal occupation of the city, began encouraging fugitive slaves there to come under federal army protection. Like General Hunter, Phelps started organizing the male runaways into military companies. On this occasion, General Benjamin Butler, who was in overall command of the occupation, stepped in to deter Phelps before Lincoln learned of this latest breach.

Even as he took action against Phelps, however, Butler himself remained unconvinced that Lincoln's original policy was a good one. A Massachusetts native, Butler had in fact been the first federal commander—while he was stationed at Fortress Monroe, Virginia, in August 1861—to afford a group of runaway slaves federal military protection, shrewdly but flexibly reinterpreting the familiar legal term "contraband," referring to enemy property, to include the fugitives who made their way to the U.S. army's lines. Over the months to follow, Butler's action in Virginia helped open the door to his own and others' reconsiderations of the relationship between black Americans and the U.S. army. Perhaps it should not be surprising, then, that less than a year after Butler welcomed three "contraband" slaves at Fortress Monroe, and within a few weeks of reprimanding General Phelps in New Orleans, Butler himself accepted for federal military service the First, Second, and Third Regiments of the Louisiana Native Guards, made up of *free* black men who had originally volunteered their services to the Confederacy for the defense of their state, but who now enthusiastically took up the federal cause.[7]

Clearly, by the time Butler engaged the former Louisiana Native Guards for federal service, the climate was changing in Washington with respect to the question of black enlistment. By the spring of 1862 federal commanders such as Hunter, Phelps, and Butler had joined a host of black men who were eager to serve the nation, in putting serious pressure on President Lincoln and the War Department, under the leadership of Secretary of War Edwin M. Stanton, to accept black Americans' offers to enlist in the U.S. army. Congress that summer added its own weight to the effort by passing the Militia Act on July 17, in which it authorized the use of black men (fugitive slave or free) for "any military or naval service for which they may be found competent." From this point on, black regiments formed steadily, their enlistees recruited and organized into units by individual white officers such as the one with whom Fleetwood first met the following year, William Birney. Once President Lincoln issued the Emancipation Proclamation, arguably the culminating act in his steady abandonment of his original "soft war" approach to dealing with the Confederacy, the creation of black regiments accelerated. For the proclamation not only freed the slaves in any states (or parts of states) still in rebellion against the federal government but also made explicit the principle that those among the newly emancipated who were determined to be fit for duty would be welcomed into the U.S. army.[8]

In May 1863, the War Department established the Bureau of Colored Troops to provide for the ongoing development and overall administration of the black regiments. Over the course of the war, approximately 180,000 black men enlisted in the United States Colored Troops (USCT), accounting for roughly 10 percent of the federal army. According to the first scholar to write a history of black soldiers in the American Civil War, George Washington Williams, himself a USCT veteran, these black Americans served—often with great distinction—across the theater of war in close to 150 regiments, participated in 450 different engagements, and suffered almost 37,000 casualties. Black federal soldiers were among the first troops to enter and occupy the Confederate capital of Richmond when it collapsed in April 1865. In the course of their military service, more than a dozen soldiers of the USCT earned the Congressional Medal of Honor.[9]

Just over a year after he enlisted in the U.S. army at Baltimore, Christian Fleetwood would become one of those Medal of Honor winners. But in the fall of 1863, in the early weeks of his military service, what is most noteworthy is that Fleetwood's duties with his regiment greatly diminished the amount of time he had to write in his diary. Simply put, the regiment and Fleetwood were busy becoming soldiers. In the process they faced some opposition from white Baltimoreans who either disliked the idea of arming blacks, like many white Americans, or were hostile to Union forces on their soil, period. On September 22, Fleetwood noted that some days earlier his regiment had paraded through the streets of Baltimore "winning the praise of even our enemies," but clearly not all of them. "Almost a fight between the 4th & the citizens," he wrote at the end of the entry.[10]

On September 29, Fleetwood's regiment left Baltimore, sailing on the *Nellie Plenty* for Benjamin Butler's old stomping grounds at federally held Fortress Monroe, in Virginia, and from there continuing about twenty miles up the James River to Yorktown, some sixty-five miles southeast of the Confederate capital at Richmond. For the next nine months, Fleetwood and the Fourth—joined in mid-October by the Sixth U.S. Colored Infantry Regiment, which had been organized in Pennsylvania—remained in and around Yorktown, marching, drilling, parading, foraging, and doing target practice and fatigue, picket, and guard duty. On one occasion, in December, the regiment underwent a review by General Butler, but for the most part, Fleetwood's diary for this period reflects the boredom, discontent, and discomfort he shared with most Civil War soldiers. Late in January 1864, he noted feeling "more low spirited and inclined to be unsociable than I remember to have been since enlisting." "Completely broken down," he wrote a few days later, and then, on the next day, "intirely [sic] disgusted." Still, Fleetwood's education paid good dividends during this period: he entertained himself by reading, and in early February he reported having made his way through volume one of *Les Misérables*. He also had found time to reflect on the meaning of the work in which he was engaged. "This year," Fleetwood had written at the end of 1863, "has brought about many changes that at the beginning were or would have been thought impossible. . . . May God bless this cause and enable me . . . to forward it on."[11]

Early in May 1864, Fleetwood's regiment was on the move again, transferred to City Point, just over twenty miles southeast of Richmond.

Two months earlier, Lieutenant General Ulysses S. Grant had assumed command of all the federal armies, then stretched across a thousand-mile-long line of battle, and the departure of Fleetwood and the Fourth U.S. Colored Infantry for City Point was in fact a preliminary undertaking in Grant's grand strategy to coordinate all of the armies' movements in order to bring the bloody Confederate rebellion, now into its fourth year, to a close. By this stage in the war, many of the greatest battles—Shiloh, Antietam, Fredericksburg, Stones River, Chancellorsville, Gettysburg, and Chickamauga—had already been fought, claiming more than 200,000 casualties on the field. Still, much more carnage lay ahead: the ghastly harvest from battles like the Wilderness, and from Spotsylvania, Cold Harbor, Franklin, and Nashville. When he summoned Grant to Washington in March 1864 and appointed him the U.S. army's general in chief, Lincoln knew full well the scope of the task he was entrusting to the man he had assigned, just five months earlier, to the successful command of the war's western theater. Now Lincoln relied on Grant, and the roughly one million black and white soldiers under his authority, to crush the Confederacy at whatever cost, save the Union, ensure the destruction of slavery, and make possible the "new birth of freedom" Lincoln had promised Americans at Gettysburg the preceding November.

And so it was that early in May, as Fleetwood and his regiment received their orders to move out, Grant launched an important component of his wide-reaching plan. With his eye on Richmond, Grant ordered the thirty thousand troops of the newly designated federal Army of the James—which was under the command of Benjamin Butler and included Fleetwood's as well as several other black regiments—forward from Fortress Monroe up the Virginia peninsula. Butler's assignment was twofold: to use his substantial force to menace (or, even better, invade) the Confederate capital and to obstruct reinforcements from fortifying the Confederate army. At that moment, the main Army of Northern Virginia, commanded by General Robert E. Lee, was engaged in a vicious contest with the federal Army of the Potomac approximately sixty miles to the north. As it turned out, Butler, whose wartime battlefield record was significantly less impressive than his commitment to black rights, badly bungled the job. Instead of boldly attacking the capital, Butler ordered the army to advance cautiously, so cautiously in fact that it never reached Richmond at all. Moreover, where the men might have done serious damage to the railroad connecting Richmond and the agriculturally rich Shenandoah Valley, which was crucial to the provisioning of Lee's army, they failed to tear up or disrupt much of anything. And instead of keeping the Confederacy's focus on defending its capital, Butler allowed Confederate General P. G. T. Beauregard to dispatch seven thousand soldiers he soon realized he could spare to Lee's aid.[12]

Although Butler failed in the end to meet Grant's objectives, black soldiers were nevertheless heavily engaged in the effort to fulfill them. On June 15, the Fourth went into battle in the company of other black and also white troops, facing enemy fire most of the day and taking heavy casualties. "Up at break of dawn and underway," Fleetwood later wrote in his diary, adding bursts of phrasing that reflected the chaos and challenges of the day. "Went into action early. Charged out of woods. Cut up badly. Regt broke and retreated. Fired into by 5th Mass. . . . Took the Battery. Advanced upon

General of the Army Ulysses S. Grant, ca. 1866. *Courtesy of the Library of Congress.*

works near P[etersburg]. Lay under their fire all balance of the day advancing by degrees in line. About 7 P. M. first charge made. Seven guns taken by our Regt. Our loss pretty heavy. Slept."[13]

Butler's ineptitude as a strategist and field commander resulted in the federals' protracted siege of the heavily fortified city of Petersburg, a railroad town of about twenty thousand residents—some 50 percent of whom were black—about twenty-five miles directly south of Richmond. Over the next six months, the Fourth USCT participated actively in the siege, which was dominated by trench warfare but included the disastrous July 30, 1864, mine assault that touched off the Battle of the Crater. On that stunning occasion, having dug an underground mine leading from their own position to the Confederates', federal soldiers intentionally (though with considerable difficulty) set off an explosion that they expected to demolish the enemy's forces. The explosion did manage to kill a few hundred Confederates, but it also produced a gigantic crater into which federal troops then poured in an attempt to secure the victory. Instead, the white and black federals became captive targets for their enraged opponents. Black soldiers at the Crater, who included Fleetwood's regiment, suffered 40 percent of the U.S. army's fatalities there.[14]

Yet another of the siege's particularly gruesome confrontations occurred in late September 1864 at Chaffin's Farm (also referred to as Fort Harrison and as New Market Heights). Situated on a large open bluff on the James River that was part of the outer line of the Confederacy's Petersburg fortifications, Chaffin's Farm posed a series of daunting obstacles to the federal soldiers: a swamp, a network of trees chopped down to block their advance, and a series of trenches and breastworks. As a result, the federals' progress in their attempt to capture this site was excruciatingly slow, made far worse by the heavy rain of enemy fire the soldiers in blue were unable to escape. In the end, although the battle was considered a Union victory, federal casualties at Chaffin's Farm exceeded 4,400, and one black company suffered a casualty rate of 87 percent of its soldiers engaged in the battle.[15]

One federal soldier who not only survived but also distinguished himself at the Battle of Chaffin's Farm was Christian Fleetwood, who, with his regiment, bravely assaulted a strong line of Confederate rifle pits on the morning of September 29 and then, the following afternoon, helped cement the Union victory. Indeed, it was at Chaffin's Farm that Fleetwood earned his Congressional Medal of Honor, awarded in recognition of his unusual courage in raising and carrying forward the flag of the United States on that first day, after two previous color-bearers had been shot down by rebel soldiers. Some days later, in his usual understated manner, Fleetwood described the events to his diary:

To Hd Qrs. Got out the Regt. and after much tribulation and several unsuccessful attempts to catch a nap we embarked on board a gunboat and debarked at Jones Landing. Marched up to works. Bivouacked at Deep Bottom. Dined and supd. with the 5th U.S. C. T. . . . . Coffee boiled and line formed. Moved out & on charged with the 6th at daylight and got used up. Saved colors. . . . Retired at night, stacked arms & moved three times ending at a captured stronghold where we spent the remainder of the darkness with the usual diversions of moving.[16]

In the wake of the battle, Fleetwood's performance as a bona fide federal hero received the acknowledgment it deserved. On October 11, in an extended letter of praise, Assistant Adjutant General Edward W. Smith declared, "A few more such gallant charges" as those made by the black regiments at Chaffin's Farm,

and to command colored troops will be the post of honor in the American armies. The colored soldiers by coolness, steadiness, and determined courage and dash have silenced every cavil of the doubters of their soldierly capacity, and drawn tokens of admiration from their enemies; have brought their late masters even to the consideration of the question whether they will not employ as soldiers the

hitherto despised race. Be it so; this war is ended when a musket is
in the hands of every ablebodied negro who wishes to use one.

Later in his letter, Smith mentioned Fleetwood by name, praising the
uncommon bravery he had displayed after the two previous color-
bearers had fallen. Laying hold of the "national colors," Smith noted,
the unflinching Fleetwood "bore them nobly through the fight." For
this, Fleetwood had earned "a special medal for gallant conduct."[17]

As it turned out, Fleetwood's performance throughout this period
of the war yielded more than the Medal of Honor. It earned him a
unique petition, signed in the fall of 1864 by every commissioned—and
therefore white—officer in his regiment, requesting that Secretary of
War Stanton promote him from sergeant major to a commissioned officer's position. As Fleetwood wrote some years later, "To the best of my
knowledge and belief, this communication received favorable endorsement and recommendation through each and several of the Headquarters through which [it was] forwarded in its regular military channel, to
the War Department." Nevertheless, "I learned some time later that it
was denied for want of authority in law to commission colored men into
active command, or something to that effect." Discriminatory principles
prevailed, and Fleetwood's rank as a noncommissioned sergeant major
remained unchanged.[18]

Although the siege of Petersburg continued until April 1865, Fleetwood and the Fourth left Virginia in mid-December 1864, now as part
of the newly reorganized all-black XXV Corps. Their new orders summoned them to participate in an assault on Fort Fisher, one of a group
of forts located at the mouth of Cape Fear River, which the Confederates relied upon to defend Wilmington, North Carolina, and keep the
port open to blockade runners. In preparation for the assault, which
combined both land and naval forces, Fleetwood's regiment found itself
spending more time on shipboard than he, at least, found comfortable.
"Oh! How I long to feel solid ground again," he moaned to his diary
on December 16, noting, with wry humor, that he was "inclined to the

belief that my former fond-
ness for the ocean was bosh."
Fleetwood was pleased when
the regiment finally disem-
barked and settled in camp.[19]

Thanks in large part to
the bungling (again) of General Butler, whom Grant
subsequently removed from
command, the first expedition to capture Fort Fisher
proved a failure. A second
and successful expedition
took place in mid-January
1865, however, and once
again Fleetwood's regiment,
now under the command
of General Alfred H. Terry,
played an important role

Sergeant Major Christian A. Fleetwood, in
1865 or 1866, wearing his Congressional
Medal of Honor. *Courtesy of the Library of
Congress.*

(sadly, Fleetwood's 1865 diary is lost). Subsequently, and through the
final months of the war, the Fourth remained on active duty in North
Carolina, participating in General William T. Sherman's campaign
through the state, helping to occupy the city of Goldsboro—a key
railroad junction—and then heading for the state capital of Raleigh
around the time that Lee surrendered at Appomattox. On that day,
an unidentified correspondent from Baltimore wrote with elation to
Fleetwood, asking his whereabouts and reporting the news: "Well to
tell or describe . . . to you . . . the enthusiasm that exists in the people here would be impossible. We had the grandest illumination that
was ever seen," he wrote, referring to the practice of lighting lamps
in homes and along city streets in celebration of an important event.
Fleetwood and the Fourth were on active duty in Raleigh later in April,
too, when Confederate General Joseph E. Johnston surrendered the

last significant Confederate army in the field to General Sherman just days after the assassination of Abraham Lincoln.[20]

In the weeks and months after the Confederate surrender, the majority of USCT soldiers remained on active duty, although white volunteers mustered out. Before they returned to their homes, however, white soldiers celebrated the federal victory in the Grand Review of the federal armies in Washington, D.C. There, at 4 a.m. on May 23, 1865, bugles sounded reveille across the camps where tens of thousands of soldiers had bivouacked the night before. At 9 a.m. the well-dressed and highly polished soldiers of Major General George Gordon Meade's Army of the Potomac, numbering more than eighty thousand and led by their commander—"knightly in bearing as ever"—began their march. Their parade on this bright and sunny day lasted nearly six hours, taking them from the foot of Capitol Hill down Pennsylvania Avenue.[21]

Pennsylvania Avenue itself was bedecked for the occasion with colorful bunting and countless flags, and the soldiers of Meade's army marched before a host of military and civilian dignitaries, both foreign and domestic, as well as representatives of the press and thousands upon thousands of exuberant, flag-waving, flower-tossing spectators, who watched from their windows, porches, and rooftops, stood along the road, or were seated in grandstands, on bleachers, and in chairs extending from the Capitol to the Executive Mansion. The ranks of local residents who watched the parade were greatly augmented by many who had traveled some distance to pay tribute. In addition, local schools were closed so that children and their teachers could enjoy the spectacle, which they enhanced by singing patriotic songs, displaying banners, and throwing flowers as the soldiers passed.[22]

The next day, May 24, the Grand Review continued in weather that was equally sunny and pleasant. "The sky was wonderfully beautiful," wrote Brevet Major General Joshua Lawrence Chamberlain of the V Corps, "and the earth gave good greeting under foot." This day's parade featured the 65,000 rugged and somewhat more ragged soldiers of the Armies of Georgia and the Tennessee, who had recently arrived

Soldiers marching in the Grand Review in Washington, D.C., May 1865. From a photograph by Alexander Gardner. Originally published in *Harper's Weekly*.

in Washington after their 600-mile-long trek through Georgia and the Carolinas, led by Sherman and General Oliver Otis Howard. Many of these men were still dressed in their field uniforms. "Sherman's army made a different appearance from that of the Army of the Potomac," recalled Ulysses Grant. They were "not so well-dressed," he wrote, "but their marching could not be excelled; they gave the appearance of men who had been thoroughly drilled to endure hardships, either by long and continuous marches or through exposure to any climate, without the ordinary shelter of a camp."[23]

Like the soldiers of Meade's Army of the Potomac, Sherman's men marched for six hours to a warm welcome from perhaps as many as 100,000 spectators. "The prestige of this army that had marched from the Great River to the Sea, and thence up half the Atlantic coast, bring-

Spectators at the Grand Review. From a photograph by Alexander Gardner. Originally published in *Harper's Weekly*.

ing the fame of mighty things done afar," Joshua Chamberlain wrote later, "stirred perhaps more the hearts and imaginations of the people than did the familiar spectacle of men whose doings and non-doings had been an every-day talk, and who so often had walked their streets in hurrying ranks or pitiful forlornness and thronged their hospitals, year after year, in service and suffering, unboastful and uncomplaining." The sight, wrote Sherman himself, " was simply magnificent."[24]

Magnificent indeed, but also incomplete. Some key individuals in the federal army were absent, including General Philip H. Sheridan, the brilliant commander of the Army of the Potomac's cavalry forces. Sheridan had already been dispatched, reluctantly, to what was then known as the army's "Middle Division," covering Texas and Louisiana, to engineer the surrender of Confederate General Edmund Kirby

Smith and his stubborn troops, to prepare for his postwar assignment monitoring civil affairs there during Reconstruction, and to deal with a diplomatic crisis brewing in Mexico. Missing, too, was twenty-five-year-old Nelson A. Miles, who had led the soldiers of his various commands successfully through almost every major battle in which the Army of the Potomac was engaged, and who was now poised to embark on a long and brilliant career in the postwar army. The night before the review had begun, Miles had traveled with a cavalry detachment to Hampton Roads, Virginia, and from there to Fortress Monroe, where he had been appointed by Major General E. O. C. Ord—who had been in overall command of the XVIII Corps at Chaffin's Farm and been badly wounded there—to take charge of the military district of which the fort was the center. There Miles guarded the nation's most famous prisoner, the former president of the Confederacy, Jefferson Davis. Also absent were countless federal soldiers who were stationed so far from Washington that it was impossible for them to reach the capital in time for the Grand Review, or those on assignments that simply precluded their participation.[25]

Notable in their collective and not-so-easily-explained lack of representation in the Grand Review were the soldiers of the USCT, some of whom were already on their way with the XXV Corps to join Sheridan in the West. Others, however, were much closer: Fleetwood and his Fourth U.S. Colored Infantry Regiment were just three hundred miles away in Raleigh. It bears noting that although official orders calling for the Grand Review on May 23 and May 24 were issued only on May 18, 60,000 of the white troops under Sherman's command had made it to Washington—on foot and horseback and by train—from even greater distances. In contrast, not even a company from Fleetwood's regiment was given the opportunity. Nor were any others from among the more than 120,000 black men still wearing the federal army uniform—men like Edward Berry of Virginia, who had enlisted in the Twenty-sixth Regiment of the U.S. Colored Infantry, organized on Rikers Island in New York in 1863, and who served with the regiment, largely in

South Carolina, until October 1865. Also missing was Alfred Bradden of Alabama, who served with the Seventeenth U.S. Colored Infantry in Tennessee until April 1866, including at the massive, two-day Battle of Nashville in December 1864, which essentially destroyed Confederate General John Bell Hood's Army of Tennessee. Missing, too, was Samuel Lacey (a.k.a. Cooper), also of Alabama, who had enlisted in the Forty-second U.S. Colored Infantry at Chattanooga, Tennessee, in early 1864. A former slave who never learned to read and write, did not know exactly when he was born, and late in life refused to talk about "slavery matters," Lacey enlisted, as he put it, "very young." As a USCT soldier, he had spent many months building forts and digging rifle pits. But he refused to become bitter about being kept out of combat. Rather, Lacey

Major General Nelson A. Miles, ca. 1865. *Courtesy of the Library of Congress.*

insisted that "the Government took care of us" and that he had been too young to fight in the first place. Immensely proud of his contribution to winning the war, this young veteran rejected his "slavery name" and became Samuel Cooper.[26]

But black veterans such as Samuel Cooper, Edward Berry, and Alfred Bradden, and even Medal of Honor winners such as Christian Fleet-wood, did not receive invitations to march in the Grand Review. Indeed, on May 23 the *New York Times*, which failed to acknowledge the USCT's absence—or, for that matter, its existence—reported the presence of only one black person among the nearly 100,000 marchers on Pennsylvania Avenue. The rear of the Second Cavalry Division, commented the *Times* correspondent that day, "is most gracefully brought up by a lonely contraband on a mule, who, looking the picture of independence, receives the cheers and laughter of the crowd with great self-complacency." The second day of the parade included more black Americans, but still no black soldiers in uniform marching in formation. Accompanying the white soldiers who passed in review on the twenty-fourth, Sherman himself observed no more than a few groups of "black pioneers" armed with "picks and spades," who "marched abreast in double ranks, keeping perfect dress and step."[27]

To many white observers, these black military laborers must have seemed only vaguely different from the other "novelties" mixed into the ranks of white soldiers, such as pack mules, cows, and a smattering of freed slaves. They offered, at best, a faint reminder of black soldiers' indispensable contributions, over months or even years, to the destruction of slavery and the salvation of the Republic. More to the point, their inclusion in the parade could have little effect on advancing the claims to full citizenship of the black veterans who were excluded, the very claims that Frederick Douglass in July 1863 had insisted that black men's military service on behalf of the nation would ensure. When the *New York Times* referred to the Grand Review as a "white day in the calendar," its unintentional precision was uncanny. One could certainly argue that the effacing of black soldiers' sacrifices for and contributions to the nation's survival began here, as did many white Americans'—even white Northerners'—dismissal of the notion that blacks' military service during the war should be rewarded with their swift and uncompromising elevation to full citizenship.[28]

Interestingly enough, the Grand Review was not the first federal victory celebration to take place after the war. Indeed, three weeks earlier, black Americans in Charleston, South Carolina, had organized what appears to have been the "first collective ceremony" commemorating federal soldiers' sacrifices on behalf of both the Union and the destruction of slavery. Moreover, black Charlestonians had been engaged in Civil War memorializing even earlier. On March 29, almost two weeks before Robert E. Lee's surrender, black townspeople—former slaves, artisans, tradespeople, firefighters, and schoolchildren—had gathered by the thousands to join in a "victory parade" that included black soldiers of the Twenty-first U.S. Colored Infantry Regiment, which had been in the vanguard when Charleston was forced to surrender to federal occupation in mid-February 1865.[29]

Then, on May Day, approximately 10,000 black locals, overwhelmingly former slaves, had gathered at the town's race course, formerly a leisure space reserved for Charleston's white elite. Some of those present had helped to convert the site into a burial ground for about 250 federal soldiers (some of whom were black) who had died there as prisoners of war when it held the overflow from the ghastly Confederate prison at Andersonville, Georgia. Following the morning's official dedication of this "special cemetery," black Charlestonians had spent much of the day listening to speeches, enjoying their picnics, and watching a brigade of federal infantrymen—including USCT soldiers—parade and drill. On this occasion, which many came to consider the nation's first Decoration Day, white and black federal soldiers marched and performed together. But when the time came for the Grand Review in the nation's capital at the end of that month, black soldiers remained on duty wherever they were, to all intents and purposes unwelcome in the Washington parade.[30]

For Fleetwood and the Fourth U.S. Colored Infantry, remaining where they were meant that they stayed put in North Carolina, awaiting their final release from federal military service, which would come a full year later. A variety of reasons help to explain why, after the fighting was over, black volunteer regiments such as Fleetwood's Fourth continued in the federal army longer than white ones. Perhaps most significant from an official perspective was the fact that the black regiments had been organized later than most white regiments, which meant that their terms of service—"three years or during the war"—could be interpreted bureaucratically to prevent them from going home as early as their white counterparts did. Predictably, some serving in black regiments, including some of their white officers, protested this distinction. In late July 1865, a white officer in a black regiment who identified himself only as "E.S.W." wrote to the *Army and Navy Journal*—the U.S. military's main media organ since 1863—asking for information on the future of the USCT. "Can you inform us," he wrote, "what is to be done with the colored troops—are they to be retained to serve for the full period of three years, or will they be mustered out as soon as the Regular Army can be organized?" For E.S.W., the phrase "three years or during the war" meant "whichever came first." "We had made no calculation on serving in the Army for a longer period than the continuation of the war," he wrote, "and now most earnestly desire to be mustered out as per contract." He added, "We entered the Army for the purpose of discharging a duty to assist in putting down the Rebellion, not from any love we bare [*sic*] the military service. . . . Surely nothing is to be gained by retaining officers who are desirous of leaving the service."[31]

In late August 1865, the *New York Times* also observed that the USCT's soldiers had not yet been released: "Thus far, while the white soldiers have been disbanded, until three-fourths of the entire force have been sent to their homes, the colored military element has been retained intact." As it turned out, not only did the USCT remain largely intact, but in Kentucky, back in mid-April—around the time Johnston surrendered to Sherman under the watchful eye of Fleetwood and the

Fourth—orders had been received from Secretary Stanton authorizing local provost marshals to "continue mustering in colored recruits to fill up the colored regiments to the maximum." In light of this, the *Times* suggested a further reason why black regiments were being demobilized more slowly than their white counterparts: namely, that the vast majority of enlistees in the USCT were former slaves, and the reality of emancipation meant that many of them, once released from military duty, would face a host of new obstacles on the road to establishing their new lives in freedom. "They are not situated as the whites were, with regard to obtaining assistance from friends in civil life," the *Times* remarked, adding, "They would be in great measure helpless and friendless wanderers were they disbanded in mass as our white troops have been."[32]

At the same time, this writer put great faith in the positive effects he believed the experience of military service must have had on black men in the wake of their years in slavery: "it has greatly elevated them," he wrote patronizingly, for it had surely "aided in the formation of habits of order and promptitude," "enlarged their intelligence," and "developed in them courage and patriotism." Military service, he noted—with what might seem like an unusual degree of respect in a white man for black men's capacity for manhood—had surely "appealed to their manly instincts." Still, perhaps most important in this writer's mind was the idea that time in the ranks of the federal army had helped prepare black men to be "more efficient workers," which, he felt, would "exercise an influence for good upon the entire race" in the long run.[33]

In any case, in the wake of Appomattox, tens of thousands of USCT soldiers remained on duty (indeed, as late as June 1867, approximately twelve hundred black soldiers were still on the rolls of the USCT). Like Fleetwood and his regiment, the vast majority were stationed in the South, and like that of all federal regiments occupying the territory encompassed by the former Confederacy, their task was enormous and as challenging as any they had faced before: to defend the federal victory in the war, to maintain order, and to enforce the freedom of the former slaves against any and all efforts on the part of white Southerners to undermine it. Accomplishing these goals required what surely would have seemed like unlimited patience and discretion on the part of any federal soldier in the face of white Southern rage and resentment, but the special burdens of black occupation troops simply cannot be ignored. Put bluntly, white Southerners typically considered black men in uniform, carrying guns and bayonets, an outrageous perversion of the proper social order, and an affront to white supremacy.[34]

It comes as no surprise, therefore, that in the months after Lee's surrender, white Southerners actively pressed the federal government about the presence of black soldiers in their midst. Black soldiers, it turns out, were stationed in ten of the eleven former states of the Confederacy, and in seven of these states their numbers exceeded those of the white federals who also served. One can only imagine the intensity of the hostility that black occupation forces confronted in states like Mississippi, where in December 1865 eleven of the twelve regiments of armed federal infantry were black. Under such circumstances, it was not uncommon for Southern whites to provoke conflicts in order to make it seem that black troops were either failing to maintain order in a particular area or were creating problems there themselves. On one occasion, six black soldiers who went to a bar in Baton Rouge, Louisiana, were denied service and insulted by a white customer who also punched one of them, a sergeant. A vicious fight erupted, and in the ensuing chaos, the sergeant was wounded in the leg.[35]

That black soldiers, on occasion, initiated disputes with local whites in the South is hardly unimaginable, given their anger over slavery as an institution and the temptations of bearing arms in the presence of the institution's former overlords and supporters. Moreover, reports such as the one issued in June 1865 by Colonel Alfred S. Hartwell, commander of the black Fifty-fifth Massachusetts then stationed in Orangeburg Court House, South Carolina, add credence to the suspicion that black occupation troops occasionally abused their positions of power, and not just to punish whites. In his June 1865 report, Hartwell—known to be a strong advocate of promoting accomplished black military men to

Sketch by Alfred Waud entitled "The Freedmen's Bureau." Originally published in *Harper's Weekly* in 1868.

the commissioned-officer rank of lieutenant—spoke with stern disappointment of the "rude, brutal and ungentlemanly conduct" he had witnessed on the part of some of the men under his authority. Hartwell referred specifically to violent attacks by some of the soldiers on free black women in the area, as well as some soldiers' theft of the freedpeople's goods and their alleged encouragement that the freedpeople should steal from their former masters in the same way. Similarly, Colonel William Shafter, who had organized the Seventeenth Regiment of U.S. Colored Infantry in late 1863, and who continued to command the regiment during its postwar occupation of Tennessee, issued orders in September 1865 addressing what he called the "continual complaints" he was receiving regarding the "lawless conduct of the Colored Troops of this Command and of the frequent outrages perpetrated by them upon citizens," by which he probably meant whites, whose citizenship was assumed in a way that black Americans' was not. Shafter called for stricter constraints on the movement of black soldiers outside of their camps, and the institution of regular roll calls between 10 p.m. and 2 a.m.[36]

It is important, however, not to conclude from reports such as these, or from the numerous complaints of former Confederates about the purported behavior of armed and uniformed black soldiers in their midst, that all or even a sizable number of black federal troops in the Reconstruction South were performing (or behaving) badly. On the contrary, following a tour of both white and black U.S. troops stationed in the Department of the Mississippi, the Department of the Gulf, and the Department of Arkansas in May 1865, the army's inspector general, Randolph B. Marcy, reported that his own "critical and thorough" examination had revealed that black soldiers in those departments were "well instructed, intelligent and zealous in their discharge of their duties. . . . Their arms have generally been in excellent order and the men neatly dressed and orderly, respectful and soldierlike in their deportment." All that was necessary, Marcy went on, to turn black men into good soldiers was the careful selection and appointment of good white officers to command them, and, with regard to the troops he had just inspected, this requirement had been fulfilled.[37]

Similarly, in March 1866 Assistant Inspector General O. H. Hart wrote regarding his recent inspection of the 126th U.S. Colored Infantry Regiment, "I found the men to be of good physique . . . mostly young and athletic, neat in their general appearance, evidently taking great pride in keeping their clothing and equipments in a tidy condition." However, even these model black troops, stationed not in the Reconstruction South but in Illinois, faced considerable hostility from local whites. Noted Hart, "They are not suffered to carry any ammunition in their cartridge boxes, as there is much animosity exhibited towards the regiment by the citizens of the Post, who take every opportunity to annoy them by personal violence, while in the performance of their duties, as well as upon every other occasion." Similar sorts of provocation, as well as the demoralization of white officers eager to return to civilian life, may well have helped to undermine the discipline of black soldiers. Disgruntled about having to remain in the military, some white officers of black regiments felt disinclined to enforce wartime discipline among the black men under their command, or to demonstrate it themselves.[38]

Conflicts between black occupation forces and resentful white former Confederates were not limited to the Deep South, and requests for the USCT regiments' removal from occupation duty ranged geographically and multiplied numerically. Even the legislature of the border state Kentucky, which had remained loyal despite its status as a slave state, petitioned the federal government early on to have the black soldiers in the state replaced with white ones. In June 1865, the Kentucky General Assembly accused black soldiers of "committing many outrages upon the lives and property of many citizens" and being "a source of great irritation to their former owners and the citizens generally." Precisely what sort of "outrages" the legislature was referring to is unclear. Certainly for many whites in Kentucky, as elsewhere across the former Confederacy, the very presence of black soldiers on state soil was itself an outrage.[39]

Whether or not white provocation was the root cause of interracial conflict between black occupation forces and former Confederates, around the same time that O. H. Hart was penning his praise of the USCT troops stationed in Illinois, O. A. Lochrane of Macon, Georgia—who identified himself as one of the "warmest friends of the Government" in that state—was composing a letter to Lincoln's successor, President Andrew Johnson, warning him that if black soldiers remained on duty in Macon, there would be what he termed "collisions." Johnson forwarded Lochrane's letter to Grant, who in turn forwarded it to George H. Thomas, the general commanding the army's Division of the Tennessee, with his own comments. Grant proved not at all surprised by Lochrane's warning; indeed, he agreed in general with the principle of withdrawing black occupation troops from the South so as to avoid "unnecessary irritation and," he added, "the demoralization of labor in those States."[40]

Three months earlier, in fact, Grant had expressed similar concerns in a report to Congress noteworthy for (and misguided in) its optimism: "There is such universal acquiescence in the authority of the general government throughout the portions of the country visited by me that the mere presence of a military force, without regard to numbers, is sufficient to maintain order," he wrote. But if numbers were not an issue, race might be. "White troops," Grant went on, "generally excite no opposition, and therefore a small number of them can maintain order in a given district." He then expressed some sympathy with the concern of some of the most vehement former Confederates, that the newly emancipated slaves-turned-contract laborers, in the presence of armed black men whom they considered their heroes as well as their allies, might decide to set down their farm implements, cease to work, and engage instead in wholesale theft and destruction of their former owners' property.[41]

To his credit, in his subsequent comments to Thomas in March 1866 regarding Lochrane's letter, Grant also expressed concern about the black soldiers' own safety in the face of post-Confederate hostility. And it appears that the fact that Lochrane had suggested black troops would be in danger if they remained in place was, at least in part, why Grant urged Thomas to replace them insofar as he was able. Grant admonished Thomas, first and foremost, to protect all of his men, black and white. "It is your duty to see that no conflict shall be brought on by the acts of the Government forces or Government Agents," he wrote. "But if conflict does come," he added, "the troops must be strong enough to resist opposition," and those who opposed them must be arrested and brought to trial.[42]

Clearly Reconstruction duty was not easy for the USCT's black volunteers, especially given that they could not fully rely on the support of the army's white officers, even with Grant's stipulation that they must provide it. Moreover, the perils of Reconstruction duty for USCT soldiers became increasingly grave as the months passed and as Andrew Johnson's overly generous policies toward the vanquished South engendered a neo-Confederate upsurge. These perils had reached critical levels by the late spring of 1866 in Memphis. The trouble began on the afternoon of May 1, when a group of soldiers recently mustered out of the Third U.S. Colored Infantry, but still in town awaiting their final pay, got into a dispute with a pair of local white police officers. An exchange of angry words escalated into an exchange of gunfire, and one of the police officers was wounded. Soon large numbers of the local police force, irate local whites, and anxious blacks had gathered on the scene, armed with whatever weapons they could bring to hand. Gunfire erupted again and, as one witness described it, "for a while both parties busied themselves in discharging their revolvers as rapidly as possible." Word then went out to Major General George Stoneman, commander of U.S. forces in the Department of Tennessee, who quickly arrived with a detachment of white troops. The crowd dispersed, leaving one white and thirteen blacks dead, as well as five whites and sixteen blacks wounded.

Over the next several hours, rumors about the afternoon battle flew around the city, exacerbating antiblack sentiments already present within the city's white population. By nightfall, calls for revenge by whites upon Memphis's blacks (including discharged veterans as well as active duty soldiers of the USCT regiments) gave way to action: "Large numbers of armed citizens," including more police officers, "repaired to the scene of the [original] fight and commenced firing upon every negro who made himself visible. . . . The Police seemed to make it their special business to shoot every negro they could see, no matter where he was or what he was doing." By the time the shooting stopped in the early hours of May 2, dozens were dead, most of them black, and a number of the surviving blacks in the city—including the black soldiers—had retreated to the protection of Fort Pickering, where the soldiers were quartered.[43]

The riot was still not over. Later on the morning of May 2, whites continued to attack and kill the blacks who remained in town. Once again, white soldiers were called in to diffuse the violence, which over the course of two days had left almost fifty people, including forty-six blacks, dead. That night, white arsonists set fire to thirty houses belonging to local blacks—including the families of USCT soldiers—as well as black schools and churches, burning them to the ground. Only then did the violence come to an uneasy end, as General Stoneman issued orders on May 3 "forbidding the assembling of any bodies of armed men, black or white, except the police, so far as they are relied on to preserve the peace." Sadly, in searching for answers to why the riot began in the first place, even the generally sympathetic *New York Times* could not resist placing some of the blame on the alleged behavior of the black USCT veterans. Their reputation, wrote one correspondent uncritically, "has ever been bad. Since the muster out they have frequented whisky shops in the southern part of the city, and been guilty of excesses and disorderly conduct."[44]

The Memphis riot set a new tone for Southern whites' resistance to Reconstruction, particularly in response to the army's black occupation troops. Two months later, in New Orleans, black soldiers again found themselves in the midst of a race riot. Around noon on Monday, July 30, with the permission of Louisiana's Reconstruction governor, a group of twenty-six local representatives of the Republican Party, most if not all of them associated openly with the party's "radical" wing, convened at the Mechanics Institute Hall. Their purpose in coming together was to revisit some features of the provisional state constitution that federally occupied Louisiana had ratified in 1864, as part of its bid to regain its membership in the U.S. Congress. The 1864 constitution satisfied the demands of President Lincoln's December 1863 plan for Reconstruction (the "10 percent plan"), but not the expectations of the so-called Radical Republicans in Washington and across the country who hoped that, in addition to the political reunion of the rebel and loyal states, Reconstruction would transform the South socially, and might even bring about something resembling black equality. One of the issues concerning many Radical Republicans, including those gathered at the Mechanics Institute Hall in late July, was that of black men's voting rights, which they considered an essential tool for securing black Americans' freedom in any meaningful way. By July 30, tensions over the electoral question, and the overall texture and scope of Reconstruction as a whole, had reached an explosive level, pitting local Republicans of varying perspectives against both each other and local Democrats, many of whom were former Confederates dedicated to protecting white supremacy.[45]

The convention provided the fuse for these tensions in New Orleans, not least because the gathering itself was accompanied by a procession, complete with "martial music and national flags," of between a hundred and two hundred black supporters, many of whom were armed veterans of the USCT. When the marchers entered the hall—presumably to hear, and perhaps encourage, the discussions going on inside—white police attempted to stop them by making arrests. The marchers resisted, and their resistance quickly led to chaos. Soon a mob of angry whites, including police officers, was engaged in a full-scale attack on the marchers. Meanwhile, the arrival of more members from the freed black community augmented the marchers' numbers. Together their determination to fight back—with guns, if necessary—grew fierce. Additional police were called in to stop the riot, but instead of acting as officers of the peace, they joined in the fighting. As disorder spread, blacks took the brunt of the violence: "Several arrests of members of the Convention have been made by the city Police," the *New York Times* noted, "but few negroes are being arrested, as they are being rapidly killed." As in Memphis, white federal troops were finally summoned to disperse the rioters. In addition, Brevet Major General Absalom Baird placed the city under martial law in order to prevent a resurgence of violence in the hours and days ahead. By midafternoon on July 30, New Orleans was quiet again, but not before almost forty blacks and three whites had been killed, and perhaps as many as a hundred other residents of the city, mostly black, had been wounded.[46]

It bears repeating that the riot in New Orleans arose specifically out of local disputes over the question of black male suffrage—a proposition that seemed particularly offensive to many, if not most, Southern whites (and many Northern whites, too). Because the march featured armed veterans of the USCT stationed in the city, it implicitly made a case for full black citizenship as a reward for their service in the nation's army over the course of the last three years. It is easy to see why interracial fury erupted. Indeed, as the *Army and Navy Journal* pointed out almost apologetically in the wake of the riots in both Memphis and New Orleans, white resistance in the South was entirely understandable, even if it was not ultimately to be tolerated. Former Confederates who had sacrificed so much to sustain the institution of slavery as well as antebellum free blacks' subordination could not be expected to surrender readily to black political and social equality just because the shooting on the battlefield had stopped. "[T]o believe that the Southern people . . . could," explained the *Journal*'s editorialist,

> in a twelve-month, reverse the current of their sentiment on national topics, is to offer them a gratuitous insult, and one which their gallant and obstinate conduct in the field for four years does not deserve. Congressional Committees who . . . pretend astonishment at finding the so-called "rebels" still defending the motives which led them to take up arms, ought rather to rejoice at the frankness and candor with which those sentiments are avowed; or, rather, ought to have learned as much from general knowledge of human nature, without their foolish questionings. . . . Considering the intensity and extent of its late hostility to the Union, its fierce local prejudices, and its inherited views concerning the true position of the negro race, the wonder is not that there has been so much political disturbance [in the former Confederacy], but that there has been so little.[47]

By mid-1866, clashes such as these between former Confederates and the occupation forces of the U.S. army had become increasingly difficult to avoid. Occupation troops generally, as the enforcers of the peace and as presumed representatives of the Radical Republicans' plan to alter the social and political balance between the races in the South—and perhaps also in the nation as a whole—provided a lightning rod for conflict. White Southerners' fury escalated when those armed enforcers were black. For as Frederick Douglass had made clear, black soldiers' uniforms, guns, and authority, combined with their years of service on behalf of the U.S. government, epitomized—in a way that their basic humanity, to whites, did not—their claim to civil and political equality, for themselves as well as for the other black Americans whose freedom they strove to protect.

Christian Fleetwood mustered out of the army in May 1866, the same month the riot erupted in Memphis. On that occasion, the commanding officer of Fleetwood's brigade, Colonel Samuel A. Duncan, described him as "an intelligent, honest & faithful man," whose military service was "full of honor" and who, "having participated in all the campaigns and battles in which the regt. has been engaged," had "conducted himself with gallantry."[48] Fleetwood garnered an unusual amount of attention and acclaim from his white officers in light of his heroic deeds during the war, especially his protection of the national colors at Chaffin's Farm. But a black soldier in the U.S. army certainly did not have to be as accomplished as Fleetwood to seek to lay claim to Frederick Douglass's 1863 promise: full citizenship on the basis of his own and other black men's contributions to the nation's survival, stability, and security.

2

Black Soldiers Go West

I propose now simply to carry them into the Army, to protect them in all their civil rights, to make them believe they are men in the eyes of the law and in the eye of their Maker, to enable them to ameliorate their own condition, and to reach the highest possible point of elevation their nature is capable and susceptible of. When we have done that and they have done that, both of us will have discharged our duty.

—Senator James H. Lane of Kansas,
January 1866

S ERGEANT MAJOR CHRISTIAN A. FLEETWOOD MUSTERED OUT OF THE U.S. army for good in May 1866, but his personal pride in having served in the USCT endured, as did his dedication to Frederick Douglass's 1863 promise about the potential implications of black men's military service for uplifting the race. Just over a year after he returned to civilian life, Fleetwood took note of the creation in North Carolina—where his regiment had been stationed at the end of the war—of a state branch of the "Colored Soldiers' and Sailors' League." The state organization's president described the league's members as being pledged "to combine and connect ourselves together, that we may at this present, as well as in the future, preserve our great blessing, the ballot-box, as we did the United States muskets which the Government placed in our hands" during the recent war. "I feel constrained to use every effort in my power to aid my comrades in arms to preserve those rights which we have fought for, which we have bled for, and for which many have died."[1]

Such words vividly expressed Fleetwood's own feelings as he settled in Washington, D.C., married Sarah Iredell, fathered two children (only one of whom, Edith, reached adulthood), set about building a reasonably successful professional career based on his abundant clerical and bookkeeping skills—taking a job as an "extra clerk" at the U.S. Supreme Court, becoming an employment agent for the Freedmen's Bureau, and later working for what was called the Freedman's Savings and Trust Company—and resuming the same sorts of social activities that had enriched his antebellum life. Through it all, Fleetwood's experience with the USCT, and the sacrifices he and almost 200,000 other black men had made on the nation's behalf, remained fundamental to his self-understanding, even as they contributed to his growing reputation and prominence among black Washingtonians.[2]

Meanwhile, the victorious federal government continued the demobilization of the army's white volunteers and, much more slowly, its black ones. At the same time, the government and its military arm engaged in a series of wide-ranging and often contentious debates concerning the size and shape the postwar Regular army should assume. As these debates got underway, the long-term future of black Americans' participation in the federal armed forces remained unclear, despite their disproportionately high representation in the occupation forces stationed across the former Confederacy. Over time, however, matters of practicality competed with other concerns, including such basic issues as how to harness sufficient manpower to complete the military's numerous postwar tasks. These considerations unavoidably led the politicians and military men involved in the debates to consider the possibility of carving out a permanent role for black men within the Regular army, although opinions varied on precisely what that role might be. If the postwar army opened its doors to black men, should black men be enlisted as soldiers or only as laborers? Should they be allowed to serve as commissioned officers, or should they be held to noncommissioned status, as even the most talented, like Fleetwood, had been? Should black men, if enlisted, be confined to segregated units, or should they be integrated into biracial regiments?

With over 100,000 black soldiers still on occupation duty in the former Confederacy, as early as June 1865 one "H.C.M." wrote from Savannah, Georgia, to the editor of the *Army and Navy Journal* to convey his thoughts. Expressing admiration for the USCT's veterans, H.C.M., who was probably a white officer, urged that as many as 75,000 black men now be granted access to the postwar military, whose size, he predicted, would surely be about 125,000 (it actually turned out to be less than half that, at 54,000). Black soldiers' "endurance and valor" had already been proved; indeed, "unprejudiced minds" could no longer question their "equality with the average of white troops" on numerous fronts, especially in cases, he noted—echoing a familiar refrain—where black soldiers operated under the authority of high-quality white officers. H.C.M., it seems, envisioned the creation of a postwar equivalent of the USCT: a "Corps d'Afrique," as he called it, whose foundation would ideally be composed of "picked" USCT veterans.[3]

The very next month, "N" dispatched a letter of protest to the *Journal*, arguing that, "till it can be shown that they have rendered *better* service than our white troops," the postwar army's doors should be closed to blacks. He continued, "[T]here are serious objections to keeping up a large army of men whose mental faculties are undeveloped. . . . As we must have a large Army for some time to come, let us have one composed of men who can read and think for themselves—men who know right from wrong . . . and who have too much independence of character to be *too* 'obedient.'" Moreover, given that it was only proper for at least "a certain proportion" of the promotions in the army to be "made from the ranks," N went on to point out that the enlistment of black soldiers in the postwar army might eventually mean that white officers would be forced to associate directly with them. Worse still, white soldiers (including officers) might find themselves commanded by black officers of higher rank. In the end, he concluded, was it not really best to deploy all black men—who appeared, after all, to be "naturally" suited to the climate anyway—into Southern agriculture instead of military service?[4]

Conflicting proposals such as these developed in the shadow of congressional and high-level military debates on the same questions. One very important U.S. army officer who chimed in was Ulysses Grant, who seems to have been decidedly ambivalent. Grant did not deny that the soldiers of the USCT had served competently and even heroically during the war, but in keeping with his variable opinions regarding the use of black soldiers as occupation troops in the former Confederacy, he had some concerns about opening the Regular army to long-term black enlistment. Writing to the chair of the Senate's Committee on Military Affairs in early 1866, Grant explained that, while he favored authorizing President Johnson "to raise twenty thousand colored troops if he deemed it necessary," he did not recommend creating permanent regiments of "colored" soldiers. As he put it, "our standing army in time of peace should have the smallest possible numbers and the highest possible efficiency." Grant may well have considered white soldiers fundamentally more "efficient" than black ones. More likely, he feared that allowing blacks to enlist on a continuing basis in the Regular army would limit the army's overall effectiveness, especially if the racial tensions evident in the Reconstruction South arose in other places requiring the military's presence. In the event that black troops did become a permanent component of the Regular army—to which Grant admittedly did not express a strong objection—he supported their segregation into separate units.[5]

If Grant was ambivalent about the prospect of creating permanent black Regular army regiments, Senator James A. McDougall of California was not. "I wish to express my thought," he declared during the same congressional hearings Grant had addressed, "that the people of my country," by which he clearly meant *white* people, "are able to maintain themselves, and do not need to be maintained by an inferior race." For clarification, McDougall added his considered opinion that, "to place a lower, inferior, different race upon a level with the white man's race, in arms, is against the laws that lie at the foundation of true republicanism." One of McDougall's fellow Democrats, Senator Willard Saulsbury Sr. of Delaware, concurred, drawing on the evidence of growing tensions between white former Confederates and USCT occupation troops to make his point. "If the object of Congress is, and certainly it should be, to restore kind feelings and friendly relations between the different sections of the country," he argued—again, clearly referring only to the white people of the "different sections"—"they should do nothing which in itself is calculated to aggravate feelings already excited or to arouse feelings which may now be dormant. What would be the effect if you were to send negro regiments into the community in which I live"—namely, border-state Delaware, which had about eighteen hundred slaves at the beginning of the Civil War—"to brandish their swords and exhibit their pistols and their guns? Their very presence would be a stench in the nostrils of the people from whom I come."[6]

Still, as had been the case during the Civil War, a number of leading politicians unequivocally supported the idea of establishing black regiments. Among them was the Republican senator Benjamin Wade of Ohio, one of the "radicals" in the party who, like many other supporters, defended the idea of permanent regiments of black soldiers on the basis of the USCT's performance and reliability during the war and since. "I am informed," Wade declared, "that while we lose greatly by desertion all the time from the white regiments . . . there is scarcely anything of the kind among the colored troops." Responding specifically to Saulsbury's point about the need to avoid further aggravating white Southerners, many of whom were becoming ever more violently bitter about emancipation and blacks' service as occupation forces, Wade added, "If it is necessary to station troops anywhere to keep the peace in this nation, I do not care how obnoxious they are to those who undertake to stir up sedition. . . . I care but little whether the insurrectionists like the kind of troops that we station there to keep them in order or not."[7]

Also supportive of black enlistment in the postwar army was the Republican senator James Henry Lane of Kansas, who, as a brigadier general during the war, had—like David Hunter and John W. Phelps—begun recruiting and organizing black troops for federal army service as early as 1862, even before Lincoln and his government were prepared to do so. Now Lane pointed out that, upon being presented with the proposed Army Reorganization Bill, Secretary of War Stanton, Generals Meade and Sherman, as well as Generals Thomas and Grant had essentially given their approval. "Colored troops," Lane argued, "are sufficient for these grand leaders who have led your armies to victory and suppressed the rebellion." On what basis, then, could they possibly be excluded from postwar military service? And while Lane made it clear that he did not believe that blacks and whites were equal in every way, he conceded, "After three hundred years of oppression the white race would be very different from what they are now." Like so many others in his time, Lane also erroneously believed that blacks could tolerate the climate in the South, and the diseases endemic to it, "a great deal better than the white troops." But this was hardly his main reason for supporting black enlistment.[8]

By midsummer of 1866, the question of black men's immediate future in the U.S. army was decided when Congress passed its "Act to increase and fix the Military Peace Establishment of the United States" (the Army Reorganization Act). Although we do not have access to Christian Fleetwood's response to this momentous development, it is safe to assume that he would have been pleased. For this bill, signed into law by Andrew Johnson on July 28—just two days before the bloody riot erupted in New Orleans—"opened a new chapter in American military history." Of the sixty regiments (forty-five infantry, ten cavalry, and five artillery) the act mandated for the 54,000-man army—which was more than three times the size of its antebellum predecessor—six (the Ninth and Tenth Cavalry and the Thirty-eighth through the Forty-first

Senator James H. Lane of Kansas, ca. 1866. *Courtesy of the Library of Congress.*

Infantry regiments) were to be reserved for black soldiers. Cavalry and artillery regiments, black as well as white, were to be made up of twelve companies each (called "troops" in the cavalry and "batteries" in the artillery), while each infantry regiment would consist of ten companies. For all three branches of the service, a company (or troop, or battery) could enlist up to sixty-four men, who were eligible for promotion to the noncommissioned ranks of corporal and sergeant. Each of these groups of soldiers came under the command of a commissioned captain, first lieutenant, and second lieutenant. Each regiment, in turn, came under the command of a colonel, a lieutenant colonel, and from one to three majors. Beginning in March 1869, subsequent reorganizations of the army reduced the total number of infantry regiments to twenty-five and consolidated the four black infantries into two, redesignating them the Twenty-fourth and the Twenty-fifth. But these changes did not affect the internal organization or size of the regiments themselves. Black soldiers remained around 10 percent of the U.S. army until the end of the nineteenth century, and totaled about 25,000 during this period.[9]

Significantly, although the July 1866 act did not so stipulate, it was widely understood that the six new black regiments would have white men as their commissioned and commanding officers, a pattern established previously with the USCT that even the most enthusiastic white supporters of black enlistment seemed unwilling to alter. To be fair, in the summer of 1866 there were few potential recruits with the qualifications of someone like Fleetwood, in other words, the education, training, and experience of command considered necessary for any army post above sergeant. Because the teaching of reading and writing to slaves had long been a crime in the South, the vast majority of the men who first enlisted in the new black regiments were severely undereducated and, in many cases, illiterate, which meant that in the early years of the black Regular regiments, white commissioned officers found themselves doing much of the administrative work usually delegated to subordinates. "I beg to call especial attention to the great labor thrown upon the officers of the colored regiments," wrote Lieutenant Colonel James H. Carleton early on, after an inspection of the black Twenty-fifth Infantry, "in being obliged to make all rolls, returns, accounts, and keep all books with their own hands. There should be employed under authority of law, an educated clerk, white or black . . . whose duty should be to do all of the official writing in the books, and on the rolls of the company, and be obliged to teach the men to read and write." Anticipating this problem, the July 1866 act assigned to each black regiment a white chaplain explicitly for the purpose of running a school for the enlisted men. Still, as Carleton's observations make clear, the results of these efforts were hardly immediate; the upshot was that most white officials early on were disinclined to challenge previous discriminatory practices, and black soldiers' exclusion from the commissioned officers' ranks continued.[10]

As General Grant and Secretary of War Stanton sorted through the likely candidates to command the new black regiments, with the help and advice of Generals Sherman and Sheridan, they therefore considered only white men, specifically veteran officers of the federal army who had sparkling Civil War records. They made their selections with care, and in the end, all of their choices were good ones, though some were more enduring than others and a few missteps occurred along the way. Among the veteran officers who initially came under consideration for command of a black Regular regiment was George Armstrong Custer, whose stunning performance during the war—he was only twenty-one when the Civil War broke out—had led to his promotion to the rank of major general of U.S. volunteers by the spring of 1865. Still, like so many accomplished veteran officers, Custer found his place in the postwar Regular army uncertain because of demobilization and downsizing. One thing is clear, however: Custer believed himself much too good for an assignment with a black regiment, and thus he vigorously turned down the lieutenant colonelcy of the black Ninth Cavalry, inadvertently setting up his subsequent appointment to command of the all-white Seventh. As it turned out, this crudely racist decision by the "dashing 'boy general'" ultimately redounded to the Ninth's benefit, not least because of the catastrophe that awaited Custer and the Seventh Cavalry in their confrontation with the Sioux at Montana's Little Bighorn River in 1876.[11]

Of all the new black regiments, it was the Tenth Cavalry that ended up benefiting from the greatest stability at the top. Benjamin Henry Grierson became the Tenth's colonel and went on to spend the bulk of his postwar career in the regiment's command. Not unlike Colonel Samuel A. Duncan, who had offered such warm praise to Christian Fleetwood at the time of his mustering out from the Fourth U.S. Colored Infantry, Grierson firmly believed that a black man could be "intelligent, honest

& faithful," could provide military service to the nation that was "full of honor," could "conduct himself with gallantry," and deserved rich opportunity, acknowledgment, and reward for doing so. From 1866 to 1888, Grierson contributed with unusual vigor and dedication to making his case on black soldiers' behalf.[12]

That Grierson would end up giving so many years of his life to the U.S. army, however, was hardly self-evident in his youth. Born on July 8, 1826, in what was then the frontier town of Pittsburgh, Pennsylvania, Grierson was the sixth and youngest child of Irish immigrants. When Benjamin was a little over two, his family moved to Youngstown, Ohio, where the future cavalry commander at the age of eight narrowly escaped death when a skittish horse kicked him in the head. The injury left Grierson with a long scar on the side of his face and, he claimed, a lingering fear of—or perhaps it was respect for—horses.[13]

As a youth Grierson was described as having a mild, uncombative temperament and a love of music; over time he became proficient with a number of different instruments, including the drum, piano, violin, guitar, and clarinet, and played in the Youngstown band. After graduating from the Youngstown Academy, Grierson took a job as a clerk in a local store, but he continued to pursue music on the side, teaching and repairing instruments and also organizing a minstrel band. It was music that first drew him,

Major General Benjamin H. Grierson, ca. 1865. *Courtesy of the Library of Congress.*

ironically, into the military, as a bugler for a regiment of cavalry in the Ohio state militia.[14]

In 1849, when Grierson was twenty-three years old, his family's quest for economic opportunity led them to Jacksonville, Illinois, not far from Springfield. There Grierson lived with his parents, making a modest living as a musician and bandleader. Five years later, he finally struck out on his own, marrying the schoolteacher Alice Kirk. The Griersons' first child, a son they named Charles Henry, arrived less than a year after their wedding; not long afterward, they moved about twenty miles away (but still in Illinois) to Meredosia, where Grierson tried his hand at mercantile pursuits and became active in the Illinois Republican Party. Grierson's commitment to the party's antislavery principles riled some in his overwhelmingly Democratic community, but enhanced his stature among local Republicans as well as party luminaries. In 1858, Abraham Lincoln himself spent a night at the Grierson home.[15]

When the Civil War broke out, Grierson got to work right away helping to organize a company of soldiers for the Tenth Illinois Infantry. In May he accepted an unpaid post as aide-de-camp to Benjamin Prentiss, the commander of the Illinois state troops stationed at Cairo, and at the end of October, Grierson received his first commission, as a major in the Sixth Illinois Cavalry. Worried that his lack of a West Point education might put him at a disadvantage—after all, since 1802 the U.S. Military Academy had been the nation's primary academic venue for training its army's commissioned officers—Grierson immersed himself in books on military tactics. Then, in late November, he joined the regiment in Shawneetown, Illinois, where he found the camp conditions dreadful, matériel and horses in extremely short supply, the troopers themselves virtually untaught, and the commanding officer, Colonel T. M. Cavanaugh, absent.[16]

Faced with these circumstances, Grierson took it upon himself to transform at least his own recruits into first-class cavalrymen and their bivouac into a manageable environment. By the end of the year, his troopers were displaying discipline, organization, and military skill, as well as improved morale, thanks to the upgrades he was able to engineer in their living situation. Impressed with Grierson's ongoing dedication to the well-being and preparedness of the men and the cleanliness and order of their camp (especially in the face of Colonel Cavanaugh's lack of interest), in early April 1862 almost forty of the regiment's other officers signed a petition to the Illinois governor demanding Cavanaugh's replacement by Grierson as the Sixth's colonel. In a matter of days, the governor effected the change. Within a few weeks of assuming command, Grierson made sure that the regiment was fully supplied with weapons. Although Grierson's supposedly "mild" personality hardly seemed to predispose him to face so unblinkingly the challenges of military leadership, his success in confronting one obstacle after another, effectively and without hesitation, boded well for his future with the black Tenth Cavalry after the war.[17]

In mid-June 1863, Grierson took five companies of his own regiment and four of the Eleventh Illinois Cavalry into action in a successful raid on a Confederate guerrilla encampment in Mississippi. It was the first of a series of raids for which he would become famous, and whose effectiveness impressed General Sherman so much that he rewarded Grierson with a silver-plated carbine and declared the former music teacher with a lingering distrust of horses to be his finest cavalry commander. Grant, too, developed great confidence in Grierson's skill, and in mid-April 1863, after several failed attempts to capture the Confederate stronghold at Vicksburg, he selected Grierson to divert Confederate attention away from Grant's own operations. On April 17, Grierson and his 1,700-man brigade moved out from La Grange, Tennessee, and over the course of the next sixteen days, with minimal losses, traveled six hundred miles while fighting small battles, killing and wounding enemy soldiers, capturing others, seizing animal stock, and destroying rail and telegraph lines, enemy weapons, and other supplies. When Grierson and his exhausted raiders, who had done much more than just create a diversion, resurfaced at Baton Rouge, Louisiana, on May 2, both Grant and Sherman were wonderfully impressed. In the wake of the raid, Grierson enjoyed promotion to brigadier general, along with newfound fame as a national hero whose picture appeared on the cover of *Harper's Weekly* and other popular publications.[18]

Toward the very end of 1864, Grierson led another major raid—a 450-mile, sixteen-day ride into Mississippi involving 3,500 white troopers, 50 black laborers, and a bare minimum of supplies. Like that in 1863, the raid in 1864–65 was a triumph, in the course of which the

Harper's Weekly cover, celebrating Grierson's 1863 raid. *Courtesy of the Library of Congress.*

raiders attracted a following of about 1,000 slaves, eagerly claiming their freedom. The raid, during which Grierson's men managed to burn, in just one evening, more than thirty railroad cars and two hundred wagons full of supplies destined for the Confederate forces, led to Grierson's brevet promotion to major general of volunteers, as well as personal interviews with Lincoln, Grant, and Stanton in Washington. At the end of the summer of 1865, he took command of the District of Northern Alabama, where he found himself in overall authority over several regiments of black occupation troops, although he seems to have had little direct contact with the men.[19]

Grierson's Reconstruction duty in Alabama lasted less than half as long as Christian Fleetwood's in North Carolina; Grierson's mustering-out orders arrived in mid-January 1866. Like Fleetwood's, however, Grierson's Civil War service had confirmed his love of the military—particularly its cavalry arm—and his aptitude for command. It had also provided him with direct experience of the horrors of slavery, while enabling him to act in a most satisfying way upon his Republican, abolitionist sentiments. At the same time, as war gave way to Reconstruction, Grierson not only briefly worked (admittedly at a distance) with black troops but also witnessed firsthand the many ways in which white Southerners aimed to undermine the war's promise for black Americans. For these reasons and more, it was to the benefit of many of the black men who sought to follow the footsteps of United States Colored Troops into the black regiments of the postwar Regular army that Grierson's period of separation from the military was brief, and his tenure with the Tenth Cavalry long.

The postwar Ninth Cavalry also enjoyed considerable stability, thanks to the appointment of the able veteran officer Edward Hatch, a native of Bangor, Maine. Hatch had been the Second Iowa Cavalry's colonel during the war, before being promoted in 1864 to brigadier general and put in command of a cavalry division, with which he served to great acclaim later that year at the Battles of Franklin and Nashville, where he witnessed the USCT troops' admirable performance.

Hatch was pleased after the war to accept the colonelcy of the Ninth and remained in command of the regiment until his untimely death in April 1889, at the age of fifty-eight. After his death, Hatch was replaced by Colonel Joseph G. Tilford, a West Point graduate and Civil War veteran who, by the time he replaced Hatch, had spent twenty years with the Seventh Cavalry.[20]

To command the new black Thirty-eighth Infantry, Grant and Stanton turned to William Babcock Hazen of Vermont, an 1855 graduate of West Point who had served during the Civil War in every major action in the western theater, from Perryville through Sherman's march through the Carolinas, and who by war's end had been brevetted to the level of major general. For the Thirty-ninth they chose Joseph Anthony Mower, also of Vermont, who had accumulated a Civil War record as impressive as Hazen's, commanding first a regiment (the Eleventh Missouri), then a brigade, a division, and a corps, and earning Sherman's enthusiastic endorsement as "the boldest young soldier we have" in 1863, when he was only thirty-six years old. For the Forty-first they selected Ranald S. Mackenzie of New York, valedictorian of West Point's class of 1862, who served in both the eastern and the western theaters and was, while colonel of the Second Connecticut Heavy Artillery, instrumental in challenging Confederate General Jubal A. Early's raid on the federal capital in July 1864. Later, Mackenzie served under Sheridan in command of a cavalry brigade in the Shenandoah Valley, and subsequently a cavalry division in the siege of Petersburg, in which Christian Fleetwood and the USCT had performed so well. Mackenzie was also active in the Appomattox campaign.[21]

One veteran officer who seemed particularly pleased to be chosen for a colonelcy in any postwar Regular army regiment, black or white, was Nelson Miles, who since May 1865 had been serving unhappily as Jefferson Davis's jailer at Fortress Monroe. Appointed to lead the new black Fortieth Infantry, Miles came to the post, like Grierson and the others, on the heels of a highly celebrated Civil War career, which culminated in his command of an infantry division during the Appomattox campaign. When he wrote to Miles in August 1866, Secretary of War Stanton made clear his esteem and his determination to keep Miles in the army: "I shall spare no effort to obtain for you one of the new regiments as a just acknowledgment of your distinguished service and gallantry."[22]

Grierson, Hatch, Hazen, Mower, Mackenzie, and Miles: these six experienced and highly respected veteran officers of the U.S. army became the founding commanders of the postwar army's black regiments. As it turns out, however, in contrast to their counterparts in the cavalry units, not one of the four infantry commanders remained at his post for very long. To some extent this was a function of the March 1869 consolidation of the four infantry regiments into two, in conjunction with Congress's attempt to further diminish the size and cost of the Regular army. "We cannot play the part of empire-founders, of continent-absorbers," grumbled the *Army and Navy Journal*, in response to this downsizing, "without being prepared to keep up an Army more than 25,000 to 30,000 strong. The sentiment of our people, tired of war though it may be, yet sets strongly toward the acquisition of territory. The timidest thinkers admit that it is but a question of time when Canada and Mexico and the 'Isles of the Sea' shall gravitate to the American Union." Still, Congress pressed forward, with the result that the Thirty-eighth and the Forty-first Infantry regiments became the Twenty-fourth under Colonel Mackenzie, while Hazen transferred to the white Sixth Infantry. When the black Thirty-ninth and Fortieth became the Twenty-fifth Infantry under Colonel Mower's command, Miles took charge of the white Fifth Infantry.[23]

Because structural changes in the army itself propelled Hazen and Miles into other assignments, it would be unfair to jump to the conclusion that they had found the command of black troops distasteful. Indeed, Miles, for one, had a long history of antislavery sentiment, and he seems to have taken an earnest and dedicated approach to his leadership of the Fortieth Infantry, which earned him, in 1869, an official recommendation from North Carolina's Reconstruction governor,

William W. Holden, that he be promoted to brigadier general. Among other things, Miles displayed a strong commitment to training and maintaining discipline among his soldiers. He also expressed concern, on more than one occasion, that the black soldiers under his authority (and enlisted men generally) be treated fairly by the federal government. "At present," he wrote to Representative James A. Garfield in 1868,

> the rank and file are, in my opinion, greatly neglected in point of pay, food and instruction. . . . They are made to perform all kinds of drudgery; subsist on the coarsest of food, and, as a general thing, their quarters are anything but comfortable. . . . Would it not be better to have more intellectual training and less of this dull role of duty, which after a certain time, neither improves the soldier physically or mentally[?] . . . If the soldiers were well cared for, and there was a prospect that true merit and talent would be rewarded by promotion, and the position of a United States Soldier made a more creditable one, our Army would be filled with some of the best young men in the country.[24]

Miles cared deeply about the welfare of his soldiers; he also demonstrated a clear awareness of the socially and politically transformative implications of black men's military service in the South, and was eager to protect their voting rights. In late 1867, three years before the ratification of the Fifteenth Amendment legally guaranteeing black male suffrage, Miles insisted that "no apprehension need arise that the colored man will not use his gift with discretion." Indeed, in the fall of 1868, Miles briefly butted heads with General Meade, then commanding the Department of the South (now encompassing North and South Carolina, Georgia, Alabama, and Florida), on using the Fortieth Infantry to enforce order and enable blacks to vote in local and state elections. Miles was determined to deploy the troops, despite—or perhaps because of—the promise of white civilian opposition to their presence.[25]

Miles took his assignment with the Fortieth seriously and was committed to guarding the rights of black Americans both within his regiment and outside of it. Moreover, looking back from the vantage point of the late 1890s, he recalled the Fortieth with pride for having compiled a "reputation for military conduct which forms a record that may be favorably compared with the best regiments in the service." Still, it is also clear that Miles put up no resistance in 1869 to being transferred to a white infantry regiment, as was the case for Hazen, too. And one must wonder whether there is any significance in the fact that, in his two published memoirs of 1896 and 1911, Miles failed to mention his service with the Fortieth. One thing is certain, white regiments in the postwar period expected to see more active duty than black ones, given the persistence (or resurgence) of white leaders' doubts about black men's military abilities, the USCT's impressive deeds notwithstanding. Since active duty meant more opportunities for glory and valor—not to mention promotion—it is to be expected that an individual officer's personal ambition, which someone like Miles had in abundance, could trump even a significant degree of personal support for the new black regiments and take precedence over a professional opportunity to further the higher principles embodied in their formation.[26]

Still, although the first four commanders of the black Regular infantry units did not remain in place nearly as long as Grierson and Hatch, all six men approached their initial tasks with diligence and energy, starting with the establishment of recruiting stations in likely locations for black enlistees. By early fall, Grierson was recruiting at Fort Leavenworth, Kansas, where he also took the opportunity to explore the unfamiliar environment. On October 3, Grierson wrote to his wife about his new location: "One remarkable thing I have noticed," Grierson informed Alice, was the "*millions* of grasshoppers fill[ing] the air and in such numbers that they actually darken the sun." These Kansas grasshoppers, he added, "are impolite and curious enough" to "make their way up under the hoops and skirts of the ladies who are bold enough to promenade among them."[27]

While the Tenth began organizing among the feisty grasshoppers at

Fort Leavenworth, Hatch's Ninth Cavalry, as well as the Thirty-ninth and Forty-first Infantry Regiments, organized in New Orleans and Baton Rouge, Louisiana; Hazen's Thirty-eighth Infantry in St. Louis, Missouri; and Miles's Fortieth Infantry in North Carolina. Concerned about the quality of the recruits they might draw, commanders and their agents cast their nets wide, Miles sending recruiters as far as the Washington, D.C., area and New York City, and Grierson, who insisted that he "wanted the most intelligent men he could find," sending Captain Louis H. Carpenter all the way from Kansas to Pennsylvania.[28]

Although the new regiments began to organize more than a year before the 117th U.S. Colored Infantry finally mustered out and the USCT was completely disbanded, the hope and expectation that some black Civil War veterans might choose to remain in the nation's military service were abundantly fulfilled. About half of the more than 4,500 enlistees who responded to the first calls to join the postwar regiments were USCT veterans, men like Pollard Cole of Georgetown, Kentucky, who had enlisted in October 1864 in the twelfth U.S. Colored Heavy Artillery, mustered out in April 1866, and now joined the Tenth's H Troop, for which he served as a farrier—the caretaker of the regimental horses' hooves and shoes. John Sample of Fredericksburg, Virginia, was another USCT veteran who went on to become a black Regular. Born a slave, Sample had spent two years with the 108th U.S. Colored Infantry doing guard and garrison duty in Kentucky and Illinois. In January 1867, Sample enlisted as a private in the Fortieth Infantry's Company E. Also a veteran of the USCT, and a former slave, was James W. Bush of Lexington, Kentucky. Bush had served two years with Company K of the famed Fifty-fourth Massachusetts, whose soldiers included Frederick Douglass's sons Lewis and Charles, and which had bravely stormed Fort Wagner in Charleston Harbor in July 1863, sustaining casualties of over 40 percent. In the course of his service with the Fifty-fourth, Bush rose to the rank of first sergeant and was also wounded quite severely in the leg, possibly at Fort Wagner. As Bush recalled thirty years later, when he enlisted in the Ninth Cavalry in December 1866, "I was yet

young," and had "a great desire to remain a soldier serving this government," so he kept the information about his injury during the Civil War
to himself.[29]

As recruiters for the new black regiments sought to fill their units
with men like Cole, Sample, and Bush, they frequently operated under
far less than ideal conditions. Such was the case for the Ninth Cavalry's
recruiters in New Orleans, which was still recovering from the riot that
had taken place there in July. Predictably, recruiters in the Crescent
City confronted strong but by no means exceptional resistance from
local whites who were still smarting from the riot and its implications
for social revolution and who considered farm labor the only appropriate work for a freed slave or even a veteran of the USCT. Of course,
recruiters were not the only ones who endured challenges in the early
days of the new regiments; enlistees suffered gravely, too, and not just
from former Confederates' opposition to their joining the postwar military instead of plying their shovels and hoes. According to the historian
Frank N. Schubert, in New Orleans,

> Ninth Cavalry recruits found themselves crowded into unsanitary
> and badly ventilated industrial buildings where steam engines run
> by slaves had once pressed cotton into five-hundred-pound fifty-
> inch bales for shipment by sea to textile mills. There the men slept
> and cooked their meals over open fires while a cholera epidemic
> raged around them. Nine soldiers died in October [1866], fifteen
> more in November, and another five in December.

Other daunting and unanticipated obstacles also arose. Five companies of the Fortieth Infantry were shipwrecked on March 1, 1867, and
although none of the men died, they lost the bulk of their uniforms,
supplies, equipment, weapons, and ammunition.[30]

White civilian resistance, inadequate facilities, crowded conditions,
raging illness, and unreliable forms of transportation were just some
of the problems recruiters, officers, and enlistees faced as they worked

together to create the new black regiments. They persisted, however, and gradually the regiments came together. New enlistees found themselves engaged in the intensive training necessary to transform them from recruits into soldiers, including, among other things, the most fundamental skills associated with "military courtesy, marching, and marksmanship." For new cavalry troopers, basic training was even more complicated: in addition to everything else, they needed to learn how to ride without thought, and while fighting with sword and gun. Veterans of the USCT such as Pollard Cole, John Sample, and James Bush undoubtedly provided leavening to the rest of the greener men as they struggled to master the art of war. Veterans also brought with them, and surely shared with their new brothers in arms, the expectations and aspirations they had developed during the Civil War regarding the army as a means to social and political uplift, both for themselves personally and for black Americans generally. As Schubert notes simply, "Black soldiers appreciated the significance of military service as a way to stake their claim to citizenship."[31]

In the spring of 1867, between 250 and 300 of the earliest black Regulars learned that they were about to begin putting their military training into practice, as they received their orders to reoccupy the U.S. army's post at Fort Davis in Texas, some two hundred miles southeast of El Paso. Built in 1854 in a mile-high desert canyon and surrounded by hills rich in both alpine and desert flora as well as pronghorn antelope, javelina, and lizards, Fort Davis—like the mountains into which the post was nestled—was named in honor of Jefferson Davis, who was secretary of war when the fort was constructed. Before the war, Fort Davis functioned as part of an elaborate network of military installations, staffed with 3,000 soldiers, that extended across much of Texas. During this period, white soldiers of the Eighth Infantry stationed at the fort had provided escort services for frontier settlers passing through the region, guarding them and their goods from raids by the region's Native inhabitants.[32]

During the war, Fort Davis—like other Texas posts—was initially

Fort Davis in the late 1880s. *Courtesy of the National Park Service: Fort Davis National Historic Site, Texas.*

occupied by Confederate forces, but it was abandoned as the war's escalation drew the soldiers east into the heart of the national crisis. For the next five years the post remained uninhabited. In 1867, the federal government decided to restore the now dilapidated fort, reoccupy it, and resume the army's services protecting white settlers heading west. The first soldiers assigned to perform these tasks were the black soldiers of Edward Hatch's Ninth Cavalry. Among them was a former slave who would later become particularly well known for the dramatic contours of his two decades of service in the U.S. army, but who was then just a "bright-eyed, hard-nosed, intelligent, well-spoken, and wiry" eighteen- or nineteen-year-old, Emanuel Stance. When the Civil War ended, Stance had initially turned to agricultural labor in the wake of emancipation. In October 1866, however, like so many other young black men in the South, he chose to leave behind the harsh realities of contract labor and sharecropping in favor of the army and its apparent promise, enlisting at Carroll Parish, Louisiana. By the time Stance and the troopers of the Ninth headed west to Fort Davis, he had already been promoted to corporal.[33]

Stance and his comrades were the vanguard for the thousands of federal soldiers who came west over the next three decades to serve in Texas. Moreover, soldiers from all of the postwar black regiments found themselves stationed at Fort Davis at some point between 1867 and 1885 (the fort was finally taken out of service in 1891), and portions of different regiments frequently overlapped there. Benjamin Grierson, who lived there from 1882 to 1885 when Fort Davis was the Tenth Cavalry's headquarters, described it to his wife, Alice, upon first visiting it: "The climate is much cooler here than at [Fort] Concho," another army post, located about three hundred miles to the northeast. "The surrounding mountains make a beautiful picture, look in whatever direction you may." However, Grierson added, "The post is not located as I would have placed it had I had charge of the matter. It has an appearance of being crowded into or between two hills or mounds and I felt . . . like taking hold of it and pulling it out and away from a position where . . . an enemy might with ease take possession of the hilltops and fire down upon the garrison." Despite Grierson's concerns, Fort Davis steadily regained its centrality to the nation's military operations in the Southwest. At the same time, across the state of Texas—which had the distinction of being both a former Confederate and a frontier state— and elsewhere in the Southwest, numerous other forts were soon either reoccupied or built from the ground up.[34]

The soldiers of the Ninth Cavalry who were posted to Fort Davis in the spring of 1867 began their journey from Louisiana in March, under the able command of the regiment's lieutenant colonel, Wesley Merritt. Born in New York City in 1834, Merritt had spent much of his youth in Illinois, but he returned to his home state in 1855 to attend West Point, from which he graduated in 1860 and of which many years later, from 1882 to 1887, he would be superintendent. Like the six men originally tapped for the colonelcies of the postwar black regiments, Merritt was propelled steadily upwards thanks to his superior Civil War performance, mostly with the Army of the Potomac; he rose from lieutenant in 1862 to major general of volunteers by war's end, at which time he was acting as Sheridan's second in command. It bears recalling that George Custer was the first man to be offered the post that

Merritt later occupied. Although he shared Custer's impressive military record, Merritt brought a significantly more moderate temperament to the position.[35]

Making a journey that other black Regulars and their white commissioned officers would soon duplicate, the troopers first traveled by steamer to the Gulf Coast town of Indianola, Texas, whose location clearly associated it more with Texas's Confederate than its frontier identity. Interestingly, in contrast with the virulent expressions of resistance to the presence of black troops to which other former Confederates had steadily given vent, a group of citizens from the town had written to Brevet Brigadier General James Shaw Jr. just a few months before the Ninth arrived in Indianola to offer their strong praise of the USCT's Seventh U.S. Colored Infantry soldiers, who had served as federal occupation forces there under his command. "The undersigned," these Texans wrote,

> After the surrender of the forces of the Confederate States . . . in good faith at once gave our allegiance to the Government of the United States, believ[ing] that in doing so there was no necessity for the quartering of troops in our midst. But the authorities thinking otherwise, we have to congratulate ourselves in being so fortunate as to have had your command stationed in our place. . . . While in many other sections of our state difficulties and discords have been engendered between citizens and soldiers even to the destruction of life and property, in your command at this place everything has been smooth and tranquil, even beyond our most sanguine hopes . . . for which you will carry with you in your retirement, our sincere and lasting gratitude.[36]

Given the relative friendliness of the white citizens of Indianola toward black soldiers, it may have been unfortunate that the Ninth did not remain there. Instead, it proceeded to march a distance of about 160 miles to San Pedro Springs, just north of San Antonio, where they remained pending further orders. While they waited, a bloody incident shook the regiment from within, involving E Troop's black first sergeant, Harrison Bradford of Kentucky. A veteran of the 104th U.S. Colored Infantry, Bradford—like Emanuel Stance—had already demonstrated a number of the skills deemed essential for noncommissioned officer status, including an ability to read and comprehend written orders, and to write out, issue, and enforce orders in turn. As a result, he had been rapidly promoted in his first months of service, first to corporal and then to sergeant.

Although his position afforded him structural authority over other soldiers, like all good officers, Bradford surely knew that the loyalty of one's subordinates had to be earned every day. And whereas Bradford seems to have done the necessary work to earn his troopers' fidelity, the white man who was in immediate command of E troop, twenty-three-year-old Lieutenant Edward M. Heyl, had not. Instead, Heyl, himself a Civil War veteran of the Third Pennsylvania Cavalry and the only commissioned officer at that point assigned to E Troop, had revealed himself to be not just a harsh disciplinarian but also a sadistic bigot. Early on he took to abusing the enlisted men, sometimes striking them with his saber even to the point of drawing blood. Already before the regiment had reached San Pedro Springs, Heyl's cruelty, stoked by his consumption of excessive amounts of alcohol, had become, to many of the enlisted men and clearly to Bradford, virtually intolerable. On April 9, Sergeant Bradford gathered some of the soldiers of E Troop with the intention of confronting Lieutenant Colonel Merritt in an orderly but collective manner and persuading him to intervene on their behalf.[37]

Bradford and the others had not yet reached Merritt's quarters when, seeing the men passing his tent, Heyl ordered them to halt and explain their actions. Within moments the two officers were fighting. Shortly thereafter, Heyl fired two shots at Bradford, wounding him badly, but not so badly as to prevent Bradford from lashing out with his sword at another white officer who had just arrived on the scene, and who later died of his wound. Still another white officer approached, quickly pulling the trigger on his revolver and killing Bradford, finishing the job that Heyl had begun. Meanwhile, a number of the enlisted men who came with Bradford had joined in the melee, but as soon as Merritt appeared, they scattered in the direction of their own quarters. Some, indeed, kept right on going in the direction of Louisiana.[38]

The Heyl-Bradford incident is only one instance of the enduring antagonism black Regulars in the postwar period experienced from some of their white officers, as had also been true for their USCT predecessors. Even the best, most supportive, and most racially progressive commanding officers—like Hatch, Grierson, and Merritt—could not always control the behavior of their subordinates when they were on their own with the enlisted men and noncommissioned officers, and the historical record contains many more instances of similar conflict, including at least one more involving the Ninth Cavalry. In that case, the white commander of K Troop, Captain Lee Humfreville, handcuffed, by pairs, a group of several enlisted men whom he then tied to an army wagon and pulled over four hundred miles across Texas during a nineteen-day period. Along the way, Humfreville sharply limited the men's rations and also deprived them of the right to warm themselves by the campfire at night. As it turns out, this was only the culmination of a long period of abuse: some days before their long journey from Fort Richardson to Fort Clark began, Humfreville had struck Privates Jerry Williams and James Imes on their heads, first with a carbine and then with a club, before tying them to a tree and taunting Williams with the words "What did you do when you was a slave?" Later, as he marched his handcuffed soldiers toward Fort Clark, Humfreville displayed no hint of mercy. According to one account, "When the troop forded streams, they were dragged through the frigid water with no chance afterward to change clothes or dry themselves," and when the train stopped for the night, "each had to carry a twenty-five-pound log" and walk around in circles until midnight." To the army's credit, Humfreville was courtmartialed, found guilty, and dismissed from the service.[39]

Although both of these incidents involved the Ninth Cavalry, this regiment was not the only one whose enlisted men endured abuse from some of their white officers. In June 1871, near where C Troop of Grierson's Tenth Cavalry was encamped at the time in New Mexico, privates Luther Dandridge, David Adams, and George Garnett led a rebellion of about eighteen black enlisted men against the troop's white second lieutenant, Robert W. Price, who seems to have made a name for himself, like Heyl, by treating the black enlisted men poorly, especially when he had been drinking heavily. On this particular day, a clearly inebriated Lieutenant Price heard a group of soldiers laughing and thought they were laughing at him (perhaps because, as the subsequent court-martial revealed, he had been "entertaining" a young civilian boy in his tent). The enraged lieutenant called to First Sergeant Shelvin Shropshire, who was black, and said, "[I]f they are laughing at me, I will give them a dead nigger to laugh at." According to Shropshire, a semiliterate native of Alabama who went on to serve with the Tenth for thirty-three years, Price then returned to his tent. Soon, however, Shropshire recalled at the court-martial, Price "came back to where I was, and walked down the Picket line near the lower end of the Company street," discharged his weapon, and fatally wounded Private Charles Smith. Price then turned to Shropshire and said, now "there was something to laugh at."[40]

If Lieutenant Price had hoped to subdue the men under his command, he failed. Instead, Dandridge, Adams, Garnett, and others gathered their weapons and threatened to kill him. No doubt hoping to stave off a bloodbath, Shropshire attempted to intervene, demanding that the troublemakers put down their arms and return to their quarters. Asked by the soldiers whether they could have Price arrested, Shropshire informed them that "it was out of an enlisted man's power, to arrest an officer." But he urged them to abandon their rebellion. Rather than listening to Shropshire, however, the excited soldiers mounted their horses and proceeded to gallop about the camp, yelling, shooting off their guns, and threatening to stampede the rest of the troop's herd. Price, meanwhile, tore through the camp brandishing two revolvers and displaying a clear willingness to do more damage. Eventually, though, the uproar came to a close, and the men who had initiated the mutiny came to trial. Thanks in part to Sergeant Shropshire's testimony, the enlisted men were all found not guilty and returned to duty. What sort of punishment Price received, if any, is not known.

Such incidents demonstrate the implacable racism of some white officers in the postwar period toward the black Regulars they were meant to lead. At the same time, they offer examples of black soldiers like Bradford, who struggled courageously—as the USCT's soldiers had also done—to stand up for themselves in the face of arbitrary cruelty and injustice. In addition, these events provide occasional examples of how at least some white officers and key figures in the federal government could be counted on to actively denounce such ill-treatment and to support black soldiers' civil rights and personal dignity. In the Heyl-Bradford case, for example, Lieutenant Colonel Merritt speedily demanded a complete investigation into Heyl's conduct, after he had already reprimanded Heyl severely. Moreover, although a court-martial found nine of the black troopers involved in that mutiny guilty and sentenced them to death, when he reviewed the court-martial proceedings later, the federal government's chief of military justice, Judge Advocate General Joseph Holt, pointed out that Heyl's brutal behavior toward the men had provoked the situation in the first place, and he recommended that Heyl be court-martialed instead and the black troopers' sentences be reduced.[41]

In overall command of the military district in which the Heyl-Bradford incident occurred, General Philip Sheridan, too, denounced Heyl's behavior, concurring with Holt and Secretary of War Stanton that the enlisted men's sentences should be diminished. Within six months, all of the court-martialed soldiers were released from their confinement. Unfortunately, for reasons that are not known, Sheridan ultimately refused to order a court-martial for Heyl, and before long, because of the army's rigid system in this period of promoting on the basis of seniority alone, Heyl was elevated to the command of M Troop within the same black regiment, a position he retained until he transferred to the Fourth

Cavalry, a white unit, in 1870. While no other racial incidents were recorded after he left the Ninth, Heyl is said to have renamed his horse "Nigger."[42]

Beyond the issue of problematic white officers, traveling through and subsequently being stationed on the western frontier meant that black soldiers regularly came into contact with white American frontier settlers and, for soldiers in the Southwest, Mexican civilians, who sometimes welcomed the black soldiers and at other times greeted them with the same sort of suspicion and animosity—even violence—black occupation forces had experienced in the Reconstruction South. A sign of some locals' resistance to having any direct interaction whatsoever with the black Regulars can be found in the fact that black soldiers serving as stagecoach guards—work they otherwise enjoyed because it offered an alternative to the dull routines of garrison life—were often refused access to return transportation and found themselves having to walk back to their posts. Such inconveniences seem trivial, however, in light of more violent examples. The Tenth Cavalry private John Burnett was killed by the civilian Pablo Fernandez after he attempted to bring a fight under control in the neighborhood just beyond Fort Stockton's boundaries, not far from Fort Davis. On another occasion, three troopers of the Ninth Cavalry—Privates Anthony Harvey, John Hanson, and George Smallow—were killed for no clear reason by local cattle herders near Cimarron, New Mexico. In cases such as these, it is difficult to exclude racial and ethnic tensions as a motive for murder.[43]

As in the Reconstruction South, it sometimes was the behavior of the soldiers themselves that provoked local civilians' rage: in January 1869, Private John O. Wheeler came before a court-martial to face charges that while serving as an escort and guard for the mail service in and around Fort Quitman, Texas, he had become drunk, causing him to be careless with his weapon, steal money and clothing from some local residents, and attempt to rape a Mexican woman, Rufina Humes. Found guilty, Wheeler was dishonorably discharged and confined at hard labor for seven years. Several months later, the Forty-first Infantry's Charles

Jackson was court-martialed for stealing a watermelon from Francisca Ortiz's husband and, after the husband took it back, attacking him. Francisca reported Jackson to a superior officer, after which Jackson threatened to kill her with a wooden rod. The court found Jackson guilty. In another case, Private Henry Jenkins of the Twenty-fifth Infantry, Company E, was found guilty of stealing a revolver and overcoat from a Mexican citizen living near Fort Davis and beating him up with the help of perhaps a dozen other soldiers and threatening to kill him with an ax. "I was spitting blood for two days" after the attack, Pioquinto Alracon testified at Jenkins's court-martial. One witness characterized Jenkins as inveterately hostile toward the local Mexican population: "God damn you," Jenkins reportedly said to a soldier who spoke in Alracon's defense on the night the incident took place, "you want to take up for the Mexicans, don't you?" In the end, the court found on behalf of the civilian, and Jenkins was dishonorably discharged, fined, and sentenced to two years' imprisonment.[44]

Some interactions between black Regulars and local civilians turned truly ghastly: in January 1869, the Leavenworth, Kansas, *Commercial* reported that a white man had been murdered at Hays City by three of the Thirty-eighth Infantry's black enlisted men. In turn, a vigilante committee sought out the alleged murderers, who had already been arrested and were awaiting trial. The vigilantes succeeded, and late one night before the soldiers' trial could take place, the men were abducted from prison and hanged from the branches of some nearby trees. Fortunately, soldier-civilian encounters were frequently much less noxious than this one, and some black soldiers made strong and lasting connections with their neighbors both during and after the completion of their military service on the frontier. George McGuire, who enlisted in 1869 and was honorably discharged from Fort Davis in 1874, remained in the area working as a civilian teamster for the post. He married a half-Mexican, half-Apache woman, Eduarda Rodriguez, with whom he subsequently had ten children. As one local in the mid-twentieth century described the town in the aftermath of the black soldiers' arrival there, "Fort Davis became a regular melting pot. Foreigners . . . married Mexican women; Negroes married Mexican women; and occasionally a white man—who forgot his skin was white . . . [did, too]. . . . I knew one Mexican woman who married a white man . . . while her aunt was married to a very black negro. An Irish girl married a Jew and her brother a Mexican girl. Fort Davis had a regular crazy quilt population."[45]

Even as they were striving, and occasionally failing, to get along with local civilians, soldiers on the frontier also had to learn how to get along with one another in close quarters at what were almost invariably remote locations, often hundreds of miles from another post or town. Indeed, court-martial records are replete with stories of conflict within the regiments, even when the soldiers occupied different ranks and sometimes, one suspects, precisely because they did. In a world in which authority overwhelmingly wore a white face, individual black soldiers' visions sometimes collided when it came to the question of what constituted acceptable behavior between and among black men, who typically shared a past as slaves but who now wielded different degrees of power on the basis of their skills and the effectiveness of their subordination to white officers. Although the black enlisted men in Sergeant Bradford's company had respected and been loyal to him, such was not always the case. In December 1868, for example, Private Edmund Durotte and First Sergeant Felix Olevia of the Ninth Cavalry's H Troop came close to killing each other at Fort Quitman after Olevia demanded that Durotte return money he had borrowed, and then threatened Durotte with a saber for refusing to do so. According to testimony given in the January 1869 court-martial, Durotte, who insisted that he owed Olevia nothing and, furthermore, that he resented Olevia's attentions toward his (Durotte's) wife, at this point "picked up a carbine and threw it" at Olevia, who dodged it. Then, testified Olevia, "the accused ran back and picked up an axe . . . and attempted to strike me with it." Pulling rank, Olevia ordered Durotte to the guardhouse, but Durotte refused to go until he was forced to do so by two other soldiers Olevia had ordered to escort him. At the court-martial, Durotte was found guilty of attacking Olevia, but in the end the finding was disapproved and his sentence reduced.[46]

An equally dangerous disagreement took place in July 1869, also at Fort Quitman, between Private John Baptiste of the Ninth Cavalry's I Troop and his company's Corporal Taylor, which similarly led to a court-martial. On this occasion, Baptiste was driving a team of unruly mules carrying a load of wood when he stopped briefly at his quarters to get a drink of water. Apparently Taylor, who had given Baptiste the job to do in the first place, thought the private was neglecting his duty, and confronted him shortly after Baptiste got the team moving again. According to Baptiste, he never heard Corporal Taylor order him to stop the team, which he characterized at the trial as "wild," "green," and hard to control. In contrast, Taylor said Baptiste heard but refused to stop the team and, instead, cursed Taylor saying, "You are the damndest fool I ever saw, to come down and talk to a man because he stopped in his quarters for water," adding, "I'll be God damned if I stop my team." It is impossible to know who was telling the truth; what is clear is that one or more of the mules promptly ran right over Corporal Taylor. Although he does not seem to have been badly injured, the court found in Taylor's favor and ordered Baptiste dishonorably discharged.[47]

Black enlisted men on the frontier who shared the same rank got into fights with each other, too, as was the case with Privates Robert Scott and Reuben Ash of the Tenth Cavalry's D Troop. In December 1869, Ash appeared before a court-martial convened at Fort Sill to answer the charge that he had tried to kill Scott after the two had gotten into a dispute over a pair of trousers, which Ash claimed Scott stole. Ash might have succeeded in shooting Scott dead but was prevented from doing so by Sergeant William West, who seized Ash's loaded carbine just as he pulled the trigger and sent the charge into the air. In the end, Ash was found not guilty, and Scott came before another court on the charge of stealing Ash's pants (among other things). He, too, was found not guilty.[48]

In contrast with Ash and Scott, who escaped punishment for their dangerous squabbling, Private William C. Alexander of the Tenth Cavalry's L Troop was found guilty of the charge that he did "follow, attack, assault, and beat with rocks and stones, the person of Private William H. Miller," also of L Troop, "without just cause or provocation." Apparently, Alexander had determined to steal Miller's pay from him; when he attacked Miller, Alexander injured him so severely that Miller could no longer perform his duties as a soldier. Found guilty, Alexander was dishonorably discharged and sentenced to imprisonment at hard labor for eighteen months.[49]

Disagreements among black Regulars arose from a host of causes and circumstances; one common source of tension was the men's conflicts over women, with whom contact was clearly (and no doubt frustratingly) limited, especially at remote frontier locations. In May 1871, at Fort Quitman, Private James Fisher and Sergeant James W. Bush (the USCT veteran mentioned earlier), both of the Ninth Cavalry's I Troop, came to blows after Bush and another of the regiment's noncommissioned officers, one Sergeant Gordon, found Fisher hanging out at the home of a Mexican woman who lived near the fort and with whom Gordon claimed to have a personal relationship, which the woman herself denied. Hoping to avoid trouble, Fisher returned to camp, but the following day, the still angry Gordon provoked a dispute with Fisher while Fisher was in the company kitchen attempting to complete his various chores for the day. Soon Bush also became involved, calling Fisher a "black son of a bitch" (Bush, of course, was also black) and knocking him to the floor. To defend himself, Fisher grabbed an ax that was hanging on the kitchen door, hitting Bush "a light lick," or so he later claimed. Yet another black noncommissioned officer in the regiment, Sergeant Andrew Carter, grabbed the ax from Fisher, but in doing so banged himself with the handle over his left eye. The potentially tragic fight came to a close with minimal injuries. In a subsequent court-martial, Fisher was found guilty of a series of charges pertaining to the events, though how he was punished for his offenses is not known.[50]

Negotiating the complex interpersonal dynamics of the mixed racial and ethnic environment in which they found themselves, while at the same time learning about military life, discipline, and order, proved more difficult for some new black Regulars than for others, though probably no more so overall than for white soldiers. Not long after his enlistment in 1867, Private William Alexander of D Troop, Tenth Cavalry, was court-martialed and sentenced to ten days' punishment— sitting on the head of a barrel in clear view of his fellow soldiers from 9 a.m. to 4 p.m. each day—for selling his government-issued overcoat to buy a jug of whiskey. At Fort Gibson in Indian Territory, Private John Burns of Company C, Twenty-fifth Infantry, paid a stern price for demanding a meal at an irregular hour: when Burns attempted to get the company cook, Private James Jones, to provide him with his midday meal after the others had already eaten, Private Jones rightly refused. In response, Private Burns cursed the cook, brandishing a razor and threatening to hurt him. A court-martial found Burns guilty of "conduct to the prejudice of good order" in the regiment and sentenced him to four months' confinement and forfeiture of pay for the same period. At Fort Brown, Texas, Private John H. Williams of the Ninth Cavalry's G Troop simply wandered away without leave from his post as sentinel over the troop's horses while the horses were quietly grazing. Rather than spending time with the horses, Private Williams seems to have sought some time—"one hour, more or less"—with one of the regiment's laundresses. When he came before a court-martial three months later, Williams offered no defense of his actions and was found guilty, fined four months' pay, and sentenced to confinement at hard labor for that same period. Being lax in guarding a regiment's animals from thieves was a persistent problem, which some new soldiers seem to have had ongoing difficulty recognizing: in September 1869 at Fort Sill, in Indian Territory, Corporal Robert Anderson of the Tenth Cavalry (B Troop) had similarly failed in his charge to guard the troop's horses, allowing the sentinel on duty to walk away from the herd and take up a leisurely conversation with him under a tree.[51]

Clearly, as they moved out on to the western frontier, soldiers in the new black regiments necessarily devoted considerable time and energy to working out the details of living peacefully and productively together and with their white officers and the local civilians. Undoubtedly, the inevitable isolation and frequent boredom of frontier service made interpersonal relations more difficult, especially when combined with the challenges of coming to grips with military discipline and military life generally. Some new soldiers in the black regiments never did manage to adjust, and found their way out at the end of their terms of service or through dishonorable discharges. Desertion also offered a potential means of escape, although as Senator Benjamin Wade had noted in 1866, with regard to the USCT troops serving on occupation duty, the desertion rates of black Regulars were significantly lower than the rates for white soldiers during this period.

Still, some recruits took what seemed (but rarely proved to be) the easy way out. Such was the case with the Tenth Cavalry's Privates James Reed and Frank Wilson, who were caught trying to board an eastbound train at Hays City, Kansas, in late May 1868. In July 1869, Private Wesley Abbott also tried to desert the Tenth Cavalry; when he was caught at Leavenworth City, Kansas, a year later, he pleaded guilty. Echoing the complaints, if not the attempted solution, of other black Regulars, Abbott insisted that it was the harsh treatment he had received at the hands of his black noncommissioned officers that had driven him off. In a written statement he prepared in conjunction with his August 1870 court-martial, Abbott declared, "I enlisted with the firm determination to do my duty and serve my time but was so brutally treated by the non commissioned officers . . . for no offense whatever . . . that I determined to escape from their clutches." It is quite possible, of course, that Abbott was just not prepared for the rigors of military discipline. In any case, he was found guilty, and in the end paid a high price for his decision to run away. Although he pleaded for a light sentence, the court dishonorably discharged him, denied him all back pay, and imprisoned him at hard labor at Fort Leavenworth for a year, during which time a weight was attached to his left leg with a five-foot-long chain. The court also demanded that Abbott be branded on the left hip with a 1.5-inch-long letter D, a brutal punishment to which white deserters from the army were also subjected.[52]

When Private Jackson Askins of E Troop, Ninth Cavalry, was brought before a court-martial at Fort Clark and charged with desertion, he explained that his decision to abscond was rooted in his inability to get along with a superior officer, in this case, his troop's white commander, one Captain Hooker. According to Askins, Captain Hooker had more than once informed him, for whatever reasons, "I do not want you in my company." Finally, Askins had decided to take Hooker at his word, leaving his troop and his regiment behind and taking a job in Austin. It was only after several months that Askins was arrested, at which point Hooker, who had known all along where to find him, preferred charges. At his trial Askins insisted that over the course of his three years of service he had "endeavoured to be a good soldier and never did the idea of deserting enter my head . . . [until] I was forced by my Company Commander [and] positively ordered by him to leave the company and encampment." Only then did he leave, he continued, knowing that if he did not, Hooker "would make it so hard for me that it would be worse than dying to serve out the balance of my time in the service." The unsympathetic court found Askins guilty and dishonorably discharged him, adding a sentence of two years' confinement at hard labor, with forfeiture of pay during that period. But a subsequent review of the court's proceedings and the evidence led to Askins's exoneration—presumably on the basis of corroborating material pertaining to Captain Hooker's active dislike for him—and he was returned to duty.[53]

As it turns out, though, just about a month later, Private Askins was in trouble again, this time for "deliberately and with malicious intent" setting loose two of E Troop's horses, which he then allegedly allowed "to run at large, thereby endangering their safety and that of the other horses in the stables," and also for using "violent, profane, abusive, and obscene language" when speaking with Private McElroy McGill. McGill was on duty guarding the E Troop's stables and demanded that Askins go and retrieve the horses. According to Askins, E Troop's commander—most likely still Captain Hooker—had told him to leave the horses alone. Then, when Private McGill told him to go get them, Askins weighed his options and initially decided to do as his company commander had told him. At this point, Private McGill tried to strike a bargain: if Askins would admit to having let the horses loose in the first place, McGill would not report Askins to Hooker. Once again Askins weighed his options and finally decided to "confess." Askins was arrested immediately. At his court-martial, Askins was found guilty, fined, and sentenced to prison. As happened in his previous trial, however, a subsequent review overturned the verdict and sentence and restored Askins to duty. Private Askins may well have had difficulty staying out of trouble, but it seems that on balance those who took ultimate responsibility for judging his behavior determined that his weaknesses as a soldier were less significant than his strengths.[54]

It must be noted that the complicated challenges black enlisted men faced in adjusting to postwar military service at places like Fort Davis and elsewhere on the frontier were compounded by their regular exposure to devastating illness and injury. Soon after Lieutenant Colonel Merritt and the first four troops of the Ninth Cavalry arrived, for example, Fort Davis experienced a medical crisis as a result of rampant scurvy and dysentery. That August, Texas and Louisiana had also been struck by yellow fever, and dysentery with its accompanying diarrhea remained frequent throughout the years the fort was in operation, exacerbated by periodic smallpox outbreaks. Some soldiers, like Private Silas Jones of Grierson's Tenth Cavalry, fell sick repeatedly: over the course of his thirty years in the army, Jones's medical record indicates that he suffered from a host of complaints, including acute diarrhea, headache, "catarrh," mumps, colic, orchitis (a testicular inflammation), constipation, tonsillitis, bronchitis, rheumatism, and neuralgia, among other conditions. None of this, however, interfered with Jones's determination to remain in the service, or with his being recognized upon his discharge as "an honest and faithful soldier." Black Regulars, like soldiers in all times and places, also

"Marching on the Mountains," by Frederic Remington. Originally published in *Century Magazine* in 1889.

suffered from a variety of sexually transmitted diseases, including gonorrhea and syphilis. For some, like Private Lewellen Young, who was discharged on account of "syphilitic mania" and committed to a government asylum in Washington, D.C., disease brought a painful end to their military careers, if not their lives.[55]

If staying healthy was a perennial problem at the widely scattered western posts where black Regulars were stationed, so was sustaining a sufficient supply of rations, not just for the soldiers but also for the cavalry horses and livestock on which the men, in turn, depended. According to one source, at Fort Davis a cavalry horse required fourteen pounds of hay and twelve pounds of grain each day. As for the men, they subsisted largely on the same sorts of rations that had sustained their Civil War predecessors, including hash, a stew known unappealingly as "slumgullion," baked beans, hardtack, salt bacon, coffee, bread, and beef. On a typical day at Fort Davis, the baker George Bentley and others prepared at least 560 loaves of bread for the soldiers stationed there.[56]

Keeping isolated posts such as Fort Davis supplied with even the nutritional basics was an ongoing challenge, and learning to endure shortages was, for both animals and men, a necessity. Hardly unrelated was the matter of maintaining good mounts for the cavalrymen, which sometimes posed serious problems: in October 1868, Benjamin Grierson received a letter from Lieutenant Henry Alvord, the Tenth Cavalry's adjutant, who had been inspecting the portion of the regiment stationed at Fort Arbuckle in Indian Territory. Although he had few complaints about the troopers themselves, Alvord expressed considerable concern to his commanding officer about the horses: "I shall condemn at least fifteen horses," he wrote, "and leave several for another time. Seven have died since you were here." Six months later Grierson wrote to his wife, Alice, from Camp Wichita in Kansas, indicating that problems similar to those that Alvord had addressed earlier remained to be solved:

A CAMPFIRE SKETCH.

"A Campfire Sketch," by Frederic Remington. Originally published in *Century Magazine* in 1889.

"Having no forage I have had to keep the Cavalry horses out 12 to 13 miles from Camp, grazing night and day in order to keep them alive, or a portion of them rather as many have died for want of food." In addition to the horses, Grierson worried about the manpower drain that having the horses so far from camp entailed. "Have had an officer and about 50 men constantly in charge of herding them," he wrote.[57]

Moreover, life and work at a frontier post, even before a soldier engaged in any government-sanctioned fighting, could be dangerous. While serving at Fort Davis, Private Andrew Emery—who spent part of his time as the post's librarian—was in the process of helping to herd about 160 of the regiment's horses when a number of them were inexplicably spooked and two of them ran over him, injuring his back, his shoulder, and his head, knocking him unconscious and causing internal damage. In the aftermath of the incident, Emery spent about four months in the post hospital. Even after his release from the hospital, he remained severely debilitated, surely contributing to his decision to leave the army sooner than he might have otherwise. Nevertheless, when Emery applied later for a government pension on the basis of his injuries, the regimental chaplain T. H. Weaver appended a letter of support describing Emery as having been "thoroughly reliable in every respect," and urged that the government reward him for "his faithfulness as a soldier and his worth as a man."[58]

Similarly, when the Tenth's Henry Walker applied for a federal pension, he did so—like Emery—on the basis of injuries he had sustained while on duty, in his case working as a blacksmith. In the course of his work, which included turning out horseshoes and a host of other regimental equipment, a piece of iron struck Walker in the right eye, permanently blinding him and causing his left eye to suffer in its attempt to compensate. Private Charles M. Farrell of the Tenth Cavalry's M Troop repeatedly saw hard action against hostile Indians after his enlistment in September 1867, but it was while he was off duty hunting quail in Texas that he lost his left hand as the result of an accident with his shotgun. Private William Allen, who served with the Tenth Cavalry at Fort Davis, also suffered an accidental gunshot wound when his revolver fell out of his pocket, hit the edge of a table, and fired, sending a bullet through his chest and breaking two ribs. And at some point during his enlistment in the Tenth Cavalry's C Troop, Saddler George France, a former slave from Virginia, was kicked so hard in the leg by a cranky company mule while he was on horseback driving the mules to a watering hole that he not only fractured his shin but also fell from the saddle, hurt his back, and had to be carried back to camp on a stretcher. The extremes of weather on the plains created their own problems, too. The frostbite on his feet that Private Benjamin Bard of the Tenth Cavalry's H Troop suffered while doing guard duty for a wagon train on a particularly stormy winter night led to a hospital stay of more than three months' duration, followed by the premature end of his military career.[59]

Joining the military posed many dangers for black enlisted men. Long after the new black regiments were formed, some enlisted men still struggled, and some failed. At his 1885 court-martial for desertion, Private John Alexander of D Troop, Ninth Cavalry, explained that he was young, and he was sorry, but he just "did not find the army what I expected it to be . . . so I decided to leave." One cannot help wondering whether the difficulty of making sense of military life on the nation's frontier contributed to the desperate decision of the Twenty-fifth Infantry's Private Walker Brown to commit suicide by shooting himself.[60] Still, it bears noting that, unlike this young man, most men who enlisted in the black regiments did not give up, did not desert, did not express their frustrations in violent ways against their comrades-in-arms either black or white, did not, in short, buckle under the myriad stern challenges that postwar military service presented to them. Rather, they worked long and hard to transform themselves into good and disciplined soldiers, companies, and regiments, and to fulfill their new and complex responsibilities.

✤3✤

Doing the Nation's Work
on the Western Frontier

Once we were happy in our own country and we were seldom hungry, for then the two-leggeds and the four-leggeds lived together like relatives, and there was plenty for them and for us. But the Wasichus [white people] came, and they have made little islands for us and other little islands for the four-leggeds, and always these islands are becoming smaller, for around them surges the gnawing flood of the Wasichu; and it is dirty with lies and greed.

—Sioux leader Black Elk (1932)

THE STRENGTHENING OF THE FORT SYSTEM IN TEXAS, AND INDEED all along the nation's western frontier, and the posting of active-duty soldiers at Fort Davis and a multitude of other military installations in this vast region, constituted a key component of the army's response to its postwar charge. Now that the Confederate rebellion had been suppressed and the South had been, in theory at least, reclaimed for the Union, a task of primary strategic importance for the united nation—though, in the eyes of many then and now, a morally questionable one—was to "pacify" the remaining unsettled land and Native people located within the boundaries of the United States in preparation for the advance of "American civilization." The black Regulars were to play a key role in this process.[1]

In his early-1866 argument for enlisting black soldiers in postwar Regular army regiments, Senator James Henry Lane of Kansas had emphasized their fundamental capacity for military service, as demonstrated by the USCT during the Civil War, as well as their supposed tolerance of high heat and humidity. At the same time, Lane had insisted that black soldiers could be put to good use preparing and defending a path for the construction of the transcontinental railroad lines that were deemed necessary not just for commerce but for dispersing the Native people who continued to resist civilization's advance. According to Lane, black Regulars, like their white counterparts in the postwar army, could participate effectively in securing the West for settlement and for what the black Fortieth Infantry's first colonel, Nelson A. Miles, would later describe as "the transformation of the wild wastes and the desolate, unproductive regions of our country to the scenes of vast industries, progressive civilization and universal prosperity." Senator Henry Wilson of Massachusetts agreed with these assessments. "We have some colored regiments west of the Mississippi that were raised in Kentucky," he noted, referring to units of USCT veterans still in the service at the time. These veterans, Wilson pointed out, had proven themselves to be "admirable riders" who "understand the management of horses as well as any men in this country." Given their skills on horseback, not to mention the low rates of desertion among black enlisted men, Wilson reasoned, did it not make sense to employ black cavalry regiments on frontier duty? "I think," he argued, "it is a great matter of economy to put some of these colored regiments into the field in the Indian country, in the mountains, and in sections of the country where white men desert," in part because white men are drawn "to the mines where temptation is very great."[2]

Clearly, although the July 1866 act that restructured the Regular army for postwar service defined the institution it was rebuilding as the "Military Peace Establishment of the United States," the end of the Civil War did not find the nation entirely at peace. In the spring of 1865, even as the federal armies celebrated their victory over the Confederate rebellion in the Grand Review in Washington, civilian and military leaders alike were busy pondering the dangers posed to the nation's security and progress by the nearly 300,000 Native people still present within its borders. The federal government considered roughly two-thirds of these Native people "friendly," or at least unlikely to cause much trouble to the government, the military, or the frontierspeople, if only because their resistance to white encroachment had been broken down steadily through treaties and assimilation. At the same time, the government—specifically the army and the Department of the Interior, which had housed the Bureau of Indian Affairs since 1849—deemed about 100,000 Indians "hostile" on account of their refusal to accept containment of any sort, even when they had signed treaties in which they had, on paper at least, "promised to dwell forever in peace with the white man and with one another and to allow the white man to build roads and forts in their country."[3]

But these Indians never understood or accepted the concept of dwelling "in peace" with white people as also encompassing the obliteration of their cultures and communities, or the surrendering of their independence. In short, some 100,000 Indians bore the label "hostile" because of their insistence on remaining free, and their determination to counter the spread of "American civilization," with all of its trappings, which they knew would ensure their own destruction. In 1865 on the Great Plains, the Sioux, Cheyenne, Arapaho, Kiowa, and Comanche still had the capability to resist westward settlement. In the Rocky Mountains, the Nez Percé, Ute, and Bannock did as well. The Paiute and Modoc remained strong in the Northwest, and in the Southwest the Apache had yet to be suppressed. By mid-1867, just two years after the Civil War ended, and while the Reconstruction South, in actuality, remained thoroughly unpacified—yet another race riot occurred in Mobile, Alabama, that May—more than half of the army (including some 4,000 black and white soldiers who were stationed in western Texas alone) could be found on duty in the West in connection with the effort to subdue the Native people once and for all. The portion of the U.S. army dedicated to western duty continued to climb in the years ahead, approaching 100 percent even before Rutherford B. Hayes's ascension to the presidency in March 1877 led to the complete withdrawal of U.S. forces from the South.[4]

In short, the U.S. army's success in subduing the Confederacy on the battlefield did not complete the federal government's struggle for hegemony on the continent, or the final consolidation of America's nationhood. As one writer in the *Army and Navy Journal* commented as early as July 1865, "The question of the treatment of our old and natural enemies, the Indians, begins again to assume the importance and interest which it lost when the strength and energy of the Nation were engrossed with the war against the Rebellion." Looking toward the future of the country, another asked, "Where will be the Indian at the dawn of the new century? How many tribes will represent his family on the continent?" And he added hopefully, "This present attack on him, or of him on us,—as you choose to put it—may prove 'the beginning of the end' to his race." Just about a year later, on June 2, 1866, still another correspondent insisted to the *Journal*, "It is quite time that the policy proper to be pursued toward the savages who roam on the vast plains and mountains of the West should be thoroughly discussed and righteously settled. There is scarcely any practical question of our public policy that more imperatively demands attention."[5]

It bears noting that the conflict between the U.S. army and the Native Americans, which dated back to the earliest days of the nation's history, had by no means been put on hold during the Civil War. Indeed, during those years, federal soldiers had clashed repeatedly with the Indians in frontier areas. Prewar friction, writes the historian Francis Paul Prucha, was "aggravated by the weakening of federal authority in the West as regular troops were withdrawn and replaced by volunteers, who were often few in number, inexperienced in Indian control, and too frequently imbued with frontier hostility toward Indians." In some cases, wartime clashes between the army and the Native people were directly related to the federal attempt to suppress the Confederate rebellion, as in the battle of Pea Ridge, Arkansas, in March 1862, which preserved Missouri for the Union. At Pea Ridge, federal troops confronted a mixed force of Texas cavalrymen and their Cherokee and Creek allies from the Indian Territory. While the federals were victorious, many of them left the battleground stunned by their first and quite unexpected encounter with Native warfare, which included scalpings and mutilations of the bodies of the federal wounded and dead.[6]

More often during the war, conflict between the U.S. army and the Native Americans arose from the federal government's ongoing struggle to lay claim to contested land that various groups of Indians argued was still—or should be—theirs. One such eruption came to be known as the Great Sioux Uprising. Minnesota, with a white population of approximately 200,000 (most of them German and Scandinavian immigrants), had become a state in 1858, but much of its land still served as the hunting and trapping grounds of the Sioux, Winnebago, and Chippewa. Indian-white tensions had been rising for some time because of persistent white encroachment, exacerbated by an untold number of broken government promises of remuneration and restitution—in the form of money, food, and supplies—for the Indians' reluctant cessions of territory. In mid-August 1862, Sioux patience collapsed. A quarrel between four young Sioux hunters and a white shopkeeper in Acton, a frontier settlement the Sioux men passed on the way to their home, escalated into violence, including the fatal shooting of a teenage white girl by one of the Indians. Word of what had happened at Acton spread quickly, as did the violence. Panic, fury, and a desire for revenge on both sides engulfed southern Minnesota over the course of the next several weeks. Enraged Native war parties attacked white settlers, destroying their property, burning them in their homes, taking captives, raping young women and girls, and chopping their victims to pieces while the army attempted to get the situation under control. Whites fled in terror, many of them seeking safety at the army's Fort Ridgely.[7]

Meanwhile, thanks in no small part to sensational reports in the nation's press, news of the events in Minnesota spread around the country. Perhaps predictably, eleven hundred miles away in Washington, D.C., false rumors circulated of a "Confederate-fomented diversion" on the Northern Plains, although the Confederacy had nothing to do with the "combination of ineptitude and deceit, cultural and racial arrogance, and obscene cheating and greed" of the federal government, white traders, and frontier settlers that had "pushed large numbers of the Sioux—especially the proud young warriors—beyond their limits of endurance." In any case, hundreds of whites and Native Americans in Minnesota were dead by the time peace, of a sort, was restored in late September 1862, thanks to a combination of federal military might (including officers and men from five Minnesota infantry regiments as well as state militia units and other volunteers), negotiation, dissension among the different Indian groups involved, and exhaustion on both sides. In December, thirty-eight Sioux were executed in connection with the uprising, and in March 1863, the Sioux were, by congressional order, removed beyond the borders of the state to lands in what would become Nebraska and South Dakota. In the weeks, months, and years ahead, violence erupted again on the Northern Plains as the frustrations and tensions expressed in Minnesota found new outlets elsewhere.[8]

One of the most grotesque examples of conflict between the U.S. military and the Native Americans during the Civil War took place in the Colorado Territory in late November 1864. Since 1858, when gold was discovered in the region, more than 100,000 white prospectors had crowded into Colorado. For the most part, the Arapaho and Cheyenne, whose lands these migrants and other settlers passed through, let the intruders go peacefully. In addition, in February 1861, the year Colorado officially became a U.S. territory, a number of Cheyenne and Arapaho chiefs who understood the long-term implications of the whites' rush to the region signed the Treaty of Fort Wise, in which they ceded a vast amount of land to the federal government. In return they accepted the promise of a small but permanent "homeland" in the southeastern portion of Colorado and fifteen years' worth of annuities, a portion of which was to be used for the supplies they would need in their quest to become, like many white Americans, successful farmers.[9]

What the Native signers of the Fort Wise treaty seem to have misunderstood is that Americans—government officials as well as miners and settlers—never meant to let them continue to hunt beyond the bounds of their new "homeland." As this became clear, U.S.-Indian friction increased. At the same time, disease and hunger—in large part a consequence of the declining buffalo herds and the poor quality of the land on which the government expected the Native people to live—contributed to worsening conditions for the Indians, leading some to engage in raids on white property. To make things even more difficult, after 1862, in the wake of the Sioux uprising in Minnesota, rumors spread among whites in the Colorado Territory that the Cheyenne and Arapaho planned an alliance with the Sioux farther east to initiate a full-scale war. In April 1864, the heightened anxieties exploded in gunfire near Fremont's Orchard, on the South Platte River, between Lieutenant Clark Dunn and a detachment of soldiers from the First Colorado Cavalry and a group of Cheyenne who the lieutenant later claimed had stolen livestock. There were fewer than a dozen casualties, half on each side, but the fragile general peace was shattered.[10]

Over the next six months, additional violent incidents took place, stoking the rage of Colonel John M. Chivington, who was in overall command of the Colorado volunteers and who believed passionately and unswervingly that the Indians were at fault in every case. Finally, Chivington lost his temper. Early in the morning on November 29, 1864, he took about seven hundred soldiers from the First and Third Colorado Cavalry Regiments and marched them to the sizable camp of the Cheyenne chief Black Kettle, a longtime advocate of peace between the whites and Indians and an original signer of the Fort Wise treaty.

Black Kettle and his band of five to six hundred Cheyenne were camped on what was known as Sand Creek, where the presence of a large American flag flying from a lodgepole indicated that the Indians there considered themselves friendly to the government and its civilian and military agents. Indeed, Black Kettle himself, alerted to the troops' arrival, called out to the Cheyenne to remain peaceful and clearly indicated to the troops, by displaying an additional white flag, that they did not plan to fight. Yet over the next four hours Chivington and his soldiers killed, and in some cases—having appropriated some of the Natives' own techniques—scalped and mutilated perhaps as many as two hundred Indians, more than half of whom were women and children. "Lack of discipline, combined with heavy drinking of whiskey during the night ride, cowardice, and poor marksmanship among the Colorado troops" allowed some of the Cheyenne, including Black Kettle, to get away. The troops themselves suffered only nine dead and thirty-eight wounded.[11]

Once the firing ceased, the soldiers ravaged and torched the village, took possession of the livestock, and searched for the runaways. Subsequently the troops made for Denver, where they were received as heroes and treated to a parade through town. Learning of Chivington's actions, the U.S. Congress's Joint Committee on the Conduct of the War, to its credit, expressed horror, declaring that Chivington had "deliberately planned and executed a foul and dastardly massacre which would have disgraced the veriest savage among those who were the victims of his cruelty." As was true in the aftermath of the Great Sioux Uprising, repercussions in relations between the U.S. and the Native people from the Sand Creek Massacre, as it came to be known, echoed for many years across the Great Plains.[12]

In light of such events—for which they appropriately feared that Native Americans would retaliate—and their desire to continue expanding the nation's sovereignty over the land and people encompassed by its borders, key players in the federal government and the army after the Civil War understood the military to have two intertwined and inseparable goals. One was sustaining the United States' fragile victory over the Confederate rebellion in the South; the other was subduing the Indians who obstructed national consolidation in Texas, on the Plains, and elsewhere. As for whether black soldiers had any role to play in this nation-building work, that question was settled in the affirmative by the 1866 Army Reorganization Act. At the same time, however, despite Frederick Douglass's 1863 pronouncement regarding the essential link between black men's military service on behalf of the nation and their rights to full citizenship, it remained uncertain what these new responsibilities meant in practice for their own and their community's social and political advancement, and for their claims to equality in postwar America.

As we have seen, not long after Appomattox, increasingly vigorous Southern white opposition made occupation duty for the black soldiers in the former Confederacy less and less tenable. To send the black Regulars west, therefore, must have seemed to many not just a practical maneuver but also a perfect solution for rising racial tensions in the South. Moreover, Native tempers in the West were already heating up, and it was clear that the black Regulars would have plenty of work to do. Indeed, as early as the summer of 1866, just as Grierson and the others were beginning to recruit men for the new regiments, trouble was already brewing along the Bozeman Trail in Wyoming and Montana, which was used by gold seekers and frontier settlers. Sioux, Cheyenne, and Arapaho in the area, who were determined to close the trail and thereby stymie white advancement across their valued lands, took to attacking both civilians and soldiers along its course at every opportunity. That fall, the Indians attacked in the area surrounding Fort Phil Kearny, which was being built along the trail at the eastern base of the Bighorn Mountains, in the heart of the prime hunting grounds of the Sioux and Cheyenne. They also began stalking supply trains that were bearing wood for the post's construction as well as stampeding stock and attacking anyone who was caught outside the fort's protection.[13]

After several months of frustration, in December 1866, just a few months before the new Ninth Cavalry received its orders to reoccupy

Fort Davis, Colonel Henry B. Carrington, commanding the white Eighteenth Infantry at Fort Kearny, attempted to strike back against the Indians' persistent depredations. To do so, he sent Captain William J. Fetterman and a detachment of around eighty soldiers, two additional officers, and two civilians to go to the relief of a supply train that the Indians had attacked. In consequence of his bumbling efforts, however, a force of several hundred Sioux ambushed and, in less than an hour, killed and mutilated the bodies of Fetterman and his entire command, the Indians taking about two hundred casualties themselves. Like the Sand Creek Massacre of November 1864, word of the "Fetterman disaster"—which the Sioux called the Battle of the Hundred Slain—spread quickly, provoking white rage and inspiring new degrees of determination among those who aimed to get the Indians under control. White settlers and military men cried out for retaliation, and in some cases for the complete extermination of the Native people. General Sherman called for a response characterized by "vindictive earnestness." One direct consequence of the Fetterman disaster was that hundreds of recently enlisted black Regulars—including the Ninth Cavalry—now went west, to "pacify" angry Indians such as those who had wiped out Fetterman's command, despite their being people of color like themselves. "How the red men and the black will get along together, we shall discover in due time," declared the *Army and Navy Journal*, acknowledging that the U.S. army was "pitting color against color with a vengeance."[14]

Over the next two decades and more, black Regulars who were sent west worked hard and at great peril to their own lives participating in actions associated with all of the major conflicts between the army and the Indians in the regions where they were posted, including "General Hancock's War," which amounted to a series of clumsy and ineffective defensive actions against Native raiders in and around Kansas in the spring of 1867; the various conflicts with the Sioux, Cheyenne, and Arapaho in west Texas and across the Southern Plains in 1868–69; the Red River War of 1874–75 against the Kiowa, Comanche, Arapaho, and southern Cheyenne in the Texas Panhandle and the Indian Territory, which ultimately broke the back of Indian resistance in this region; the contest with the Apache leader Victorio and his followers extending from the late 1870s until his death in October 1880; and the pursuit and capture of Geronimo in the mid-1880s, which brought an end to Apache resistance. They also fought with smaller, less organized, but equally angry groups of Indians on a regular basis when they went on scouts and patrols, on mapping expeditions, or simply on assignments to guard the mail or the railroad, or to escort overland migrants, or even when the soldiers went hunting.[15]

Indeed, it was not long before some of the earliest groups of black Regulars dispatched to the frontier had their first costly experiences in trying to fulfill their obligation to "pacify" the Native people who continued to resist the nation's expansion and their own communities' constriction. "That there will be a general bloody Indian war this Spring and Summer you may rest assured," one writer had warned the *Army and Navy Journal* in May 1867. That very summer, John Randall, an original member of the black Tenth Cavalry's G Troop, was wounded in action against some Cheyenne near Fort Hays, Kansas. Two months later, in October, the *Journal* issued another warning. "The Indians," it reported, "demand the discontinuance of roads through their country, and the removal of military posts and white settlers." And sure enough, that very month, a party of Kickapoo ambushed and killed two soldiers from the Ninth Cavalry's D Troop—Corporal Emanuel (or possibly Samuel) Wright and Private Eldridge T. Jones—while they were escorting the mail to Fort Stockton. Two months later, in December 1867, a detachment from the Ninth's F Troop successfully rescued a stagecoach heading east from El Paso that was being attacked by about a hundred Mescalero Apache, a confrontation in which one soldier was killed and four horses were wounded. Just days later, a motley group of approximately nine hundred Indians, Mexicans, and disgruntled whites attacked K Troop's encampment about 170 miles from Fort Davis at Fort Lancaster; the resulting three-hour fight left twenty Indians dead, many more of them wounded, and three of K Troop's enlisted men missing.[16]

By the summer of 1867, in fact, fighting was underway all across the Great Plains, and black Regulars found themselves in the thick of the conflict. That summer, the black Thirty-eighth Infantry's commander, Colonel William B. Hazen, wrote to the *Army and Navy Journal* warning that "the Indians now, feeling pressure equally from the west and east, seeing roads and lines of forts run across all their country, have become desperate and determined to fight it out. . . . This [is] the beginning of the great and last Indian struggle for his existence." In conjunction with this "great and last Indian struggle," which would occupy the army for the next twenty-five years, Benjamin Grierson now ordered three companies of his Tenth Cavalry from Fort Leavenworth, Kansas, into Indian Territory. On Sheridan's orders, he sent still more of his men, including the Tenth's F Troop, deeper into Kansas, where it was well known that hostile Indians were planning to make a stand. Soon after the Tenth Cavalry's F Troop reached its Kansas post, on August 1, 1867, the company, commanded by Captain George Armes—who, a dozen years later, was responsible for the death of an enlisted man, Private William Simmons, whom he locked in the barracks when Simmons was suffering from dysentery—fought a six-hour fight with approximately seventy-five Cheyenne. This battle produced the regiment's first combat death, that of the free-born Pennsylvanian private William Christy. According to one recollection of the events, Christy, an original member of the Tenth, was scalped and his scalp then "tied to a lance" and waved threateningly by one of the Cheyenne at the remaining troops, as if to warn them of their own danger.[17]

Over the course of their postwar service on the frontier, black soldiers occasionally found themselves collaborating with their white counterparts in their actions against the Indians, and sometimes they did even more, as was the case for a group of Tenth Cavalry troopers in the fall of 1868. On that occasion, Major George Alexander Forsyth, a

Civil War veteran and former aide to Sheridan, was in command of a company of fifty white frontiersmen who were camped along the south bank of the Arikaree fork of the Republican River, about sixty miles northwest of the western railhead of the Kansas Pacific, just across the border from Kansas in Colorado Territory. Many of Forsyth's motley but all-white command were "veterans of the Union or Confederate army, seasoned plainsmen, and average to excellent marksmen," armed with Spencer repeating rifles and revolvers. Forsyth himself later recalled that he had

> little trouble in obtaining capable and competent men for my new command. Hundreds of men who had served through the bitter civil strife of 1861 to 1865, either for or against the government, had flocked to the frontier and were willing, and even anxious, to assist in punishing the Indians, while many a frontiersman was only too glad to have an opportunity to settle an old score against the savages.

It seems that one thing many white veterans of the blue and gray could agree on soon after Appomattox was the need to "punish" the continent's Native people.[18]

The immediate task facing George Forsyth's command in the late summer of 1868 was to help secure the railroad line. Ground for the Union Pacific had been broken in 1863 in Omaha as well as in Sacramento, where the Central Pacific had begun heading east to meet it. By the time Forsyth's men took up their position on the Arikaree, the Kansas Pacific extended over three hundred miles along a path from the eastern border of the state to the vicinity of Fort Wallace. Meanwhile, plans were maturing in the army for a winter campaign against the Cheyenne, Arapaho, and Sioux, who still ranged across the Southern Plains. In conjunction with these plans, Sheridan had also concentrated the troopers of Custer's white Seventh Cavalry on the Arkansas River, less than a hundred miles south of the railroad. "We all agreed that the nomad Indians" in the region "should be removed from the vicinity of the two great railroads then in rapid construction," Sherman recalled in his memoirs. They needed to "be localized on one or other of the two," actually three, "great reservations south of Kansas and north of Nebraska." The reservation system to which Sherman referred aimed to place the Indians on specific plots of land where in theory they could live free of any of the vices associated with uncontrolled white intrusion (such as alcohol abuse), while also having the benefits of missionary instruction to help them become Christians, agricultural training to help them become self-sufficient farmers, and clothing, annuities, and other provisions—for a time—to help them get started. In return, the Indians were expected to surrender all rights to any territory they claimed beyond the reservations' boundaries, except for hunting grounds, while they were making the transition to the pastoral life (and while the buffalo lasted). Significantly, the Native people were also expected to halt all acts of resistance against white settlement, the military, and the railroad.[19]

In connection with the plans for the winter campaign and in addition to Sheridan's deploying to the region not just the Seventh Cavalry but also Forsyth and his frontiersmen, Benjamin Grierson had dispatched troopers from his Tenth Cavalry, whose headquarters at the time were over five hundred miles away at Fort Gibson in Indian Territory, to help cover the Republican. Both Grierson and Sheridan knew that many of the Indians who lived in the area were not "ready to abide by the white man's rules." As Forsyth himself explained it, by the late summer of 1868, "the Indians, who had grown confident in their own strength, were greatly exasperated; and the ongoing construction of the Union Pacific Railroad . . . directly through their hunting grounds, drove them almost to frenzy." Raiding parties routinely disrupted the railroad's construction and also caused the loss of settlers' lives and property.[20]

Then, at dawn on September 17, some six or seven hundred Oglala Sioux and Cheyenne surprised Major Forsyth and his frontiersmen in their camp. The Indians were led by a Cheyenne warrior named

Roman Nose, in Forsyth's words, "the very beau ideal of an Indian chief . . . mounted on a large, clean-limbed chestnut horse . . . and save for the crimson silk sash knotted around his waist and his moccasins on his feet, perfectly naked." Some shots were exchanged, but soon Forsyth and his men realized that they were outnumbered and surrounded. In desperation, and having already lost the command's pack mules in the engagement, Forsyth ordered the men to saddle their horses and seek protection on a small, sandy, brush-covered island in the middle of the Arikaree. There over the course of the day the white men, deep in their rifle pits, fended off three frontal charges by the Indians. In the process, however, Forsyth's command sustained roughly 50 percent casualties (six dead and fifteen wounded), and even more among their horses. One man who died in the fight was the Third Infantry's Lieutenant Frederick Beecher, a nephew of Henry Ward Beecher and Harriet Beecher Stowe and a survivor of the Battle of Gettysburg, who had been serving as Forsyth's executive officer. In honor of his death, the battle on September 17, 1868, came to be known as the Battle of Beecher's Island. Roman Nose, too, died in the course of the fighting, along with perhaps a hundred other Indians. Forsyth himself suffered a head wound, a thigh wound, and a broken leg.[21]

By evening on the seventeenth, Forsyth's command was frantic. In addition to coping with their mounting casualties, the surviving white men remained surrounded by hostile warriors, and their rations and medical supplies had run out. Their attackers, at least, had finally stopped shooting. That night two of Forsyth's number—Jack Stilwell and Pierre Trudeau—managed to slip away under cover of darkness. For the next four days, they struggled to make their way on foot back to Fort Wallace, about eighty-five miles away, to get help. Finally, at about noon on the twenty-second, they encountered two black soldiers from the Tenth Cavalry's H Troop who were on a mission carrying dispatches from the fort. Grierson's troopers raced off to find their company and its senior officer, Captain Louis H. Carpenter, who had been with the Tenth Cavalry since its formation. Hearing the news, Carpenter and his men, camped on the Sandy Creek about sixty miles from Fort Wallace, immediately headed out to find Forsyth and his frontiersmen. As one participant in the rescue later recalled, "The whole command was eager to do all that was in their power to crown our efforts with success. Not a man, horse, or mule but did all that was required of him."[22]

Finally, on September 25, eight days after Forsyth and the others had taken cover on the island, Carpenter and thirty of his black soldiers, with a

Battle of Beecher's Island, or "Defeat of Roman Nose by Colonel Forsyth." *Courtesy of the Library of Congress.*

wagon full of food and supplies, found them. The men of the Tenth soon drove the remaining Native attackers away from the stranded white soldiers, who had been surviving the ordeal by eating the flesh of their dead horses and drinking the horses' blood and their own urine. "It is impossible to describe the meeting that now took place," wrote a white survivor of the battle. "Men rushed into each other's arms; some cried, some danced and sang; the wounded set up a faint cheer as they once more saw horsemen among them, realizing that they were saved." Recalled Reuben Waller, a former slave and member of the Tenth Cavalry, "[W]e all cried together as we helped them out of their starving condition."[23]

The situation for Forsyth and his men remained dire: maggots infested the wounds of the injured men and animals, and the strong odor of decay led Carpenter to move the living as far away as possible before beginning to dress their wounds. But the arrival of the black troopers of the Tenth Cavalry meant that the end of the white men's agony was near at hand. Moreover, as another survivor of the battle later recalled, the rescuers' kindness and generosity continued all the way back to the fort, as they shared their rations cheerfully. Major Forsyth, who in a report just a few months earlier had written that "it is a difficult undertaking to make good cavalrymen of colored men and requires labor, patience, and time," may well have thought it was time to revise his opinion. Still, twenty years later in his published recollection of the events of September 1868, Forsyth failed to mention that the Tenth Cavalry's troopers who saved his all-white command were black.[24]

If Forsyth did not divulge his thoughts about the merits of black men's military service for the nation's work in general, or their white comrades in particular, others did, including Henry Carpenter, an enlisted man in the Tenth Cavalry who some months before the events on Beecher's Island had written from Kansas to the *Christian Recorder*, a black newspaper in Philadelphia. Carpenter was deeply concerned about white Americans' refusal to recognize and demonstrate sufficient respect for what black soldiers had continued doing on their behalf, and the nation's, since the Civil War. "It seems," wrote Carpenter, "that some persons try still to make it appear that the colored man is a curse to the country, and try to cheat us out of our rights as citizens. I, for one, feel that I have been wronged, and I appeal to every generous-hearted white whether we have been a curse." Addressing the issue of black men's military service specifically, Carpenter rhetorically demanded to know whether enlistees of the USCT had been conscripted and forced to fight, to which he answered, "No! We offered our services when this once distracted country was in great danger of being overthrown by rebel renegades. . . . We responded to the President's call and rallied round the good old flag!" After the Civil War ended, Carpenter continued, black men such as "Grierson['s] boys in blue" had volunteered again, this time "cheerfully respond[ing] to the call to assist in driving the savage foe from Kansas," in the course of which some had already been killed, many had been wounded, but all had demonstrated their fearlessness. "We have come out to Kansas to fight, and, if need be, to die to save that flag which gave us freedom," and to "defend our white brethren of the far West . . . from the scalping-knife of the blood-thirsty savage." Unfortunately, Carpenter pointed out, such efforts by black soldiers were rarely and insufficiently rewarded: "We know that some white men hate to see us free, but we are free, and will die free." In his mind, the only reward black men should consider acceptable was "universal suffrage," by which he likely meant universal *male* suffrage. "There must," Carpenter concluded, "be no distinction on account of color."[25]

Black soldiers such as Carpenter were hardly alone in continuing to contemplate black Americans' claims to an equal place with whites in the social order. Just a year after the battle on Beecher's Island, Frederick Douglass gave a speech in Boston in which he offered an inclusive vision of a new, post–Civil War America grounded in the principles of universally shared human rights and social justice. "Until recently," Douglass declared, "neither the Indian nor the negro has been treated as part of the body politic. No attempt has been made to inspire either with a sentiment of patriotism." Instead, "the hearts of both races have been diligently sown with the dangerous seeds of discontent and hatred," when both races should be warmly accepted into the embrace of the American national family. Douglass proposed that white Americans in particular should strive toward greater tolerance—especially now that another nonwhite "race" was making its way to the nation's shores. Here Douglass referred to immigrants from China, whose numbers, he predicted, would soon reach to the millions, especially if white Southerners, frustrated by the supposed intractability of the former slaves as laborers, could find a way to cheaply harness Chinese labor instead.[26]

For his part, Douglass saw nothing particularly troubling about Chinese immigration. He declared, "There are such things in the world as human rights," and in his mind Chinese people deserved human rights as much as anyone else did. The key was for Americans of all sorts to rejoice in and make an international example of what he called their "composite nationality." "Our geographical position," Douglass pointed out, "our relation to the outside world, our fundamental principles of government, world-embracing in their scope and character, our vast resources, requiring all manner of labor to develop them, and our already existing . . . population, all conspire to one grand end, and that is, to make us the [best] national illustration of the unity and dignity of the human family that the world has ever seen." America's greatness could best be expressed only by ensuring "perfect civil equality to the people of all races and of all creeds." Civilization itself demanded nothing less. "It is no disparagement to Americans of English descent," Douglass insisted, "to affirm that much of the wealth, leisure, culture, refinement and civilization of the country"—and he might have included "security"—"are due to the arm of the negro," by which he surely meant the labor of black Americans, including black soldiers, in war as well as peace.[27]

In late October of the year Douglass articulated his vision of an inclusive national identity, emphasizing the contributions of black Americans to the nation's ongoing development, detachments from six companies of the Ninth Cavalry, under the command of G Troop's Captain John M. Bacon, participated in an expedition designed explicitly to curb Indian raiding in Texas and implicitly to further the advance of American civilization on the frontier. On this occasion, the black cavalrymen, who were accompanied by some white Fourth Cavalry troopers and twenty Tonkawa Indian scouts (the Army Reorganization Act of 1866 had authorized the army to employ up to a thousand Indian scouts), were caught by surprise while in camp by about five hundred Kiowa and Comanche warriors in an attack that descended into hand-to-hand combat and left several of the soldiers wounded and forty of the Indians killed. Just a couple of months later, six companies of the Ninth Cavalry under the command of D Troop's Captain Francis Dodge rode north from Fort Davis into the Guadalupe Mountains on the Texas–New Mexico border, where they engaged in what might be called a mission of intimidation: they attacked an Apache encampment, killed at least ten of its inhabitants, and captured supplies and about two dozen ponies.[28]

Although many of the expeditions the black Regulars undertook were intended to subdue through violence any Indians deemed hostile, it was hardly uncommon for their efforts to yield only frustration. Indeed, during their years at Fort Davis, black cavalrymen "literally rode their mounts into the ground over thousands of dusty miles in blistering heat, pursuing war parties that seemed everywhere and yet nowhere." Still, even when the results of their labor were not always immediately apparent, their work contributed importantly to the national goals. Black Regulars in Texas, as elsewhere, "sweated, bled, and died to make life and property secure on one of the most turbulent and strife ridden frontiers in the history of American westward advance."[29]

Not all of the soldiers' military assignments involved actual combat. They also performed an abundance of noncombat work in and around their posts that was of crucial importance to national consolidation and expansion and to the spread of "civilization" across the continent. This work, too, was frequently grueling and dangerous. Moreover, such activities as building and restoring military posts, laying telegraph wire and guarding the construction of the railroad lines, escorting the mail service and watching over westering migrants often produced results more tangible and more recognizably enduring than any single incident of actual Indian fighting. Some of the black Regulars' assignments also took them deep into unfamiliar country, more for future navigational and mapping purposes than for the purpose of directly challenging Native people. In the spring of 1869, for example, some two hundred soldiers of Colonel William B. Hazen's Thirty-eighth Infantry who were then stationed in New Mexico engaged in a lengthy expedition to explore and map the southwestern portion of the territory. Over the course of more than sixty days, these infantrymen traveled more than 1,200 miles across land that perhaps only Native people had traversed before, mapping its features and making it accessible to future settlers.[30]

Similarly, in 1871, William "Pecos Bill" Shafter led approximately seventy enlisted men of the Ninth Cavalry and the Twenty-fifth Infantry on a 500-mile, monthlong expedition to explore the area around Fort Davis and as far south as the Big Bend mountains. This expedition greatly expanded the nation's geographical knowledge of the region and provided crucial information that would help both civilian and military groups maneuver through the region more easily in the future. Four years later, Shafter led another four hundred black Regulars on a four-month campaign, during which they covered some 2,500 miles, observing and charting the region they were traveling through and revealing its potential for settlement, agriculture, and ranching. In short, in addition to their responsibilities for subduing the Indians, black Regulars—at great peril to their health and lives—were expected to develop the nation's infrastructure, essential work in the postwar nation-building enterprise.[31]

But success in this enterprise depended perhaps first and foremost on overcoming the obstacles posed by recalcitrant Native Americans, and as Shafter himself explained it, one option for the armed forces in any given region was simply to displace the Native people, which, in the case of Texas at least, he believed was best accomplished by "thoroughly scour[ing] the country with cavalry." In keeping with this approach, in the summer of 1871, three companies from the Ninth pursued the Apache into the White Sand Hills of the Staked Plains (Llano Estacado), a particularly arid and harsh 37,500-square-mile area encompassing western New Mexico and part of northeastern Texas. According to one participant, this fifteen-day expedition, which saw no armed encounters with the Apache, was "an extremely wearisome one," which "severely tested the powers of endurance of both men and animals" and led to the deaths of two soldiers from exposure.[32]

Some routine patrols by black Regulars that were not necessarily expected to involve immediate conflict with hostile opponents did so anyway. On May 20, 1870, the Ninth Cavalry's Emanuel Stance—who had been among the first black Regulars sent to Fort Davis to restore and garrison the post, and who was now a sergeant stationed at Fort McKavett—set out on a scout with nine or ten other troopers from the regiment, keeping an eye out for some Kickapoo known to have been engaging in raids on white settlements in the area and to have captured two white children back on May 16. After traveling about fourteen miles, the soldiers caught sight of a small group of Indians leading some horses. Believing they might be the ones who had captured the children, Stance and the other soldiers attacked. The Indians escaped, but in doing so, they released their horses, which the soldiers soon brought under control.

The following morning, the soldiers, having decided to take the captured horses back to Fort McKavett, encountered another party of approximately twenty Indians who seemed to be threatening a small wagon train along with some government horses. Again, Stance and his men assumed the offensive. In his official report, Stance later wrote, "I immediately attacked [the Indians] by charging them. They tried hard to make a stand . . . but I set the Spencers to talking and whistling about their ears so lively that they broke in confusion" and "fled to the hills," again leaving behind some of the horses. A while later the Indians returned, perhaps to reclaim the horses, and the struggle resumed, but once again the soldiers drove them off without taking a single casualty of their own or inflicting any, either. For his performance in this encounter, and for his detachment's capture of fifteen horses, and even though the detachment did not recapture the kidnapped little girls or even locate them, the troop commander Captain Henry Carroll recommended Stance for the Congressional Medal of Honor, the same medal Christian Fleetwood had earned for his courage at the Battle of Chaffin's Farm in the fall of 1864. Two months later, "For Valor in the Battle of Kickapoo Springs" in addition to four previous engagements, Emanuel Stance received his medal, the first to be awarded to a black Regular in the postwar period. On July 24, the medal was presented to him in front of the entire garrison at Fort McKavett. That day, Stance expressed his pride and gratitude in a letter to the army's adjutant general, noting that he would "cherish the gift as a thing of priceless value and endeavor by my future conduct to merit the high honor conferred upon me." Stance continued to serve with the Ninth until 1887.[33]

One black Regular whose military career, like Stance's, spanned much of this period was John F. Casey, born in 1850 or 1851 in Missouri, the child of a slave mother and a white father who was probably his owner. Nothing is known about Casey's life in slavery, or about his experiences during the first years after he gained his freedom at the end of the Civil War. What is clear, however, is that in September 1872 this fair-skinned former slave enlisted at Kansas City, Missouri, in H Troop of Grierson's Tenth Cavalry, the same troop whose men had rescued Forsyth's command on Beecher's Island four years earlier. Casey spent fifteen of the next sixteen years in the Tenth Cavalry (he took a half year off between his discharge in September 1877 and his reenlistment in March 1878), rising through the ranks to the position of first sergeant in his troop on account of his being, as one commissioned officer described him, a "good efficient" soldier and, as another put it, having "always discharged his duty in a very satisfactory manner" and not having "neglected any duty . . . in the slightest degree." Casey also demonstrated superior skill as a marksman. As he later recalled, "When I was in the service I [was] a sharp shooter for several years and [was] with three department rifle teams. From this you can see that at that time I [had] very good eyesight."[34]

Regrettably, Casey's dedication as a soldier seems not to have been paralleled by his behavior in private life. For one thing, Casey was known to gamble recklessly on occasion. He also had a reputation as a womanizer, despite having been married for several years and possibly already having fathered two children (it is not clear when the children were born). During his third enlistment, Casey's failings finally got him into trouble, and he was court-martialed on the charge of having consorted with prostitutes near the fort. According to one statement presented at his trial by the regimental chaplain, Casey and another soldier had obtained passes, as well as a wagon and a team of horses (or perhaps mules), for the purpose of going on a hunting expedition. Along with their equipment, however, the two men had loaded onto the wagon "two women of the town, as a necessary appendage of their hunting equipment, to the disgust of the entire enlisted force of this post." Found guilty, Casey lost his stripes and six months' pay, although the record indicates that less than two years later he had been promoted again to the rank of corporal, and soon after that regained the rank of sergeant.[35]

The unhappy incident of his court-martial aside, however, Sergeant Casey's record as a soldier was a solid one, and he appears to have been involved in several of the key encounters between his regiment and the Indians in Texas. In his 1892 application for a veteran's pension, Casey recalled in particular an event at Fort Sill in Indian Territory (then the headquarters of the Tenth Cavalry) in the spring of 1873 in which several thousand impatient Kiowa and Comanche from the nearby reservation had surrounded the fort, probably seeking redress of a legitimate grievance. Eager to communicate with the government Indian agent (who was located about three miles away) in order to diffuse the tension without bloodshed, Colonel Grierson called for a volunteer to serve as a messenger. Casey accepted the challenge and, as he later recalled—perhaps with some dramatic embellishment—took the sealed envelope and "charged right through the Indians who lined the road and all the surrounding country," delivering Grierson's dispatch safely. Not long thereafter, Casey returned as he had gone, now bearing the agent's response, which seems to have served its immediate purpose; within hours the Indians were dispersing peacefully. Justifiably proud of his accomplishment, Casey declared that he had completed his dangerous mission "without firing a shot," which, he noted wryly, "would have been futile" anyway, "as the Indians were in great numbers and had their bows and arrows pointing at me as I rode through."[36]

The near-crisis at Fort Sill in 1873 that John Casey described in his pension application was not the first of its kind at the post. A similar event had taken place two years earlier, in 1871, a year before Casey even enlisted in the regiment. On that earlier occasion, the black Regulars of the Tenth Cavalry not only faced down a large group of angry Indians but made the difference between life and death for a military figure far more elevated than any one of them could ever hope to be. That spring, in response to numerous reports of serious problems on the Texas frontier, Sherman, then the commanding officer of the U.S. army, had made a tour of the state to evaluate the situation for himself. Sherman, it appears, hated Washington and the political scene there and was pleased to have an excuse to get away to the West for a time. Little did he know, when he arrived in San Antonio, how close he was about to come to losing his life.

Sherman reached San Antonio on April 28. On May 2 he set out with Inspector General Randolph B. Marcy, two staff officers, and a carefully chosen escort of seventeen Tenth Cavalry troopers. The group proceeded to visit a series of Texas posts, including Forts McKavett, Concho, and Griffin. Although regaled throughout their sixteen days of traveling with stories of dreadful Indian attacks, they encountered no Indians. They were lucky, for on May 18, just a few hours before they arrived at Fort Richardson—the final point on their expedition and now the headquarters of the white Fourth Cavalry's Ranald S. Mackenzie, who had been the original commander of the black Forty-first Infantry—they crossed Salt Creek Prairie, near where some one hundred Kiowa were hiding. These Kiowas, who reportedly included war leaders like Satanta, Satank, Big Tree, Eagle Heart, and Big Bow, might well have attacked Sherman, Marcy, and the black troopers right then, had it not been for the misguided prediction made by one of their number that there was "still richer prey" to be taken.[37]

Arriving safely at Fort Richardson, Sherman and Marcy were prepared to conclude that much of the trouble they had been hearing about in Texas was either past or imaginary. That night, however, they were compelled to change their minds when a civilian teamster named Thomas Brazeale stumbled into the fort covered with blood. Brazeale explained that his wagon train had been attacked about twenty miles to the west and seven other teamsters had been killed. Immediately, Sherman dispatched Mackenzie and 150 of the troopers stationed at Fort Richardson to locate the site and determine the accuracy of Brazeale's report. The report proved horribly true: "Seven bloated and mutilated bodies were found, including one that had been chained to a wagon pole and burned to a cinder." In addition, "Five dead mules were found, but forty-one others were missing."[38]

Sherman then set out for Grierson's Fort Sill headquarters, about 115 miles away in Indian Territory, arriving on May 23. At Fort Sill, which also served as the Indian Bureau's agency for the Kiowa-Comanche reservation, Sherman confronted the local bureau agent, Lawrie Tatum—described in one source as a "balding, big-framed Iowa farmer of great courage and tenacity"—demanding to know which Native leaders might have inspired, ordered, or even perpetrated the attack on the wagon train. Tatum was deeply troubled by the news of the violence, and on May 27, when the Kiowa began to come in to the agency for their seasonal allotment of rations, he demanded information. Among the Kiowa who had gathered there was Kicking Bird, a leader generally considered to be supportive of the government's various peace initiatives, but also present was Satanta, who had been with those who almost ambushed Sherman and was known for his threats against white settlers encroaching on his people's hunting grounds. Satanta spoke up and took credit for the attack on the wagon train, at the same time scolding Tatum for the United States' many wrongs against the Kiowa. In addition, Satanta accused Tatum of cheating the Indians out of the goods and supplies they were due. He then demanded guns and ammunition. Infuriated, Tatum contacted Grierson, who ordered that Satanta and other guilty parties be arrested.[39]

Presumably to facilitate the capture and arrest of Satanta, and perhaps also to provide the "hostiles" with an opportunity to display their goodwill and avoid arrest altogether, Sherman, Tatum, and Grierson called the gathered Kiowa to meet in council at Grierson's house at the fort. Not certain what to expect, Grierson ordered troopers of the Tenth, as a precaution, to mount their horses and take up designated positions around the house and the grounds of the fort in order to prevent the Kiowa leaders from escaping should they attempt to do so. Additionally, Grierson positioned about a dozen black cavalrymen inside the house, facing the porch where Sherman, Tatum, and Grierson were expected to greet the arriving Kiowa. These black Regulars stood directly behind the windows, before which the shutters were pulled shut.[40]

Tensions were already high when Satanta and other Kiowa representatives arrived at Grierson's house, and they came close to escalating into violence when the hot-tempered Sherman directly confronted an equally hot-tempered Satanta, declaring him under arrest and announcing that he and all the guilty parties would be held in confinement and then sent to Texas for trial. Becoming enraged, Satanta reached for his gun, hidden under the blanket he had wrapped around himself. Before Satanta could shoot the general, however, Sherman barked out a command and suddenly the black troopers hidden inside the house flung the shutters open and aimed their weapons out the windows. At the same time, Lone Wolf, another Kiowa war leader, appeared, bearing guns, bows, and arrows, and handing them to others among the gathered Indians while maintaining possession of one gun himself. Meanwhile, the mounted men of the Tenth's D Troop, led by Lieutenant Richard Henry Pratt, and those of H Troop, led by Captain Louis Carpenter (who had led the Beecher's Island rescue), moved in closer to the house, making escape impossible.[41]

Satanta and others were soon arrested, and the immediate danger to the life of General Sherman was averted. On this occasion, when a single shot from a gun on either side might have resulted in disaster all around, the black troopers had performed brilliantly, with "crisp coolness and disciplined restraint," arguably saving not only Sherman's life but also at least some of their own, not to mention the lives of their

Satanta, ca. 1875. *Courtesy of the Library of Congress.*

commander, Grierson, and Agent Tatum. Surely many of the Kiowa would also have been wounded or killed. Instead, the crisis passed without injury. "I am satisfied the Kioways [*sic*] will be more careful in the future," wrote Sherman to Grierson from Fort Leavenworth about a month after the events. He added, "I regard your Post as one of the best if not the very best on the frontier."[42]

Cavalryman John Casey was not present for the excitement at Fort Sill in 1871, but he was there in 1873. And although the Kiowa and Comanche who surrounded Fort Sill in 1873 had scattered after Sergeant Casey brought calming news from the government's local Indian agent, their frustrations soon swelled once more, ultimately gaining full expression in what came to be known as the Red River War, which lasted from the summer of 1874 to the spring of 1875 and during which black Regulars were actively engaged. By the time the war erupted, the Native people in the Indian Territory and the Texas Panhandle had already been suffering for years on their reservations, often making do with inadequate rations, suffering arbitrary punishments for purported but unproven offenses, and watching the buffalo herds upon which they depended decline, at least in part because of the wasteful practices of white hunters. Indeed, already during the winter of 1873–74, these tribes of the Southern Plains had begun preparing to fight. And in this context, troopers of the Tenth Cavalry were among those U.S. forces sent in pursuit of the Kiowa leader Lone Wolf—who had been among those threatening Sherman's life in 1871—and other regional Indians who seemed bent on following him into war.[43]

Casey's account of his experiences before and during the Red River War provides a glimpse of the harsh conditions soldiers on the frontier encountered during this campaign. In the course of its wintertime operations in 1873–74, for example, the Tenth's H Troop found itself snowed in for ten straight days with virtually no rations except some hardtack and a little coffee, while the troop's supply train wandered blindly in the snow unable to locate where the men were camping. Casey also recalled being assigned that same winter to go with a detachment of men to the rescue of some buffalo hunters who had come under Indian attack. For this five-day expedition, Casey wrote, "each man was only allowed to carry one blanket and his poncho"—no overcoats—and as a result, "we nearly froze."[44]

Soon the members of Casey's detachment also found themselves with very little to eat, as their fuel for cooking—buffalo chips—had been destroyed by the rain and snow they encountered along the way. Fortunately, although the rest of the troop had struck camp and moved on by the time Casey's detachment returned from its rescue mission, they had left a wagonload of provisions behind: hardtack, bacon, beans, and coffee. Casey and his hungry comrades ate heartily before heading off again—still without their overcoats—in the direction the rest of the troop had gone. Twenty miles later, at around midnight, Casey and his detachment finally reached the others, now encamped in snow half a foot deep. "In this," he wrote, "we had to lay down to sleep with our clothes and blankets wringing wet." The weather "remained very cold during the entire time we were there, which was ten days or more," and once again rations grew scarce, for the horses as well as the troopers: "We had to go one-half or a mile to cut down cottonwood trees and carry the limbs for the horses to eat. This was all the food they had during the whole ten days and [we] had to carry wood and build log heap fires in the rear of our horses, night and day, to keep them from freezing to death." Many of them perished anyway.[45]

By the summer of 1874, the Red River War was fully underway, and over the course of the next several months, some twenty violent engagements took place in the region between various groups of determined Indians and portions of the military and its auxiliaries, with the army slowly but steadily encircling the Native fighters until they surrendered, gave way in the face of bad weather, or grew so hungry and desperate that they were incapable of further resistance. In the spring of 1875, the war finally wound down, a key marker of its end being the capture and removal of over seventy of the male leaders of the region's Native war factions—including Lone Wolf—under the authority of the Tenth Cavalry's Lieutenant Richard H. Pratt, who had been present at Fort Sill when the black troopers saved the life of General Sherman. In late April, by wagon and by train, Pratt escorted these men in chains all the way to Fort Marion, located in St. Augustine, Florida, where he would spend the next several years attempting to "civilize" his prisoners while also pondering the implications of the Indian wars for race relations in America. Meanwhile, Casey and the Tenth Cavalry's H Troop transferred from Fort Sill to Fort Davis, where Casey served for the ensuing ten years.

In Casey's memory, his years at Fort Davis were spent constantly scouting. These expeditions took various shapes: sometimes the men operated "as a whole company," ideally about sixty-four men; some-times they operated in smaller detachments, ranging in size from ten to twenty men. Casey also recalled being summoned in the middle of one May night in 1877 to mount up with a number of others and go to the rescue of a "band of men"—it is not clear whether they were civil-ians or soldiers—who were under siege at a place called Musker Can-yon. "When we got to the canyon," wrote Casey, "we had to file in and charge the Indians in columns of fours, the canyon being so narrow we couldn't deploy." It was also so dark that "we could not see one from the other and there was danger of falling into a subterranean lake."[46]

As it turned out, Casey's horse, on which he was leading the rest of the detachment, did fall "into a partly filled up well or spring," and as in a highway pileup, two other horses fell in succession, at least one of them landing on Casey and dislocating his shoulder. Only when he was able to return to Fort Davis six days after the accident did Casey receive medical attention for his injury. Perhaps as a result of the delayed treat-ment, or perhaps because the treatment itself was inadequate, Casey never regained full use of his shoulder. Moreover, further injuries and ongoing exposure to the severe conditions of military service on the frontier compounded his disability. By the time he applied for his pen-sion years later, although he was only about forty years old, Casey per-suasively claimed to be unable to perform manual labor, having been "completely broken down physically" by his time in the army.[47]

Like many black Regulars, John Casey suffered considerable physical strain over the course of his active duty service on behalf of the nation's postwar agenda. But there were others who suffered more, including the forty troopers of the Tenth Cavalry's A Troop who were forced—in large part because of the incompetence of the white officer command-ing the detachment, Captain Nicholas Nolan—to go without water for eighty-six hours while on a scouting expedition on the brutally hot and arid Staked Plains. In the summer of 1877, Nolan, the troopers, twenty-two buffalo hunters, at least one other white officer, and a guide named José had set out to pursue hostile Comanche. Things went reasonably well until the party moved out at midafternoon on July 26 from a site about twenty-five miles south of Lubbock, without taking enough water for the next few days and without sufficient knowledge of the terrain or of the availability of fresh water along the way.[48]

At the time the party broke camp, the temperature was already above one hundred degrees Fahrenheit. Most of the soldiers were soon out of water; some would not drink water again until dawn on July 30, having sustained themselves as best they could as they scattered and wandered about for more than three days, covering at least fifty miles of dry, hot land. As an officer in the regiment later wrote, echoing the experience of Forsyth's command on Beecher's Island, during that time they were compelled "to drink their own, and their horses' urine and the blood of their played out horses." One member of a detachment sent in relief of the lost soldiers described the troopers' mouths and throats as "so parched that they could not swallow the government hard bread; after being masticated, it accumulated between the teeth and the palate, from whence it had to be extracted with the fingers. . . . Vertigo and dimness of vision affected all," and they "had difficulty in speaking," their voices having grown weak and their ability to comprehend when spoken to having deteriorated dramatically.[49]

In the end, four of the soldiers died (Privates John T. Gordon, Isaac Derwin, John Bond, and John Isaacs), along with some twenty horses and five pack mules. In a bizarre twist of "justice," in September, four troopers who had participated in the expedition, including one non-commissioned officer named William Umbles, faced courts-martial for desertion and other offenses. All were found guilty and sentenced to lengthy prison terms, reductions in rank, denial of pay and other allowances, and dishonorable discharges. To his credit, General E. O. C. Ord, then in overall command of U.S. forces in Texas, saw to it that their sentences were reduced and that they were returned to duty.[50]

Sergeant John Casey was fortunate not to be on the nightmarish and deadly 1877 expedition. But as we have already seen, his years on the frontier, like those of the other black Regulars with whom he served,

Victorio, ca. 1880. *Courtesy of the National Park Service: Fort Davis National Historic Site, Texas.*

were hardly idle. At the end of the 1870s, Casey found himself participating in one of the U.S. army's most significant postwar campaigns in the Southwest, the so-called Victorio campaign. Not unlike the Native people who had fought in the Red River War of 1874–75, by the late 1870s, Mescalero Apaches on the reservation near Fort Stanton in New Mexico Territory had become increasingly unhappy and internally factionalized as a result of their miserable living conditions—inadequate rations, shoddy supply goods, unpaid annuities, and unyielding land—as well as disputes with white ranchers who now occupied their preferred hunting grounds. Victorio, a Warm Springs Apache, had for the past two years successfully resisted federal government efforts to move him and his followers onto the San Carlos reservation, across the border in Arizona Territory. Now, in 1879, Victorio meant to unite his Warm Springs followers with those among the Mescalero who were most discontented. He led his mixed band of about a hundred warriors and their families off the reservation, out of U.S. territory, and out of U.S. army jurisdiction into Mexico. They did not depart quietly, either: "Their trail into Arizona, back through New Mexico into old Mexico," recalled one veteran of the white Sixth Cavalry in the 1890s, "was marked by burned ranches, forest fires, dead cattle and sheep, and the bodies of murdered human beings."[51]

Over the next several months, Victorio and his followers (their numbers increased by angry Comanche and Navajo they encountered in their travels) continued to trouble American forces as they undertook a series of raids on U.S. soil from Mexico. With support from others in Grierson's Tenth Cavalry and Joseph H. Potter's Twenty-fourth Infantry (and still more from various white regiments also stationed in the region), black Regulars from Edward Hatch's Ninth Cavalry—which had been transferred from Texas to New Mexico in September 1875—struggled to stop, capture, or kill the fugitives before they melted back across the nation's southern border and out of reach. At the same time, Hatch attempted to disarm the Mescalero who had remained on their reservation, a job for which he also enlisted the help of Grierson and the Tenth. "We arrived here to-day about noon," Grierson wrote to his wife, Alice, from the Mescalero Agency on April 12, 1880. "The command is in good health & condition."[52]

Four days later, on April 16, Grierson wrote optimistically to Alice that the disarming process, while difficult, had been successful up to that point: "The supply depot of Victorio & his followers has been cut of[f] & all Indians who are now out will be disarmed & dismounted when they come in, & if they do not voluntarily come in & surrender, will be hunted down & killed." He added, "Gen Hatch is greatly pleased with the earnest support I have given him in this entire matter & says that he could not have succeeded without us." The following day Grierson wrote again to Alice, noting that he and his troopers, who included John Casey, would all be glad in the next few days "when we face homeward."[53]

Unfortunately for Grierson, Casey, and the other federal soldiers on this campaign, Hatch's efforts to disarm the Apache seemed successful on the surface, but the troops had so infuriated about fifty of the Mescalero that they, too, had escaped and made their way to Victorio's Mexican stronghold. By summer, fearing more raids and more escapes, Mexican and U.S. forces agreed to coordinate their operations, though according to Grierson's son Charlie, the Ninth Cavalry's capacity for participating effectively in the operations was sure to be hindered by the regiment's horses, which he described as being "in horrid condition, nothing but skin and bones." Meanwhile, Grierson, who firmly believed that the renegade Apache would be most likely to reenter the U.S. by crossing the Río Grande into western Texas, had returned to the Lone Star State, where he held the troops under his command on alert in and around Fort Davis, posting them along the Río Grande's banks, along well-used trails, and at every known watering hole in the area. "Without access to water," Grierson pointed out, "no one, not even Victorio, could cross that inhospitable country."[54]

Grierson's hunch about Victorio's plans panned out at the very end of July, when the Apache leader and a group of his followers were seen crossing the Río Grande near Texas's Eagle Mountains, about 140 miles from Fort Davis. Grierson's Regulars fired on the Indians when they approached a watering hole, and the Indians fired back. Though few in number compared with Victorio's raiders, the soldiers prevailed, killing at least seven of the Indians and driving the rest back across the river into Mexico. On August 2, Grierson wrote to Alice about the events of the past few days: "The Indians were much more severely handled than I at first reported. They were compelled to travel back across the Rio Grande faster than they came north, and did not find Texas an easy route to travel through." Grierson expressed confidence that his black Regulars had badly crippled the Indian force. "It may seem to have been a rash and dangerous undertaking to get ready to fight Victorio and his hundred Indians with only (at first) seven men," he reassured her, "but I had looked the ground over well before going into camp, and saw clearly what a strong position I had." He expressed further confidence that Victorio's end was now in sight. "I have sent this afternoon to Col. Valle of the Mexican army," he wrote, "and I presume that he will attack them to-day or to-morrow."[55]

As it turns out, the attack by the Mexican army was several weeks in coming. In fact, in early August, Victorio tried again to cross into the United States, but black Regulars under Grierson's command drove him back a second time. As John Casey later described it, the Tenth Cavalry's attempt to gain an advantage over the fugitive Apache required the men of H Troop to travel "over an unknown trail over sage brush, sand and alkali," during which they used up all their supplies of fresh water and had to subsist on salty water for twenty-four hours until a sudden rainstorm provided relief. And still they persisted. Wrote Casey,

> We traced the Indians from Texas into Old Mexico and the Mexicans drove them back into Texas crossing the Rio Grande near El Paso, Texas. We first intercepted them at Eagle Springs, had a running fight about dark on the following day, and drove them back in toward Mexico and the Copoka mountains and thence into the Crecey Mountains in the Salt Lake Valley where we engaged in battle and drove them from the Salt Lake Valley into the mountains again, and two companies of us kept them engaged all day until about 3 o'clock in the afternoon when our ammunition ran out and . . . other troops took our place in the firing line.[56]

Looking back on the performance of Casey and the rest of his men in this grueling campaign, Grierson wrote proudly to Alice from Eagle Springs on August 22, "So far I have been very successful on the Indian campaign. I cannot now see how I could have made a better disposition of troops or accomplished more with the force available." And as if he hoped for another chance to test himself and his men, he added, "I am now better prepared than ever & if they come again into this section of the country I feel confident of my ability to whip them again." But Grierson and the soldiers serving with him in this campaign never had another chance to prove themselves against Victorio, for whom the early August crossing onto federal soil was his last. Later that fall, Mexican soldiers killed Victorio and most of his followers and, with this, the Indian wars in Texas, to all intents and purposes, came to an end.[57]

John Casey's career with Grierson's Tenth Cavalry did not end when Victorio was killed. He also participated in the long campaign to capture and subdue the last key Apache war leader, Geronimo, as the decade of the 1880s began. Although Geronimo was not a chief and was also a controversial figure even among his own people, his steadfast resistance against the United States and his brilliance as a warrior meant that he was both deeply respected and deeply feared by virtually all whom he encountered. At the time of Victorio's death, Geronimo was living relatively peacefully, or so it seemed, at the San Carlos reservation in Arizona. But like those at reservations elsewhere, the conditions at San Carlos were deteriorating, and the Apache, not known for their patience, were becoming increasingly agitated.[58]

Still, for almost a year after Victorio's death, life at San Carlos had remained relatively quiet. Then, in the summer of 1881, beginning in the northern portion of the reservation, a Native shaman known as Nakaidoklini stirred up discontent with his spiritual messages, which promised that the Apache people's recommitment to their Native religious traditions would bring the dead back to life and permit a purging of white conquerors from the land. As the weeks passed, the federal government's Indian agent at San Carlos, J. C. Tiffany, who was extremely anxious about the implications of Nakaidoklini's influence, succeeded in persuading Colonel Eugene A. Carr, commander of the white Sixth Cavalry and commanding officer at nearby Fort Apache, to order the shaman's arrest. The actual arrest went awry, however, and on August 30 Nakaidoklini was killed. Late in September, Geronimo and about seventy-five other Chiricahua Apache broke out of the agency, linking up with the remains of Victorio's band in Mexico.[59]

Over the next two years, the U.S. army, in collaboration with Mexican forces, endeavored to bring Geronimo and the other rebellious Apache back to San Carlos. Many considered Geronimo's endurance to be almost superhuman: "He could march seventy miles during a night, fight all day, and appear no more weary than an ordinary man after an ordinary day's labor," recalled one white veteran. Several times, in various places across the Southwest and then in the rugged Sierra Madre of Mexico, portions of the army, including John Casey and other black Regulars, engaged the Apache in battle. Meanwhile, the numbers of

Geronimo, ca. 1898. *Courtesy of the Library of Congress.*

Apache determined to resist federal control (and to engage in raids to supply their needs) continued to grow, as did the very real threat to the frontierspeople settled in the area. At one point, in frustration, Sherman ordered General George Crook, then commanding the Department of Arizona, to "pursue and destroy the hostile Apaches without regard to department or national boundaries." Finally, in late 1883, after an extended and exhausting struggle in the Sierra Madre, the war-weary and hungry renegades began to yield, and in early 1884 Geronimo himself surrendered and returned to San Carlos.[60]

But a year later, in May 1885, the fragile peace gave way to rebellion again as some Apache on the reservation, who had initially planned only to engage in moderate resistance to regulations they considered unfairly repressive—specifically the regulations forbidding men to beat their wives and banning the production of the highly intoxicating corn-based alcohol "tizwin"—decided to flee the reservation instead. Among the 130 or so who escaped were Geronimo and another leader known as Mangas Coloradas. Some of the Indians headed straight for Mexico; others engaged in raiding activities in New Mexico and Arizona before heading across the border. Over the course of the next few months, General Crook sent hundreds of soldiers and scouts into Mexico in pursuit, at the same time posting about three thousand of them—including sizable numbers of black Regulars—along the U.S. border with Mexico to stop the Apache, should they attempt to return. All of these efforts were to no avail. "Nearly one-sixth of our army has been pursuing between fifty and one hundred Apaches for over a year and accomplishing nothing," wrote the First Infantry's James S. Pettit in September 1886. The Apache in Mexico continued to evade capture, and some even managed to cross the border to terrorize and kill American settlers and steal property before returning untouched to their Sierra Madre base.[61]

During the long campaign against Geronimo and his followers, Grierson's Tenth Cavalry was summoned to active duty again. Once more, Casey recalled, the conditions under which the Tenth's soldiers operated were daunting. "On this campaign in the fall of 1885, we encountered a very severe snow storm. . . . We got lost in the mountains for four days being snow bound and we could not get out." Moreover, it was at this time that Casey later claimed to have contracted a bad cold, symptoms of scurvy (including the loss of some of his teeth), rheumatism, and a long-term bladder disorder, all of which would plague him in one way or another for the rest of his life. H Troop's Private Solomon Boller, a former slave from Nottoway County, Virginia, who served from 1882 to 1887 as a regimental blacksmith, similarly recalled the harsh conditions during the Geronimo campaign: "Sometimes," he wrote in his application for a pension at the turn of the century, "snow would be up to our knees and I had to shoe horses in snow and rain."[62]

In January 1886, federal and Mexican forces finally located and invaded the main Apache camp in the mountains, a development that temporarily persuaded Geronimo and others it was time to talk. But as the negotiations extended into late March, Geronimo's persistent desire for freedom gained the upper hand over the exhaustion he and some thirty remaining followers felt, and they once again slipped from the army's grasp. Discredited, General Crook resigned his command and was replaced in early April by now General Nelson Miles and his Fifth Infantry. As Miles directed the final phase of the U.S. army's pursuit of Geronimo, he continued to include black Regulars—whose abilities he had personally witnessed and encouraged as commander of the Fortieth Infantry in North Carolina from 1866 to 1869—including portions of the Tenth Cavalry. In early May 1886, under the command of Captain Thomas C. Lebo, C Troop skirmished with a number of the Apache in the Pinito Mountains thirty miles south of the U.S.–Mexico border. In late August of that year, to prevent further trouble, Miles decided to deport to Fort Marion in Florida—as had been done with the Red River War chiefs—even those Warm Springs Apache who had remained peacefully on the reservation. In conjunction with Miles's decision, several companies of the Tenth were assigned to gather, arrest, and transport more than four hundred Indian men, women, and children from the San Carlos reservation to Holbrook, Arizona, where they would board the train that would lead them into exile.[63]

Having learned of his people's deportation, Geronimo finally surrendered to Miles in early September at Skeleton Canyon, just north of the Mexican border in Arizona. Six weeks later at Arizona's Rio Bonito, troopers of the Tenth Cavalry's H Troop—John Casey's company—tracked down and forced the surrender of Mangas Coloradas and about a dozen others who had refused to come in with Geronimo. As a white veteran of the Thirteenth U.S. Infantry later recalled, "When Geronimo and his followers surrendered . . . and allowed themselves to be bundled on a train and hustled out of the territory, the curtain fell on the most picturesque and stupendous drama that was ever enacted on the American continent."[64] The Indian wars were almost over.

For their performance in the capture of Mangas's group, a number of H Troop's black Regulars earned commendations from General Miles himself, who in recalling the summertime conditions of the last part of the campaign later wrote, "One who does not know this country cannot realize what this kind of service means—marching every day in the intense heat, the rocks and earth being so torrid that the feet are blistered and rifle-barrels and everything metallic being so hot that the hand cannot touch them without getting burnt. It is a country rough beyond description, covered everywhere with cactus and full of rattlesnakes and other undesirable companions of that sort." Among the black Regulars who had endured the campaign and who were now formally recognized by Miles was John F. Casey.[65]

Black Regulars such as Casey earned official commendations for their performance in the Geronimo campaign; they earned recognition for their service in other battles on the frontier, too. Among those whose particular courage in the work of extending the nation's boundaries against its Native opponents came to their white commanders' attention was George W. Ford of Fairfax, Virginia, who was born in 1847, enlisted as an original member of the Tenth Cavalry's L Troop in September 1867, and proceeded to rise through the ranks to the position of quartermaster sergeant before he was discharged, with "character most excellent," in 1877, the year his regiment's A Troop suffered its disastrous waterless fiasco on the Staked Plains. During his decade with the Tenth, Ford served for a time as one of the regimental mail couriers, riding back and forth between Fort Arbuckle, Kansas, and Fort Gibson in Indian Territory and "fording the icy waters of the Canadian, the Washita, and [the] Wild Horse" rivers on a regular basis. Ford also participated in his regiment's military activities during the Red River War, and in August 1874 earned an honorable mention for "gallantry against Kiowas and Comanches" at the Indian Territory's Wichita Agency.[66]

Some black Regulars were recognized for their courage in situations that did not directly involve fighting with the Indians. In July 1889, for example, the Ninth Cavalry's Private James Settlers earned a commendation for "meritorious conduct" as a result of having "saved his commander from drowning while crossing Wind River, Wyoming, at the risk of his own life." And in November 1893, Sergeant John F. Buck of the Tenth Cavalry earned an official citation "for highly meritorious service" while leading a pack train from Fort Missoula, Montana, in terrible weather across the Bitterroot Mountains in Idaho. In 1891, Benjamin Burge of the Twenty-fourth Infantry was awarded a certificate of merit for heroism in action, which added two dollars per month to his salary. Burge's certificate acknowledged his "gallant and meritorious conduct" in May 1889 after he helped put down an attack by thieves while serving as part of an escort, between Forts Grant and Thomas, Arizona, for the army paymaster Major Joseph W. Wham.[67]

Black Regulars surely treasured any and all such formal acknowledgments of their labor on behalf of the nation, which were conveyed in printed official orders and thus became part of each individual soldier's (and the army's) permanent records. Surely no official acknowledgment, however, was as gratifying as the Congressional Medal of Honor. As has already been noted, some dozen USCT soldiers—the black Regulars' predecessors—had earned the medal during the Civil War. Now, in the years between the formation of the black regiments in 1866 and the surrender of Apache leaders Geronimo and Mangas two decades later, more than a dozen black Regulars took pride in earning the medal themselves, not least because it provided a tangible symbol of the ways in which their work in the postwar army echoed the courage and fortitude under fire that USCT soldiers such as Christian Fleetwood had displayed during the Civil War.[68]

The bulk of the black Regulars who earned the medal during this period came from the Ninth Cavalry, including Emanuel Stance, the first one to do so. Five years later, Private Pompey Factor and Sergeant John Ward of Arkansas, and Private Isaac Payne of Mexico, followed suit. The cases of Factor, Ward, and Payne are particularly striking in that all three were soldiers in John Bullis's regiment of Seminole Negro Indian Scouts. In 1870, four years after the postwar black regiments were created—and in keeping with a long-standing tradition of deploy-

ing different groups of Native or other oppressed people against one another on the premise that those who allied with the United States would benefit most in the end—the federal government authorized the recruitment of men of mixed African and Seminole Indian descent for scouting duty on the frontier, particularly on the U.S.–Mexico border. In 1873, thirty-two-year-old Lieutenant John L. Bullis, a veteran who had commanded USCT troops during the Civil War and was now serving with the black Twenty-fourth Infantry, took command of the unit, which was stationed at Fort Clark in Texas. He remained with the scouts for eight years. Many of Bullis's scouts were ex-slaves who had escaped to freedom in places like Texas, Florida, and Mexico, where they lived and formed kinship relations with local Native people; others among the scouts were these ex-slaves' descendants. Many if not all were fluent in Spanish, and they were widely "conceded to be the best body of scouts, trailers, and Indian fighters ever engaged in the Government service along the border." Privates Factor and Payne and Sergeant Ward earned their Medals of Honor in 1875 in connection with their participation in a charge against two dozen Comanche and Apache raiders during a fight on the Pecos River in Texas, in which they may well have saved Bullis's life.[69]

There were other proud honorees during these years, including the Virginia native Corporal Clinton Greaves of the Ninth Cavalry's C Troop—with which he went on to serve for more than twenty years—who earned his medal in 1877 for heroism in close combat with Apache in the Florida Mountains of New Mexico. According to Greaves's citation, "While part of a small detachment [sent] to persuade a band of renegade Apache Indians to surrender, his group was surrounded. Corporal Greaves, in the center of the savage hand-to-hand fighting, managed to shoot and bash a gap through the swarming Apaches, permitting his companions to break free." Two years later, in 1879, Sergeant Thomas Boyne of Maryland—who served first with the Ninth Cavalry and later with the Twenty-fifth Infantry—was recognized for two separate examples of his "bravery in action" while on duty in New Mexico during

Group of Seminole Negro Indian scouts taken near Fort Clark, Texas, ca. 1880. *Courtesy of the National Park Service: Fort Davis National Historic Site, Texas.*

the Victorio campaign. That same year, yet another enlisted man in the Ninth Cavalry, Private John Denny of Big Flats, New York, also earned the Medal of Honor in connection with the Victorio campaign, for having rescued a wounded comrade, Private Freeland, during the September 1879 Battle of Las Animas in New Mexico. More than a dozen years later, in describing Denny's courage under fire, Colonel James Biddle declared that "such acts of gallantry not only reflect credit upon the individual, but also on the organization to which he belongs, and the 9th Cavalry may well feel proud of having in its ranks a man so signally honored." The Twenty-fourth Infantry's Benjamin Brown, a Missouri native who had enlisted at Fort Leavenworth in 1881, and Virginia's Corporal Isaiah Mays, of the same regiment, earned the Medal of Honor for their courage during the same attack on paymaster Wham and his escort that earned their comrade Benjamin Burge a commendation. According to the citation that accompanied his medal, Corporal Mays, possibly wounded in the attack, "walked and crawled 2 miles" to a ranch to get help for the beleaguered soldiers.[70]

During the two decades from 1866 to the surrender of Geronimo in 1886, these and other Medal of Honor winners—along with the thousands of black Regulars who served beside them on the nation's western frontier—sacrificed much or, in some cases, all on behalf of the national agenda. From the vantage point of the early twenty-first century, the unbroken progress of overwhelmingly white westward settlement and the steady encirclement and displacement of America's Native people onto reserved and ever-shrinking pieces of only moderately productive land seem both unmistakable and inevitable. Also clear in hindsight are the crucial contributions made by the black Regulars, who courageously advanced the national agenda at great peril to their own lives, as well as to the lives, communities, and cultures of those Native people they were enlisted to suppress. It must be admitted that historians, in the words of James Leiker, can find "little evidence of a 'rainbow coalition' in our past through which peoples of color cooperated in interracial camaraderie." The black Regulars understood themselves to be, first and foremost, U.S. soldiers and as such, although "[s]ome of them probably recognized the irony and approached their tasks with trepidation," they served voluntarily (some of them over the course of several enlistments) as proud "accomplices in . . . their country's racial and imperialistic policies," even as they sought to fulfill their own claims to "advancement and citizenship," and as a result Native Americans likely saw little difference between them and white soldiers (or civilians), viewing both with "a combination of suspicion and apathy."[71]

But from the perspective of the army and the federal government, the black Regulars were simply doing the job they had been enlisted to do, and doing it well. In 1881 Benjamin Grierson calculated that in Texas alone the Tenth Cavalry and the Twenty-fourth and Twenty-fifth Infantries had constructed and maintained "over a thousand miles of wagon roads and three hundred miles of telegraph lines," and had marched almost 136,000 miles in the course of their scouting and exploring expeditions as well as their various campaigns against regional Indians, all of which, he believed, made them worthy of "some special and suitable recognition from the Government." Six years later, Nelson Miles wrote a letter recommending Grierson for promotion to brigadier general. Miles commented on Grierson's distinguished record during the Civil War and since, and praised the black Regulars under Grierson's command. Miles wrote, "His regiment has, perhaps, done as much hard campaigning against hostile Indians and built as many posts and military roads as any other regiment of cavalry in the service and is still occupying the most remote and isolated posts in the country."[72]

When Grierson replaced Miles as commander of the Department of Arizona in 1888, he finally relinquished command of the Tenth Cavalry. In words that other commanders of the post–Civil War black regiments might have echoed, Grierson proudly recalled the regiment's "splendid record of nearly twenty-two years service to the Government . . . in the field and at the most isolated posts on the frontier; always in the vanguard of civilization and in contact with the most warlike and savage Indians of the Plains." Subsequently, upon inspecting the troops newly brought under his authority, Grierson's replacement, Colonel J. K. Mizner, confirmed his predecessor's evaluation of the men: "I found the drilling and tactical instruction to be fairly good," wrote Mizner. "The majority of the men are good horsemen and understand their drill[;] expertness in field experience, as the result of experience and instruction was in some instances excellent and very creditable," though "in a few cases it was greatly lacking." But he noted, "The promptness with which some of the troops responded to an unexpected call for field service, was remarkable. In two instances it was almost marvelous, and is deserving of special notice. Troop E, commanded by Lieutenant W. H. Smith, got into the saddle and was on the march in eleven minutes after the order was delivered to the troop commander, and troop H, commanded by First Lieutenant W. E. Shipp, accomplished the same feat in just nine minutes."[73]

What all the training, hard service, and sacrifice of the soldiers of the Tenth Cavalry, as well as those of the three other black Regular regiments, meant for the nation's future security and strength (and for the

Native Americans' destruction) was clear. What all their efforts meant for their own futures—as full-fledged citizens of the United States they so bravely fought to support, expand, and defend, and as constituents of Frederick Douglass's vision of a "composite nationality" for America— remained much more ambiguous. Speaking of the Geronimo campaign many years later, the black veteran Solomon Boller of the Tenth Cavalry simply recalled, "There is where I lost my health in the line of my duty trying to protect my country."[74]

❖4❖

National Progress, Race Thinking, and Taking On West Point

[B]efore long you will be the most conspicuous boy on the American continent; . . . you will be the pivot on which a big row will gyrate; . . . there will be a deal of lying done about you and over you. . . . [Y]ou are in the path of destiny. You are one of the pieces with which desperate players and honest players and dishonest players are going to make all manner of moves. You have no idea, and probably never will have any idea, what a position the fates have placed you in.

—Newspaper reporter, speaking to Michael Howard,
the first black man appointed to attend the
U.S. Military Academy at West Point, in 1870

Well, all I want is to be left alone.

—Michael Howard's response

BY THE 1880S, THE FEDERAL GOVERNMENT'S PROGRAM OF NATIONAL consolidation, expansion, and the extension of "American civilization" across the land was going well. Just as the hard labor and personal sacrifice of the men of the USCT had helped ensure the nation's very survival during the Civil War, so had the dedication, toil, and blood of USCT soldiers on occupation duty in the vanquished South, and of the black Regular regiments on the frontier, contributed significantly to the nation's ongoing success in laying claim to the continent. Between the years 1874 and 1880 alone, Nelson Miles later recalled, "a belt of country extending from the Rio Grande or the Mexican boundary on the south, to the Canadian boundary on the north, and averaging some four hundred miles in width from east to west, was redeemed from a wild state and its control by savage tribes, and given to civilization."[1]

Indeed, one of the first key indicators of civilization's triumph had come as early as May 10, 1869, the day on which the "golden spike" ceremony at Promontory Point, Utah, marked the long-awaited meeting of the Union and Central Pacific lines and the completion of what some described as a "military highway" extending all the way from the Atlantic to the Pacific. When an "enterprise so remarkable for the vastness of its conception, the rapidity and energy of its accomplishment, and its wealth of possible results . . . is brought to successful consummation," the *Army and Navy Journal* had crowed in response, "the political, military, and strictly national importance of the undertaking tower above even the commercial advantages which it foreshadows." The article had expressed lingering concern about two ongoing problems, the Mormons and the Indians, but suggested that the "Mormon problem" seemed easy enough to solve: a government prohibition on polygamy should do the trick. (On this score, one suspects that it was more than just symbolically noteworthy that the golden spike should be driven in Utah, just a few miles outside of Salt Lake City.) As for the "Indian problem," the emigration westward that the transcontinental line now made possible would "gradually crowd the Indian out of its path." This "new highway," declared the equally enthusiastic members of the New York City Chamber of Commerce in a public letter to the *New York Times*, "will not only develop the resources, extend the commerce, increase the power, exalt the dignity, and perpetuate the unity of our Republic, but . . . will [also] materially facilitate the enlightened and advancing civilization of our age."[2]

By 1872, yet another rail line had made its way across much of the continent: Jay Cooke's Northern Pacific Railroad, which reached from Duluth, Minnesota, to Bismarck in the Dakota Territory. And it is clear that the development of these and other important railroad lines, as Miles recalled many years later, were the direct result of "the heroic services, the splendid fortitude and courage and noble sacrifices, of men"—soldiers—who had "placed themselves between war and peace, between danger and security, guarding the newly-constructed railways and protecting the towns as they rose on the plains." Also in 1872—the year that John Casey enlisted in the Tenth Cavalry—the creation of Yellowstone National Park supplied another milestone on the path of the nation's progress. Yellowstone was itself an outgrowth of what Miles called "the extension of channels of communication and commerce, and the steady westward march of settlements as the long trains of cars came laden with immigrants, not only from the East, but from all parts of Europe, and established hamlet after hamlet, and village after village, farther and still farther toward the western horizon."[3]

As it turns out, the transformation of more than two million acres of wilderness—most of it in Wyoming and the remainder in Montana and Idaho—into a national "pleasuring ground" had begun when General Henry Dana Washburn and Lieutenant Gustavus Cheyney Doane, veteran officers of the federal army who had chosen to remain in the military after the Civil War, led the first official expedition of the Yellowstone region more than sixty years after a white American had first been known to set foot there. Their original assignment was simply to provide an escort for a group of civilian explorers, presumably in anticipation of any clashes with the Native Americans in the area (no such clashes took place). In the end, however, the Washburn/Doane expedition had produced a "surprising wealth of diaries, articles, reports, and letters describing the expedition's great adventure on the Yellowstone Plateau," which in turn generated great interest in the region.[4]

Predictably, the first Washburn/Doane expedition was followed by others, and before long, the volume of information and the abundance of enthusiasm it stirred led Congress to pass bills placing under federal control roughly 3,500 square miles of territory, which would be named Yellowstone National Park. The bills' charge to the Department of the Interior was to "provide for the preservation, from injury or spoliation, of all timber, mineral deposits, natural curiosities, or wonders within said park, and their retention in their natural condition." But it seems clear that these "natural curiosities" did not include the Sheepeater Indians—Shoshone who were so called on account of their dependence on the bighorn sheep that were plentiful in the region, where the Shoshone lived year round—or the many other Native Americans who hunted on that land. Moreover, within just a few years after the park's creation, its first superintendent, Philetus Norris, constructed Fort Yellowstone close to the park's Mammoth Hot Springs entrance explicitly to "stand off the attacks of hostile Indians," of which there is virtually no evidence. Two years later Norris issued an edict declaring the park entirely off-limits to all Native Americans, and beginning in 1886 the army regularly posted cavalry troopers (none of them black) inside the park to keep the treasures of "Wonderland" safe from Native American intruders as well as white poachers. Clearly Yellowstone's establishment marked an important moment in the ongoing nation-building process, which involved mastering the nation's Native people, the wildlife upon which they depended, and the land upon which they lived and roamed, transforming all for the purposes of U.S. settlement, security, and "scenic tourism."[5]

Developments in the progress of the national agenda such as the completion of the transcontinental rail lines and the founding of Yellowstone National Park were followed by the end of the Red River War and the collapse of Indian resistance on the Southern Plains. Already by the spring of 1876, ten years before Geronimo's surrender and a century after the British American colonies' declaration of independence, the United States had much to celebrate. Indeed, that year's Centennial Exposition in Philadelphia was called for by President Grant specifically to trumpet a century of national advancement and to showcase the evidence of the country's ongoing achievements in nation building. A "monument to the 'Progress of the Age,'" the "International Exhibition of Arts, Manufactures and Products of the Soil and Mine" opened on May 10 in Philadelphia's 3,000-acre Fairmount Park, and over the course of the next six months, roughly 20 percent of all Americans—almost 10 million people (though many of these attended more than once)—attended, over 186,000 passing through the gates on the very first day. The Main Building (as it was named), built of wood, iron, and glass, was at the time the largest building in the world, measuring almost 2,000 feet in length and over 450 feet in width.[6]

The exposition's organizers, led by the Civil War veteran General Joseph R. Hawley, were highly selective about what to include among the fair's exhibits. Fittingly, given its contributions to precisely the sort of national progress the exposition meant to celebrate, the military was well represented from the start, beginning with the opening-day parade. "Through the mud and drizzling rain" characteristic of a Pennsylvania spring, wrote J. S. Ingram, author of a massive tome detailing the exposition's various displays,

> the various regiments then in the city, composing the National Guard of Pennsylvania, marched early to the place of assembling. Previous to the first trumpet-blare, Governor [and Civil War veteran John F.] Hartranft and his brilliantly-accoutred staff appeared . . . and a few minutes after . . . the signal for the start was given. Out Walnut street proceeded the rows of glistening bayonets. . . . The head of the line had scarcely arrived at the residence of George W. Childs . . . when President Grant stepped out upon the door-step. . . . Accompanied by his escort . . . he then took a position in the line.

Not only Grant but also Generals Sherman and Sheridan were present, participating in an immense procession of American and foreign dignitaries who marched through the fairgrounds. The parade highlighted the military's importance at the exposition and acknowledged its

"Bird's Eye View" of the Centennial Exposition Grounds, Philadelphia, 1876. *Courtesy of the Library of Congress.*

significance in having made the exposition possible in the first place by quelling Indian unrest and protecting settlers in frontier territories and the railroads that connected those territories to the rest of the nation.[7]

The military also had a strong presence in what was called the Government Building, over which a representative of the U.S. Ordnance Corps presided. Here the exhibits offered some indication of the government's peacetime functions, but emphasized "its resources as a war power." The War Department exhibit, for one, impressed viewers with its portrayal of the scope and technological sophistication of the Signal Service Bureau, "fully equipped and in operation, with recording instruments, telegraph wires, and printing press," as well as a "full corps of observers." The exhibit also showed off ordnance and weapons of various sorts, including a "20-inch Rodman Gun, weighing 115,000 pounds," requiring "a charge of 200 pounds of powder," and capable of throwing "a 1080-pound ball."[8]

In contrast to their emphasis on the military, the organizers of the exposition sharply minimized the contributions of others to the nation's progress and prosperity, including those of American women. They did include an exhibit called the Woman's School House and, under duress from feminists, the Woman's Pavilion, where the organizers played it safe by displaying such things as female silk weavers making fabric by means of power looms. Organizers also omitted almost all explicit representations of the centuries of black, mostly slave, labor upon which America's economic and industrial strength was founded. At the same time, despite the fair's heavy attention to the military's ongoing efforts on behalf of the nation, organizers provided for no exhibit whatsoever acknowledging blacks' costly service during the Civil War or—even as the fair itself was taking place—on the western frontier. This particular omission is even more striking given that Centennial Commission President Joseph Hawley himself had witnessed the impressive performance of black soldiers in action during the February 1864 Battle of Olustee in Florida, where he had commanded a brigade that included the Eighth U.S. Colored Infantry regiment.[9]

But evidence of black men's military service was not on display at the Centennial Exposition, echoing the USCT's overall absence from the Grand Review of the federal armies in May 1865. Indeed, the virtual erasure of black Americans generally at the fair was put into higher relief by a few troubling exceptions, one being a concession stand called "the Southern Restaurant," run by a white businessman from Atlanta, which was described in a guidebook as featuring "a band of old-time plantation 'darkies' who will sing their quaint melodies and strum the banjo before visitors of every clime." Only two black artists—Edmonia Lewis and Edward M. Bannister—were permitted to put their work on display, and only one work of art at the fair directly related to the experience of American blacks: a statue by a white sculptor entitled *The Freed Slave*.

Caricature of a black family visiting the Centennial Exposition, from *Harper's Weekly*, 1876. *Courtesy of the Library of Congress.*

As if to add insult to injury—but essentially replicating their overall lack of opportunity in the national economy—black Americans were even denied access to potentially lucrative jobs associated with bringing the exposition to life. In addition to being written out of the story of the nation's growing wealth, progress, and stability, they were, as the historian Robert Rydell has noted, "excluded from the construction crews that built the exhibition halls" despite a black unemployment rate of 70 percent in Philadelphia at the time. "Once the fair opened, the only employment available for blacks was as entertainers or as waiters, hotel clerks, messengers, and janitors." Even Frederick Douglass, who had, in fact, been invited to join a host of other dignitaries at the opening ceremonies but not to give a speech, was initially denied entrance to the park on opening day by police who failed to recognize him.[10]

Although it sidelined black Americans, the Centennial Exposition did offer some representations of Native Americans, under the guidance of Spencer F. Baird, a well-known naturalist associated with the

Smithsonian. Baird had spent two years preparing the exhibits, traveling to the West to gather artifacts from Native people who, he believed, would within the next hundred years "have entirely ceased to present any distinctive characters" and would instead "be merged in the general population." Given Baird's point of view, it should not be surprising that the displays he created were part of the War Department exhibit. In addition, fair organizers set up a small encampment of Native Americans—among them an individual described by one white observer as a "little, puckered-mouth, pug nosed Esquimaux"—for fairgoers' observation and enjoyment, and at the same time, presumably, for the Indians' own education regarding the majesty and power of white civilization and the federal government. Such displays suggested that the Indians were already part of the nation's past, not fighting for their survival in the present, as indeed the Sioux and Cheyenne were doing at that very moment in what would come to be known as the Great Sioux War on the Northern Plains. The U.S. army's largest undertaking since the close of the Civil War, the Great Sioux War spanned a region encompassing southeastern Montana and northwestern South Dakota (an area in which no black Regulars were then stationed). It was in the course of this war, and just a month after the exposition opened, that George Armstrong Custer and almost his entire Seventh Cavalry command were killed by the Sioux leader Sitting Bull and his determined followers at a site along Montana's Little Bighorn River.[11]

The Centennial Exposition closed in November 1876. Early the following year, in the shadow of the March 1877 inauguration of President Rutherford B. Hayes, U.S. occupation troops made their final withdrawal from the former Confederacy, signaling, in theory at least, the end of Reconstruction (black troops, as we have seen, had been withdrawn from the South to the West considerably earlier). That spring, in good measure through the efforts of Nelson Miles and his white Fifth Infantry, the Great Sioux War wound down, as large numbers of Indians surrendered and returned to the Great Sioux reservation, although Sitting Bull managed to survive and escape with a band of followers to

Sitting Bull, ca. 1885. *Courtesy of the Library of Congress.*

Canada. Another important Sioux leader, Crazy Horse, died in September 1877. Recalled Black Elk after Crazy Horse's death, "Our people were all sad because Crazy Horse was dead, and now they were going to pen us up in little islands and make us be like Wasichus," Black Elk's term for white people.[12]

The army's conquest of the Northern Plains continued in 1877, as General Miles unexpectedly found himself at the head of a mixed command of white infantry and cavalry chasing another group of desperate Native people—Chief Joseph and his band of about 800 Nez Percé from the Pacific Northwest—right through the middle of Yellowstone National Park, as they made a bid to join Sitting Bull in Canada, beyond the reach of the U.S. army and government. Instead of freedom, the

Chief Joseph, ca. 1902. *Courtesy of the Library of Congress.*

Nez Percé's daring three-month, 1,700-mile flight—in which about 120 of the Indians and almost 200 white civilians and soldiers died—ultimately led to Chief Joseph's surrender to Miles on October 5, 1877, at Bear Paw in Montana, about 50 miles south of the Canadian border. Then, in mid-1881, a combination of hunger, exhaustion, and persistent military threat finally drove Sitting Bull and his followers to the breaking point, and on July 19 Sitting Bull himself, along with the last roughly 200 remaining members of his band, surrendered to Major David H. Brotherton at the Dakota Territory's Fort Buford.[13]

The Great Sioux War was over, and the Northern Plains, like the Southern Plains, was to all intents and purposes at peace and under the control of the United States. Two years later, standardized time zones were established across the country, and the first telephone connection was established between New York and Chicago. In addition, whereas only four decades earlier some forty million North American buffalo had "blackened the Great Plains and fed the material, spiritual, and cultural needs" of the Native people living there, in the fall of 1883 the last of the large-scale buffalo hunts by non-Natives took place, making way for westering ranchers and their cattle. "I can remember when the bison were so many that they could not be counted," recalled the Sioux leader Black Elk many years later, "but more and more Wasichus came to kill them until there were only heaps of bones scattered where they used to be."[14]

Clearly, by the 1880s—which would also see the death of Victorio and the surrenders of Geronimo and Mangas Coloradas and their bands—the nation-building work of the post–Civil War period, however one judges it on moral grounds, was well underway, thanks in large part to the contributions of the U.S. army, including its black enlisted men. Despite the black Regulars' unflagging and costly engagement in and commitment to this national agenda, however, it is equally clear that the obstacles standing in the way of their own and other black Americans' progress toward equality and full citizenship remained plentiful and intransigent. Looking back over the same block of time during which the United States—with the black regulars' help—actively asserted its authority over the continent, one sees black Americans generally striving to assert their citizenship, with some successes, but also many disappointments.

Indeed, in the words of the historian Eric Foner, "Virtually from the moment the Civil War ended, the search began for legal means of subordinating a volatile black population that regarded economic independence as a corollary of freedom and the old labor discipline as a badge of slavery." Mere months after the Civil War's end, for example, and notwithstanding the federal (including USCT) occupation troops' determined efforts to sustain the former slaves' new freedoms, states across the South, beginning with Mississippi and South Carolina, had started developing "black codes" to undermine them. These codes denied black Americans the right to serve on juries; limited their access to public accommodations and private land; forbade their intermarriage with whites; sharply restricted their mobility, their right of assembly, and their economic choices and opportunities; and outlined a variety of often harsh punishments for a host of purported infractions. As they spread across the South, the black codes sought to restrict black Americans' rights, to reconstruct key features of the now defunct institution of slavery as effectively as possible, and to thwart emancipation as well as the Thirteenth, Fourteenth, and Fifteenth Amendments to the U.S. Constitution, which freed the slaves permanently, promised black Americans equal protection under the law as citizens and, theoretically at least, granted black men the right to vote.[15]

Some Northerners may well have criticized the states of the former Confederacy for legislating postwar black codes, but in doing so, they should have brought attention to the similar constraints on full citizenship that Northern blacks also experienced. For although far fewer in number than Southern blacks, Northern blacks, too, were typically discriminated against in the law as well as by custom, excluded from juries and denied the right to testify against whites; segregated in schools, hotels, theaters, and other institutions; and forbidden to marry across the color line. They were also denied the right to vote: in the fall of 1865, even as South Carolina and Mississippi were designing their black codes, Connecticut, Wisconsin, and Minnesota defeated state referenda designed to enfranchise black men of voting age.[16]

Meanwhile, in the South—as we have already seen—powerful white resistance to blacks' improving social, economic, and political status was evident, some of it taking shape in the form of the Ku Klux Klan, founded soon after the war's end in Tennessee by the former Confederate cavalryman Nathan Bedford Forrest and others. Within two years, the KKK had become "a hooded terrorist organization dedicated to the preservation of white supremacy," whose influence was on the rise. Moreover, the KKK was hardly the only post–Civil War organization dedicated to white supremacy; joining it were groups like the Knights of the White Camelia, the White Brotherhood, and the White League in Louisiana. It certainly seems probable that members of the KKK and organizations like it had helped to instigate the race riots in Memphis and New Orleans in 1866, and they undoubtedly played a role in the many similar race riots that erupted across the South in the years ahead.[17]

From the beginning, of course, federal occupation forces in the

South—including USCT troops—had struggled to limit white suprem-
acists' ability to operate. In addition, by 1871, President Grant and the
federal government had begun taking more rigorous steps to squelch the
KKK by means of an extensive investigation, which then led to the 1871
Ku Klux Klan Act. This act not only defined the violent intimidation
practices for which KKK activists were well known as punishable crimes
under federal law; it also gave more teeth to the enforcement of protec-
tive federal laws in the South, even by means of military deployment.
Before long, the KKK Act, and federal determination to implement it,
was making some headway toward bringing the KKK and similar organizations under control.[18]

Still, efforts to sustain white supremacy in the South and across the
nation endured, fueled by whites' desire to undermine black Americans'
determination to claim their full rights as citizens. In the spring of 1873,
Colfax, South Carolina, became the site of yet another ghastly race riot,
one that is reminiscent of the Confederate massacre of black soldiers
at Fort Pillow, Tennessee, almost a decade earlier. On Easter Sunday,
as the result of a political dispute that had been brewing for months, a
group of whites bearing rifles and small cannons murdered fifty black
Americans (many of them former USCT soldiers), although the blacks
had laid down their own weapons and raised a flag of surrender. Three
years later in Hamburg, South Carolina, an angry exchange of words
escalated into a clash between armed whites and blacks that resulted
in twenty-five of the blacks being taken into custody. Five of the jailed
black men were then murdered in the middle of the night, after which
the murderers and their allies—none of whom ever came to justice—
went on a spree destroying property in the black community. According
to one black witness, throughout the bloody events in South Carolina
(which later came to be known as the Hamburg Massacre), whites were
heard repeatedly declaring, "This is the beginning of the redemption of
South Carolina," by which they meant the restoration of white Democratic Party authority in the state.[19]

For a time in the South, the Freedmen's Bureau had served (at least in part) as a buffer between the freedpeople's efforts to lay claim to citizenship and white Southerners' efforts to virtually reenslave (or eradicate) them. In the period during which it was fully operational, the Freedmen's Bureau provided a vast range of essential services to the former slaves, including supplying immediate relief in the form of food and other necessities; helping the former slaves find paid forms of employment and negotiating wage-labor contracts; founding schools and hospitals; assisting the freedpeople in their efforts to find family members from whom they had been forcibly separated and helping them establish and protect their families through the law; serving as an advocate in court; and so forth. But the bureau's ability to function in any meaningful way declined steadily over the four years after its war-time creation. As early as December 1868, all of its operations, besides paying those freedmen who had served in the military or their estates, were shut down. Soon the bureau's remaining functions were discontinued as well, leaving more than four million black Southerners, only six years after the war's end, but after more than two hundred years of slavery, without a significant federal government agency dedicated to their assistance. No such agency, it bears noting, had ever existed for black Northerners.[20]

It would be wrong to suggest that black Americans' efforts to claim the rights of full citizenship were completely unsuccessful. Despite the many huge obstacles they confronted, black Americans after Appomattox enjoyed tangible and profoundly important social, economic, and political advances, among which the passage and ratification of the Reconstruction amendments to the Constitution were of particular significance. The 1866 passage of the Southern Homestead Act, too, had provided more than just hope to some. The act set aside tens of millions of acres of public land in Alabama, Arkansas, Florida, Louisiana, and Mississippi to be claimed, theoretically, in eighty-acre segments by the freedpeople (as well as Unionist white Southerners) who took up residence and set about cultivating the land for themselves. Although in the end, according to the historian James M. McPherson, "[f]ewer than seven thousand freedmen claimed homesteads, and only a thousand of these fulfilled the requirements for final ownership," for those thousand freedmen, landownership was a source of pride and independence unthinkable just a few years before.[21]

Moreover, in the decades after the Civil War, black literacy rates, which had hovered around 10 percent for decades, increased dramatically because of the upsurge in the proportion of black children now enjoying access to formal education. In addition, thousands of black men in these years could and did register to vote, and then turned around and used their votes effectively to elect other black men to political office. Another sign of progress was the passage of the 1875 Civil Rights Act, based on a bill that Senator Charles Sumner and others had introduced years earlier, which extended the promises of the Fourteenth Amendment by granting the federal government power to enforce the desegregation of all public spaces, including schools, transportation, and theaters, which the Fourteenth Amendment had left in the hands of the states.[22]

There is no denying that, in the years following the Civil War, despite the enormous and daunting resistance of many white Americans, the political, social, and economic status of black Americans—especially the roughly 90 percent of black Americans who had been slaves—showed important signs of improvement. "To me the wonder is," declared Frederick Douglass in 1880, "not that the freedmen have made so little progress, but, rather, that they have made so much—not that they have been standing still, but that they have been able to stand at all." Standing and, one might add, faithfully serving their nation.[23]

Indeed, the creation of permanent regiments of black soldiers in the U.S. army and their ongoing deployment to the frontier to advance the national agenda must be seen, at least in part, in a positive light. Military service in the black Regular regiments was, after all, a form of steady—if dangerous and often tedious—paid employment that offered thousands of black men a break from the long history of cruel agricultural servitude. Joining the army also meant adventure, travel, training in new skills, the possibility of a rudimentary education, the right to bear and use a firearm, and the chance to become a recognized leader of other black men. Perhaps more important, postwar military service on the frontier offered a new and welcome opportunity for black men to assert themselves as "true" Americans in light of Douglass's 1863 promise, that by fulfilling one of the key responsibilities of nineteenth-century male citizenship they might earn citizenship's full rights. At the same time, by virtue of the work they were assigned to perform, black Regulars in the West found themselves for the first time acknowledged, and even publicly rewarded, as representatives—perhaps exemplars—of American civilization, in contrast to the supposedly base savagery of the Native Americans they were sent west to suppress. For these and other reasons, black men's right to enlist in the postwar army suggests that the federal government was delegating to its military arm some of the work of redressing centuries of black Americans' legal, social, economic, and political subordination, although, admittedly, at the expense of the continent's indigenous people.

Moreover, some white army officers—typically those who had commanded black troops themselves, such as Benjamin Grierson—had since the war's end demonstrated a particular degree of concern and interest in the overall status and future of black Americans generally. Key among these was Samuel Chapman Armstrong, a Civil War veteran who had served as a commanding officer in two separate USCT regiments and whose experience with black soldiers led him to grapple with questions pertaining to the intersection of race, military service, citizenship, and justice in America. Within the limits of his own culture, circumstances, and character, Armstrong struggled to help shape a future for the nation in which whites and nonwhites could live peacefully together.

The son of an Irish Protestant missionary and his wife (of Massachusetts Puritan heritage), Armstrong was, interestingly, a naturalized white American, having been born in 1839 in Hawaii, where he lived until he traveled to Massachusetts in 1860 to attend Williams College. Beginning in 1862, Samuel Armstrong spent three years as a federal army officer,

including as the lieutenant
colonel of the Ninth U.S.
Colored Infantry Regiment
and then as colonel of the
Eighth. After the war, in
February 1866, Armstrong
became the Freedmen's
Bureau's superintendent
for the Ninth Subdistrict of
Virginia, an area extending
over nine counties in the
eastern portion of the state,
which included the village
of Hampton as well as Fortress Monroe. In addition to
serving as Jefferson Davis's
postwar prison, the fort,
as Armstrong well knew,
was located just miles from
where the first ship bearing

Brevet Brigadier General Samuel Chapman
Armstrong, founder of the Hampton Normal
and Agricultural Institute, ca. 1865. *Courtesy of
the Library of Congress.*

slaves to America had landed in 1619. It was also the federal installa-
tion at which General Benjamin F. Butler, in May 1861, had famously
declared his unwillingness to return runaway slaves to their masters,
coining the term "contraband." In the wake of Appomattox, the area
became home to forty thousand freed slaves. As such, it offered a historic and potentially fertile site for contemplating—and perhaps even
developing—new social and racial arrangements in postwar America.[24]

In connection with his work for the Freedmen's Bureau, in 1868
Armstrong established Hampton Normal and Agricultural Institute.
Hampton was not unlike other schools that were then being founded for
the freedpeople elsewhere across the South, including Howard University, founded in 1867 and named after Freedmen's Bureau commissioner
and Civil War veteran Oliver Otis Howard. In founding and develop-

ing Hampton, Armstrong translated his own personal experience with nonwhite people and the mission schools in Hawaii into an effort to contribute to the nation's racial progress by providing the former slaves with the education necessary to make their way in free society. However, neither Armstrong himself nor the staff he assembled at Hampton were unadulterated egalitarians. Even as late as 1862, Armstrong himself had expressed ambivalence about slavery: "I am sort of an abolitionist," he said, "but I have not learned to love the Negro." Two decades later, Armstrong still refused to condemn slavery outright. For all its horrors, Armstrong believed that slavery had propelled the education of blacks about civilization, and he vowed to continue this project. "I will begin in a humble way," he insisted, to "open the door for this people . . . into intelligence, self-control, manhood and womanhood, and send my pupils over all this southern land to be centers of light and love, examples of diligence and loyalty to the noblest motives."[25]

In the end, Hampton Institute proved markedly less elevated than the ideals Armstrong had initially expressed. The school was designed primarily to teach young black Americans of both sexes to read, write, do mathematics, and master the domestic and agricultural skills they needed to become efficient, or in Armstrong's words, "mechanical," laborers themselves and to teach other black Americans to do so, too. The result was that Hampton became the top vocational school for black American men in the postwar South. While it amounted to an unimaginably rich education for those who had previously been denied all forms of schooling whatsoever, it is also clear that its founder understood racial uplift through education—and, arguably, black citizenship as a whole—in distinctly limited terms.[26]

Interestingly, even as black soldiers were coming face-to-face with Native Americans on the frontier, the black students at Hampton Institute began encountering Native people on their campus. During the first ten years after its founding, Hampton Institute's student body was all black, but in 1877 Armstrong proposed to the Department of the Interior that Hampton enroll students from among the Nez Percé who had so recently surrendered to Nelson Miles near Yellowstone National Park. On October 31 of that year, the school accepted its first Native American student, a Ute named Peter Johnson who had previously taken classes at Christian Fleetwood's alma mater, Ashmun Institute/ Lincoln University. Then, in April 1878, at the urging of his fellow veteran Richard Henry Pratt, Armstrong began accepting more Native American students, initiating what came to be known as Hampton's Indian Branch, a program that remained in place for the next twenty-five years.[27]

Lieutenant Pratt was not only a white Civil War veteran like Armstrong (he had served with three different Indiana regiments); he was also a veteran officer of Benjamin Grierson's postwar black Tenth Cavalry, with which he had served since its organization in the late 1860s. Indeed, Pratt had extensive experience both with the black soldiers under his command—from whose courage and dedication he learned, as he explained many years later, that "so far as the national defense is concerned they are equal to the emergencies"—and with Native Americans. During the 1874–75 Red River War, Pratt had worked with the Tenth Cavalry's troopers to subdue the warring Native people in northern Texas and the Indian Territory, and had also been given temporary command of a company of forty-four Tonkawa Indian scouts assigned to the regiment to assist the troopers with their tasks. Then, in the spring of

Captain Richard Henry Pratt, founder of the Carlisle Indian Industrial School, in civilian dress, ca. 1890. *Courtesy of the Yale Collection of Western Americana, Beinecke Rare Book and Manuscript Library.*

1875, at the close of the Red River War, when President Grant ordered that the male "ringleaders" of the Native American forces that had been arrayed against the U.S. army be separated from their families and imprisoned at some distant location, it was Pratt who took responsibility for the transfer of these "ringleaders" from Fort Sill to Fort Marion in St. Augustine, Florida.[28]

Not surprisingly, Pratt's involvement with black soldiers as well as Native American allies and enemies had influenced his attitudes toward race in America generally. Even while he was on duty in the West, "Pratt made decisions with racial implications in a more flexible and practical manner than his superiors may have. Although on the one hand he supported the conquering of Indian peoples at any cost, on the other he could look beyond race when dealing with 'civilized' individuals." Subsequently, in a manner perhaps somewhat more progressive and egalitarian than that of Samuel Armstrong, Pratt came to see both groups as entirely capable, given proper discipline (including military discipline), education, guidance, and regular exposure to white American civilization, of sharing the rights and responsibilities of full citizenship. He further judged white Americans' denial of these rights and responsibilities for black and Native Americans to be criminal and immoral. In his memoir, *Battlefield and Classroom*, Pratt recalled a conversation he had with a white fellow officer in the Tenth Cavalry in the earliest days of his service with the black regiment, one that proved crucial in shaping his ideas about race and citizenship in America. He remembered,

> Being sworn as army officers "to support and defend the Constitution of the United States against all enemies foreign and domestic," we gave consideration to our immediate duties. The fourteenth and fifteenth amendments to the Constitution then pending before the states provided that "All persons born or naturalized in the United States, and subject to its jurisdiction, are citizens thereof." We talked of these high purposes and the Declaration of Independence, which affirmed that "all men are created equal with certain inalienable

rights," etc., and then contrasted these declarations and the proposed amendment with . . . the case of the Negro[. W]e were agreed
that when the fourteenth amendment became part of the Constitution, the Negro would be entitled to be treated in every way as other
citizens. . . . The rights of citizenship included fraternity and equal
privilege for development.

Admittedly, Pratt's view of "development" was only egalitarian in the
sense that he believed that all nonwhite Americans should and could
develop in such a way as to model and blend into white civilization and
culture. Still, in Pratt's mind, such a multiracial, if otherwise uniform,
culture was possible.[29]

For Pratt, the key was for nonwhites—as many foreign immigrants
had done over the course of America's history—to leave their languages
and cultural traditions behind and to adopt, as fully as possible, white
Protestant ways, to "go out and live among us as individual men, adopt
our language, our industries and become a part of the power that was
fast making this country so great and was sure to make it vastly greater
as the years rolled on." From Pratt's perspective, then, segregation of
the races in any form, including in the military, was wrong. "I firmly
believe," he wrote many years later,

> that had there never been separate organizations in the Army, and
> the colored man had gone into the service in white Companies, there
> would have been far less Jim-Crow-car, separate schools and other
> schemes throughout the country that build race prejudice and bar
> individual rights. Each man would have stood for his own individual
> merits, and race merit would have been far less his hindrance.[30]

Moreover, Pratt firmly believed in the principle of integration,
and he vehemently opposed lynching. "Such conduct," Pratt declared,
"smirches any claim to our higher civilization." He also dismissed as
irrelevant white anxieties about intermarriage. Toward the end of the

century he wrote in a letter to his friend and fellow veteran army officer Montgomery C. Meigs, "I must differ with you on the questions of races and the brotherhood of man. . . . In the providences of the Almighty," individuals of different races "are thrown together here in one country, and if individuals see their affinities in crossing the races, that is, in my judgment, entirely their affair." Pratt also resisted the tendency to consider the progeny of black-white unions by definition "Negro," as well as the assumption that all black Americans were somehow irremediably depraved. In alluding to the rape of black women by white men, he declared, "To say that the negro is exceptionally prone to immorality is only a guess which the millions of mulattoes and their origin contradicts." In sum, Pratt insisted that the races must be brought together for a harmonious and egalitarian America to emerge. In some ways, Pratt's views were not so different from those expressed by Frederick Douglass back in 1869, when he spoke of a "composite" American nationality and declared that "the salvation of every race in this country, is in becoming an integral part of the American government, becoming incorporated into the American body politic, incorporated into society, having common aims, common objects, and common instrumentalities with which to work . . . side by side. The further [black Americans] get apart the more we are hated; the nearer we come together, the more we are loved."[31]

Unlike Samuel Armstrong, although his sympathy, support, and vision of racial harmony embraced black Americans, Pratt focused primarily on Native Americans. Like other military men, over the course of his years with the Tenth Cavalry, Pratt had become disenchanted with the treatment afforded by the federal government, specifically the Bureau of Indian Affairs, to them. Routine neglect, spoiled and insufficient rations, and broken promises of all sorts, Pratt believed, were at the root of the Indians' refusal to remain submissive and of their regular recourse to violent raiding. And so, aware of experiments underway in the education of the freedpeople—such as Armstrong's Hampton Institute—Pratt began developing his own vision with his Indian prisoners at Fort Marion, of establishing vocational schools for Native Americans off the reservation, in lieu of the mission schools that had existed on the reservations for years. In such schools, Pratt came to believe that, as had been the case for black Americans in slavery, the cultural traditions of the Native children could be erased and replaced by the values, skills, and cultural traditions of white civilization, which would in turn prepare them for full citizenship. Moreover, by planting such schools in the midst of white communities, Pratt hoped to educate white Americans about the capacity for civilization and citizenship of the country's nonwhite people.[32]

Pratt was determined to test his theory. And so, over the three years from 1875 to 1878, while Armstrong was pursuing black industrial education at Hampton Institute, Pratt established a sort of educational boot camp for his prisoners at Fort Marion. First, he removed the prisoners' shackles, cut their hair, denied them war paint, issued them military uniforms, and had them build themselves reasonably comfortable living and sleeping quarters. Then this white officer of a black cavalry regiment (from which he remained officially on detachment) established strict regulations for his Native prisoners with regard to caring for their uniforms, their personal hygiene (including "regular bathing in the sea"), and their quarters. He also organized the men into companies, instructed them in military drill, and even assigned them as guards over each other. At the same time, local women, led by Pratt's wife, volunteered to teach the incarcerated Indians how to read and write English, purportedly in exchange for archery lessons. Gradually, the educational program at Fort Marion expanded to include other subjects, such as art, and in time, constraints on the prisoners' movement in and out of the fort diminished, with some eventually taking paid jobs as day laborers beyond the prison walls.[33]

In 1878, their three-year term of exile having expired, Pratt's charges were finally released from Fort Marion, and most of them returned to Indian Territory, although a handful went on to other locations in the East, supported by funding from various New England philanthropists who had come to admire Pratt's work. In addition, seventeen of the former prisoners traveled with Pratt to Virginia, where they enrolled in April at Armstrong's Hampton Institute. For the most part, the Indian students did extremely well at Hampton, which encouraged Pratt, who remained there for about six months, to recruit—with Armstrong's permission—another fifty students, both boys and girls, for the school's Indian program.[34]

The bringing together of black and Native American youth at Hampton produced some friction, in part a consequence of Armstrong's requirement—presumably supported by Pratt—that black and Native American students share rooms. Although the school's black students initially seem to have resisted this order, eventually all seventeen of the Indian enrollees were successfully housed. At the same time, black students were rewarded with key privileges in what turned out to be—despite the shared rooms—a hierarchical rather than an egalitarian race system. For Armstrong's willingness to bring the races together at the school was inflected by his determination to position the black students over the Indian ones, and to have them function as " 'civilizers,' hoping to make Indians more 'teachable' by exposing them to a race praised as sunny and demonstrative," not to mention cooperative.[35]

It would seem that by creating a racial hierarchy in which black students held superior positions over Native American students, Armstrong offered what may have seemed a comforting kind of symmetry to his black students for the white-over-black arrangements that prevailed in the South and in the nation, generally. Moreover, as the historian Donal Lindsey writes, the "Hampton formula of race relations" may well have helped "to ease the disappointment of blacks at the retreat from the constitutional guarantees of Reconstruction. By teaching another race new skills," black students "were made to feel proud of what they had and less resentful of what was denied them, thereby promoting contentment without social change." One can only imagine that out on the western frontier, maintaining the army's arrangement in which black enlisted men and noncommissioned officers served *under* white commanders but *over* Native American subordinates and "enemies" served the same purpose and had the same result.[36]

Perhaps not surprisingly, given Armstrong's military background, one of the ways that black students' "superiority" over Native American students at Hampton was made manifest was in the granting of the power of enforcement—specifically, the enforcement of federal regulations—to black students over their Native American "peers." Whereas black students were free to leave the school grounds temporarily or even permanently if they so desired, Native American students, as federal government wards, were under Armstrong's custody. As a result, their activities and their comings and goings were closely monitored, and if they went beyond the school grounds' boundaries, they were forcibly returned by the local sheriff or a military escort. At the school black students were assigned, essentially, as auxiliaries to local military and police forces, to keep Native American students in line. Even worse, an underground "guard house" was built to discipline recalcitrant students, though it was apparently never employed for the punishment of errant blacks. Native American students resented these features of the Hampton program—not least of all the ways in which black students were routinely given the right to serve as the school's on-site "military muscle." At the same time, black students for the most part seem to have appreciated the distinctions in power being made between them and the Indian students, which served as "evidence of their superior status and as their reward for accepting and helping to 'tame'" people whom Armstrong—though not Pratt—considered even less civilized, or civilizable.[37]

Unhappy with the racial arrangements at Hampton as they affected "his" Native American students, Pratt, who also likely just wanted his own laboratory in which to experiment, soon began to seek opportunities to establish a school exclusively for Native American children from the reservations. In the middle of 1879, in central Pennsylvania, Pratt located what seemed like a perfect site for his proposed venture, just over thirty miles from Gettysburg: a deserted military base in Carlisle.

Black and Native American students studying "mechanical drawing" together at the Hampton Institute, ca. 1895. *Courtesy of the Library of Congress.*

Pratt applied to General Winfield Scott Hancock, then commanding the U.S. army's Department of the East, as well as the secretary of the interior and the War Department, for permission to use the former cavalry post for his school. By September, permission to establish what came to be known as the Carlisle Indian Industrial School was secured. Pratt then selected a promising woman teacher, a Miss Mather, whom he had known in St. Augustine, and traveled with her to Pine Ridge (Sioux) reservation and elsewhere in the Dakota Territory to recruit his first group of students. Over the next quarter of a century, and despite his seemingly more elevated expectations of blacks' and Indians' capacity for (and worthiness of) the full rights of citizenship, Pratt—rather like Armstrong—attempted to train his students not as intellectuals but as diligent laborers, with an eye toward making their integration into white society more rapid and successful. Not unlike Hampton Institute for black Americans, Carlisle became a model of what whites such as Pratt thought education could accomplish for Native Americans. One could also argue that Carlisle embodied a vision of assimilation that amounted to nothing more than cultural genocide or "education for extinction."[38]

Even as Armstrong and Pratt were grappling with the meaning of education for nonwhite Americans, other military men were pondering what role, if any, the U.S. Military Academy at West Point should play, and specifically what the implications might be of expanding black men's opportunities within the Regular army to include access to the commissioned officers' ranks. For it must be recalled that just as they faced abundant obstacles to full citizenship wherever else they turned in the postwar period, so too did black men continue to confront stiff resistance to their complete equality within the U.S. military. Although the 1866 Army Reorganization Act had made it possible for black men to enlist as regular soldiers and earn promotion within the noncommissioned ranks (sergeant and below), it had—following the tradition of the USCT—segregated them within their own units and placed them under the command of white commissioned officers. Many whites, both within the army and outside of it, fervently opposed the idea that a black man should be permitted to serve as a commissioned officer (lieutenant and above) in the U.S. army, especially if the men under his authority might themselves be white. In short, even as the black Regulars on the frontier were doing the nation's work at great peril to their own lives, the U.S. Military Academy at West Point became a key focus for postwar clashes over how far the quest for black equality should go within the army itself.

As it turns out, the first young black man to attempt the desegregation of the academy had arrived in the spring of 1870, two years after the founding of Hampton Institute and the same year Emanuel Stance earned his Medal of Honor out on the frontier, by which point in its nearly sixty-year-long history the academy had graduated almost three thousand white cadets. A native of Mississippi, Michael Howard was

Senator Hiram Rhodes Revels of Mississippi, ca. 1870.
Courtesy of the Library of Congress.

described by a newspaper reporter as "a bright-looking boy, a little over five feet in height, slender in physique, airy and cheerful in disposition, and modest in demeanor." Howard's appointment to the academy was the work of Senator Hiram Rhodes Revels of Mississippi, a freeborn black native of North Carolina who had served during the Civil War as the chaplain of a USCT regiment. After the war, in the newly (if briefly) expansive post-emancipation environment, Revels went into politics. Shortly before he appointed Howard to the academy, Revels had taken up his duty in Washington, D.C., as the first black American elected to the U.S. Senate. Senator Revels, too, then, was a trailblazer among black Americans striving to claim their full rights as American citizens, and one of his first acts as senator was to take on West Point. When Senator Revels's appointee reported to Brevet Major Edward C. Boynton at 3:00 p.m. on Monday, May 30, 1870, he became the first candidate for a West Point cadetship in the history of the academy who was known to be black. "His advent," commented the *New York Times*, "is the sensation of the season."[39]

Howard's arrival at West Point may have been the "sensation of the season," but it was hardly the first time West Point had found itself in the public spotlight. Since its 1802 founding, the academy had been a lightning rod for controversy, critics insisting that the school was, among other things, "elitist, expensive and superfluous in a democratic society," especially a society that had a long tradition of distrusting standing armies. West Point had weathered additional blows in the wake of the Confederate attack on Fort Sumter in 1861, after which approximately three hundred of its graduates—including illustrious ones such as Robert E. Lee—forswore their allegiance to the United States in order to serve the Confederacy. In the context of the Civil War, the ambivalent performance of some federal officers who had also graduated from the academy (such as George B. McClellan, John Pope, and Fitz-John Porter) raised further questions about the value of a West Point education, especially in light of the splendid work of some commanders who had not attended, such as Benjamin Grierson and Nelson Miles, who went on, in 1895, to become the commanding officer of the entire U.S. army.[40]

But the specific challenges that West Point, its staff and students, and leading military and political figures found themselves facing as a result of Michael Howard's arrival were unprecedented. Should Howard and other young black men be admitted for training as commissioned officers? Could black cadets succeed at the school both socially and intellectually? If they managed to graduate, could they be integrated successfully into the army's officer corps? When discussing the school's possible integration, one reporter noted that even the officers at the academy, despite "having fought for the colored race . . . on the battle-field . . . speak very doubtfully of the expediency of this venture." Most troubling to many was the feasibility of even one black cadet's mixing on a level of social equality with whites in a setting like West Point, where personal interactions would be unavoidable and frequent. Underlying most early expressions of concern about mixing the races at West Point, surely, was the recognition that a black cadet at West Point who made it through just the first year of training would theoretically be in a position, beginning in his second year, to give orders to white cadets of lower rank.[41]

For Howard himself, a number of much more practical and imme-diate questions arose as soon as he arrived at the school: where, for example, was he going to sleep and eat while he waited for his room to be readied on campus? Reports indicate that finding temporary lodging near the academy was no easy task for a young man whose African heri-tage was evinced by his very dark skin. Finally, however, after making a series of inquiries, Howard was able to work out a short-term arrange-ment with a "colored family" who lived not far from the campus, to provide him with room and board for the time being.[42]

Undoubtedly an even more pressing question for Howard than that of lodging was whether he could pass the entrance examinations that would enable him to begin his officer training in the fall. These examina-tions were famously rigorous, and it was not uncommon for 20 percent or more of the students who attempted them to fail. Moreover, having spent the bulk of his early life in slavery, Howard came to West Point, as so many enlistees came to the postwar black Regular regiments, with very little formal education, though he was certainly earnest. "He says he is studying hard," commented one reporter, "and is going to do his best." The reporter was not optimistic about Howard's likelihood of success. "Wishing to get some idea of Michael's chance," he wrote, "we questioned him as to his proficiency in elementary branches, and asked him to write his address for us. He took our paper and pencil and wrote his name and residence in a fair schoolboy hand; but his answers to our

questions on arithmetic, geography, grammar, and history induced solic-
itude as to his fate." The reporter pronounced Howard a "bright" and
"good boy," but concluded that "his preparation has been deficient."[43]

Indeed it had been: according to an academy circular from the early
1870s, appointees were expected to be "proficient in *Reading* and *Writing*; in the elements of *English Grammar*; in *Descriptive Geography*, particularly of our own country, and in the *History of the United States*."
They were also expected to be competent in basic arithmetic, including
addition, subtraction, multiplication, and division, and to be acquainted
with concepts of "*reduction*, simple and compound *proportion*, and vulgar
and decimal *fractions*." It is possible, of course, that the 1870 entrance
examinations were particularly difficult: at least one source indicates
that only 39 out of the 86 appointees, or 45 percent of those who took
the exams that summer, actually passed. Howard did not, and soon
headed back home.[44]

When he left West Point, though, Michael Howard did not leave
the academy devoid of black cadets. The very next day after Howard
had reported on campus, a second young black man had also arrived at
the school to prepare for the entrance examinations. And indeed, during
the summer the two aspiring black cadet candidates had briefly roomed
together. Unlike Howard, however, James Webster Smith, a native of
Columbia, South Carolina, went on to pass the exams, the first black
cadet candidate to do so and to advance to "plebe" status. Thanks to
a white benefactor named David Clark who had brought the freeborn
Smith north after the war, Smith had spent some time at a high school
in Hartford, Connecticut, where he had excelled before moving on to
Howard University, in Washington, D.C. While at Howard, Smith
came to the attention of Congressman Solomon L. Hoge, a white federal army veteran and native of Ohio who was now representing Smith's
home state of South Carolina and who decided to nominate Smith for
the cadetship. Thanks to his academic preparation, Smith found himself in a far better position to succeed at West Point—intellectually at
least—than Michael Howard had been.[45]

Smith was different from Michael Howard in another important way, too: whereas Howard seemed to have hoped to make his way quietly through his West Point career without responding to any potential provocations—"all I want is to be left alone," he had told a *New York Times* reporter—Smith was a fighter, his natural edges sharpened even more by his isolation once Howard departed. "Since he went away," Smith wrote in late June, "I have been lonely indeed." Smith was also prone to getting into trouble. And although it is impossible to know how many of the problems he encountered were the result of his prickly personality and how many were the result of whites' discriminatory acts—and, furthermore, how much Smith's combativeness was itself a consequence of his lifetime of struggle against racial oppression—it is clear that Smith's success on West Point's entrance examinations did not give way to overall success at the academy. For the time being, however, he persisted, encouraged, no doubt, by the ongoing support he received from his own father, himself a USCT veteran. "Don't let them run you away," wrote Israel Smith to his son in the summer of Smith's first year at the academy, undoubtedly recalling his own experiences in the Civil War; "for then they will say, the 'nigger' won't do. Show your spunk, and let them see that you will fight. That is what you are sent to West Point for."[46]

Smith also enjoyed support from his D.C. alma mater's namesake, General Oliver Otis Howard, himself no stranger to challenge. Having assumed command of the Third Maine Infantry in May 1861, O. O. Howard had risen quickly to brigade command, lost his right arm during the two-day battle of Seven Pines/Fair Oaks in the late spring of 1862, and returned to duty three months later to lead a division at Antietam and later at Fredericksburg, after which he commanded a corps at Chancellorsville and Gettysburg, and again, in the war's final year, during Sherman's campaign through Georgia and the Carolinas, in which Cadet Smith's father had participated. As Freedmen's Bureau commissioner, Howard had demonstrated his strong commitment to expanding educational opportunities for black Americans, supporting the establishment of schools for black children across the former Confederacy and helping to found the university that carried his name.

Now General Howard attempted to bring his military record and his concern for black education and uplift to bear on the situation of the only black cadet at West Point. By way of doing so, in July 1870 he sent the *Army and Navy Journal* a letter he had initially written privately to Smith, who had complained to him in late June about the white cadets' frequent "insults and ill-treatment," and what he believed to be their determined attempts to "run me off." In his dispatch, General Howard declared Cadet Smith "quick, able, honest," and "noble-spirited," and he urged the young man forward: "I do hope you will never think of giving up while you have health to stand the storm." As Smith's own father had done, Howard counseled the young man to withstand whatever hostility he endured from white cadets without fighting back. "Endure the insults without any show of fear," he wrote. "A prompt and able reply . . . will sometimes avail you." Moreover, this man whose religious faith and devotion had led him to be known during the Civil War as the "Christian General" insisted, "God, who allowed you to be born and live with the blood of the African in your veins, will bear you through every trial." Having experienced sufficient defeat and condemnation himself during the war, Howard went on to counsel Smith, "To be a soldier one need not only be brave in battle, but have an abundance of genuine fortitude so as to bear up in disaster and apparent defeat. There is no real defeat for the true soldier—his soul is unconquerable."[47]

It is likely that General Howard's encouragement bolstered Smith's determination to endure his solitude at West Point with as much patience as he could muster. Surely Smith was aware of the stakes: as had been the case for USCT soldiers just a few years earlier, especially when they were permitted to put down their shovels, pick up their guns, and go into battle, and as was now the case for the black Regulars on the western frontier, the eyes of the nation were watching. Should Smith survive and succeed at West Point, both academically and socially, the doors to the academy might open a bit wider for other young black men. Should

Smith fail, the doors would almost certainly swing shut again—at least for a while. "I say now," wrote a white observer some years later after having visited West Point several times, "that the indignities heaped upon Jimmy Smith would have been unbearable to any white boy of spirit. Hundreds of times a day he was publicly called names so mean that I dare not write them." It is hard to imagine that any young man in Smith's position, even the mildest-mannered young man, could have done much better than he did. But Smith was not mild mannered; moreover, he wanted respect and justice and fair treatment at the academy, and each situation in which one or more of these things was denied him wore his patience down further. In turn, each time Smith reacted negatively to the hostile treatment to which the white cadets routinely subjected him (including Ulysses Grant's son, Frederick Dent Grant, who overlapped at the academy during Smith's first year), Smith's stock at the academy declined. "He was a proud negro," one white West Pointer remarked. "I never heard him complain, but his black eyes used to flash when he was insulted."[48]

Meanwhile, as Smith strove to make his way at the nation's oldest military academy, white army men continued to engage in a lively debate about the place of black men there. Bits and pieces of this debate appeared in the *Army and Navy Journal*, one February 1871 article declaring the whole idea "a dangerous one." The author claimed, in principle, not to be opposed to permitting black men to attend nonmilitary schools as elite as Harvard, which had awarded an A.B. to its first black undergraduate, Richard T. Greener, the year Smith began at West Point, or Yale, which accepted its first black undergraduate, Alexander Bouchet, that same year. Nor did the author object to permitting black Americans (black American men, anyway) to serve in the U.S. Congress, like Michael Howard's sponsor to West Point, Senator Revels. The problem with allowing black men to attend West Point, however, was that black cadets, he believed, would seek not just military officer training but also "social equality" with the academy's whites.

Moreover, social interaction among the cadets on a level of "common equality" was unavoidable given the nature of the campus, the curriculum, and the numerous required group military activities, such as drill, mess, and parade. White cadets who found interacting with black cadets distasteful, this contributor to the *Journal* wrote, would have no recourse, unlike white students at a nonmilitary college or university, or white congressmen, who could more easily maintain their desired social distance from black peers and colleagues. "Mr. Revels in the Senate," he pointed out, "has his political rights and his status fixed by law." Nevertheless,

> It is still the unrestrained freedom of will of [white] Senators whether they elect to bring Mr. Revels into domestic and social relations with their families; and so of the [white] students in Harvard or Yale, whether they invite the colored [students] of the colleges to unrestrained social intercourse with their families, and open the way for intermarriage of the Anglo-Saxon and African races. . . . The laws of the Army, the regulations of the Military Academy, and the very rudiments of discipline, fix unalterably the social relations of cadets, and put the Anglo-Saxon and African on equality. They must sleep together, mess together, room together, drill and march together, and associate together. This is forcing the social problem in the wrong place.

The author went on to express what seems like a faux concern, that those who would suffer most from the presumably wrongheaded policy of admitting blacks to West Point were blacks themselves. "In the nature of things," he wrote, it "must prove on trial damaging to the very purpose the friends of the African race intend to promote—the elevation of the colored race."[49]

In the end, after four turbulent years, which included a year's suspension following a court-martial for lying, a famous incident in which he purportedly hit a white cadet with a water dipper during an argument, and several unsuccessful attempts by supporters to get President

Grant to intervene on his behalf, James Webster Smith was dismissed from the academy, allegedly for academic reasons. "The colored cadet Smith," reported the *Army and Navy Journal* on July 11, 1874, "has dropped quietly out of the Military Academy without protest, or even so much as a remark, from those vigilant exponents of 'public opinion,' who have heretofore taken such careful note of every movement which in any way concerned him. The disease of 'civil rights' as applied to the selection of cadets, left to run its course, has wrought its own cure." Returning to South Carolina, Smith briefly put his military training to use as the "commandant of cadets" at the South Carolina Agricultural and Mechanical Institute at Orangeburg, an all-black school (now South Carolina State University).[50]

At the same time, Smith put his editorial skills to use writing letters to a black newspaper based in Washington, D.C., the *New National Era and Citizen*, edited by Frederick Douglass. In these letters, Smith detailed his experiences at West Point, which he summed up with this statement: "While affairs remain at West Point as they have always been, and are now, no colored boy will graduate there." In another letter Smith insisted, "I never asked for *social equality* at West Point. I never visited the quarters of any professor, official, or cadet except on duty, for I did not wish any one to think that I was in any way desirous of social recognition by those who felt themselves superior to me on account of color." That Smith should have felt compelled after the fact to publicly disavow any desire for "social equality" is in and of itself a clear testament to the antagonism he faced during his years at West Point. Perhaps, too, his struggle for justice had worn him down physically as much as it clearly had emotionally: in 1876—the year of the Centennial Exposition in Philadelphia—Smith died of tuberculosis. He was twenty-six.[51]

Not surprisingly, black Americans during this period also explicitly engaged in the debate about black men's access to the Military Academy, including one particularly angry individual who wrote to a South Carolina newspaper following Smith's dismissal from the academy and signed his letter "Niger Nigorum." "No one who has watched the course of Cadet Smith and the undemocratic, selfish, and snobbish treatment he has experienced from the martinets of West Point . . . can help feeling that he returns home to-day . . . a young hero who has 'passed' in grit, pluck, perseverance, and all the better qualities which go to make up true manhood." The problem with the academy, this writer insisted, was that former Confederates had begun to reassert themselves there, as they were doing elsewhere. Former Confederates, he went on to explain, had no desire "to meet on terms of equality" at West Point "the sons of the fathers to whom [they] refused quarter in the war and butchered in cold blood at Fort Pillow." It was up to the federal government, then, either to bring the opponents of black equality in the army under control and make West Point a more hospitable environment for young black men seeking to become army officers, or to close the academy and similar institutions entirely and resort to training military officers, black and white, in other settings. The writer concluded with an admonition: "It is the duty of every member of Congress to see that the government sanctions no such [bigoted] spirit; and it becomes every loyal citizen who wishes to avoid the mistakes of the former war to see to it that no class be excluded, and that every boy, once admitted, shall have the strictest justice dealt out to him, a thing which, thus far, has not been done."[52]

To their great credit, despite the experiences of Michael Howard and James Smith, and even as the often rancorous debate over black cadets continued, young black men persisted in making their way to the academy. In one of his letters to the *New National Era*, Smith himself mentioned the arrival of another Howard University student, Henry Alonzo Napier, the year after he matriculated. For reasons that are not known, however, Napier, who came from Tennessee, did not remain at the academy for more than a few months, although it is clear that he passed his entrance examinations. The same was also true of Thomas Van Renssalaer Gibbs, appointed from Florida in 1872. In the spring of 1873, however, Henry Ossian Flipper of Georgia arrived, and Flipper's performance at West Point changed everything.[53]

Flipper was born a slave on March 21, 1856, in Thomas County, Georgia, which later became the site of the notorious Andersonville Prison. Flipper was the oldest of five children, all boys, born to the slaves Isabella Buckhalter and Festus Flipper. At the time the Civil War broke out, Henry Flipper and his family were living in Atlanta with the estranged wife of their owner, Ephraim G. Ponder, whom he later described as "a successful and influential slave-dealer." Either through benevolence or neglect, and in violation of the law, Ponder's wife, Ellen, began allowing the black people she owned to learn to read and write, and at the age of eight Henry began his schooling under the tutelage of an older slave, a highly unusual opportunity that cemented his lifelong interest in education.[54]

By the end of 1864, the destructive passage of Sherman's army through Georgia had driven many slaveholders to abandon their human and other property in order to save their own lives, and the Flippers were to all intents and purposes free. Soon Festus and Isabella established a business cooking meals and manufacturing and repairing shoes for the federal (including USCT) soldiers occupying Atlanta. When the soldiers departed, the restaurant end of the business remained, becoming the core of the Flippers' effort to climb from slavery to lower-middle-class status. Meanwhile, they saw to it that their children continued their education by hiring, somewhat ironically, the impoverished widow of a former Confederate soldier to tutor them. As a result, by the time he was ten, Henry Flipper, according to one biographer, "was already far ahead of most Georgia ex-slave children in education."[55]

As the war gave way to Reconstruction and Northern missionaries hastened south to fulfill their own goal of uplifting the freedpeople both spiritually and intellectually, Flipper's educational opportunities expanded. By the time he received his appointment to West Point, he had already spent a year at the American Missionary Society's college in Atlanta, which later came to be known as Atlanta University. Flipper had also undergone both a physical and an academic examination to determine whether he had a hope of surviving the ordeal that lay ahead. Tall (almost six two), slender (175 lbs), healthy, and well educated, Flipper passed both of these preliminary exams, and, at the end of April 1873, the Georgia congressman James Crawford Freeman, a white Republican, nominated him as a candidate to attend the Military Academy.[56]

According to Flipper himself, in a story that may be apocryphal, by the time he learned of his appointment he was so determined to enter the academy that he "refused a five-thousand-dollar bribe from a white Atlantan who was attempting to gain admission to West Point for his own son." "I had so set my mind on West Point," Flipper explained, "that, having the appointment, neither threats nor excessive bribes could induce me to relinquish it." Flipper arrived at the school on May 20, 1873, just short of three years after the ill-fated Michael Howard had reported there, and soon took and passed his entrance examinations. By July 1, Flipper had officially become a West Point cadet. Also beginning his career as a cadet in the summer of 1873 was another young black man, John Washington Williams of Virginia. However, although Williams passed his entrance examinations—apparently with the highest score of all the appointees that year—he failed his midyear exams a few months later and was dismissed. Flipper, in contrast, hung on.[57]

For his first year at West Point, Flipper shared a room with James Webster Smith, even though they were in different classes. Almost immediately, he experienced the same sort of bigotry that Smith had endured for the past three years. Indeed, even before Flipper matriculated, Smith tried to warn him about the treatment the academy's white cadets would surely inflict upon him, in what Flipper later described as a "sad letter" Smith had delivered to the young Georgian when he first arrived. Smith was right: on his very first day at the academy, Flipper was forced to endure the jeers of numerous white cadets as he walked across campus to his barracks. Over the next four years, Flipper put up with considerable social ostracism, as well as gawking curiosity, both from his fellow cadets and the national press, which became even more pronounced once Smith was dismissed in the summer of 1874 and Flipper was left on his own. Conditions seemed likely to improve in August 1876, the beginning of Flipper's fourth year, when, by dint of his successful completion of the entrance examinations, Johnson Chesnut Whittaker of South Carolina doubled the number of black cadets attending the school. But, although Flipper once again had a black roommate and companion, Whittaker's presence in the end did little to make his time at the academy easier.[58]

Still, Flipper bore his white classmates' hostility and harassment with patience, rising to the defense of some of his attackers on the basis of their simple ignorance, and insisting that the acts of outright hostility he encountered always came from, or were inspired by, the "rougher elements of the corps." Flipper apparently believed that, in the absence of these "rougher" sorts' influence, other constitutionally more gentle and fair-minded white cadets would have treated him kindly, as they often did when they first met him, or on the rare occasions when they encountered him off campus. Moreover, in spite of his birth in slavery, Flipper seems to have been "temperamentally suited to the U.S. Military Academy, with its emphasis on hierarchy, social class, and the code of gentlemanly honor." Explains the historian Quintard Taylor,

> Like most of his fellow cadets, he believed himself intellectually superior to most Americans of the era, regardless of their racial background. He held in contempt impoverished, poorly educated Euro-Americans, whom he saw as the repositories of most racial prejudice. But he scorned equally African Americans who he believed were not prepared for social equality because of their low educational and cultural attainments.

Flipper, in short, fundamentally endorsed the principle of social hierarchy, although for him one's proper place in the hierarchy should be a function not of race but of one's academic and other (including martial) accomplishments. At the academy itself, Flipper even claimed to recognize the importance of the practice of hazing—"It would simply be impossible," he wrote, "to mould and polish the social amalgamation at West Point without it. . . . Nothing so effectually makes a plebe submissive as hazing."⁵⁹

For better or worse, this attitude enabled Flipper to praise those white cadets whom he considered "gentlemen themselves," as well as his white officers. "I am most unwilling to believe it possible that any officer would treat with injustice a colored cadet who in true gentlemanly qualities, intelligence, and assiduousness equals or excels certain white ones who are treated with perfect equanimity." At the same time, Flipper criticized

Second Lieutenant Henry O. Flipper, 1877. *Courtesy of the U.S. Military Academy at West Point.*

those white cadets whom he considered inferior underachievers, a practice that led him to be, on balance, not particularly supportive of James Smith, whom he scolded for retaliating against his white oppressors in a fashion that was "not compatible with true dignity" and was, therefore, not "manly." In contrast to Smith, Flipper chose a path more like the one Michael Howard had hoped to walk: to endure his isolation, remain quiet in the face of ill-treatment, leave the disciplining of his challengers to others, and simply do the work that lay before him. "Not even the Massachusetts boys will associate" with him, declared Flipper's hometown newspaper in June 1874, in a reference to the Bay State's legendary liberalism on issues of race. But Flipper had a different perspective:

"There is a certain dignity in enduring [prejudice], which always evokes praise from those who indulge it, and also often discovers to them their error and its injustice."[60]

And so, from summer 1873 to summer 1877, Flipper steadily and quietly made his way through the academy's intellectual and other requirements essentially on his own. He did not participate in any significant social activities with his white peers, although he did take part in a ten-day encampment of some three hundred West Point cadets at the Centennial Exposition in 1876, which he later recalled quite fondly, including the moment when he was confronted by a white visitor with the words "You are quite an exhibition yourself. No one was expecting to see a colored cadet." Regarding the regular course of daily life at the academy, however, Flipper commented, "There was no society for me to enjoy, no friends, male or female, for me to visit, or with whom I could have any social intercourse, so absolute was my isolation." At the same time, Flipper does not seem to have complained even once, openly, about being ostracized. "I have the right—no one will deny it—of choosing or rejecting as companions whomsoever I will," he explained. "Am I to blame a man who prefers not to associate with me? If that be the only charge against him, then my verdict is for acquittal." In the end, Flipper's patience, diligence, and dignity paid off: in the summer of 1877, he became the first African American cadet to graduate from West Point and assume his post as a second lieutenant—the lowest commissioned officer rank in the U.S. army, but the same rank accorded to the academy's white graduates. Flipper graduated fiftieth in his class of seventy-six, which included the son of at least one white Civil War veteran who would have been pleased to witness Flipper's success, the now congressman Benjamin Butler, who had been a friend to runaway slaves during the Civil War, an advocate of the USCT and of the enlistment of black men in the Regular army, and in fact the first congressman to nominate a black man for a cadetship at the academy, though his nominee proved unqualified.[61]

Perhaps it was the self-contained poise and composure with which he endured his West Point years that led Flipper's classmates and their visiting families during the commencement ceremonies that summer to acknowledge his accomplishment with a clear display of enthusiasm and applause. Whatever the reason for their unexpected show of support, the reaction of his classmates and their families thrilled Flipper: "Oh how happy I was!" he recalled. "All signs of ostracism were gone." Moreover, during the next few months, while he was officially on leave pending orders from the army, the satisfactions Flipper associated with his momentous accomplishment multiplied. After graduation he traveled to New York City, where he attended a large gathering in his honor of some two hundred prominent black Americans, including one of Frederick Douglass's sons, Charles Remond Douglass, a veteran of the USCT's famed Fifty-fourth Massachusetts. Subsequently, Flipper returned home to Atlanta for a few weeks, where he found himself in popular demand as a lecturer. Then, in January 1878, he headed west to Fort Sill in Indian Territory to join his regiment, Grierson's Tenth Cavalry, as A Troop's second lieutenant. The man in command of A Troop was still Captain Nicholas Nolan, who had led the disastrous, eighty-six-hour, waterless scout on the Staked Plains of Texas the preceding summer, in which four black troopers had died.[62]

It seems ironic that in the same season that the newly minted second lieutenant Henry O. Flipper was being feted in New York and Atlanta, and only a dozen years after their creation, efforts to do away with the black regiments altogether were building in Congress once more. It does not represent a great leap of faith to recognize that it was at least in part because of the army's symbolic importance as a point of entry to the rights of full citizenship that some white Americans remained keen not only to deny black men access to West Point but also to push black Americans out of the army altogether, especially given the important inroads blacks had been making in the service since 1863. As "Niger Nigorum" pointed out in his comments about James Smith's dismissal from West Point, everywhere black Americans turned in the 1870s resurgent former Confederates and their northern Democratic supporters were increasingly making their presence and their white supremacist prejudices known; the nation's capital and the nation's armed services were hardly immune. Indeed, once Democrats took control of the House of Representatives in 1875—for the first time since the war—they dedicated themselves to attacking the army and diminishing its size.[63]

But the question of the future of the black Regular regiments had already arisen in Congress in 1874 when the House Committee on Military Affairs initiated a protracted series of hearings regarding proposed reductions in the army's overall size. Early in the hearings, General Sherman had spoken out, as he always did, against any downsizing. He also took the opportunity to praise in particular the black cavalrymen who were helping to secure the western frontier. It seems likely that making explicit statements of support for black soldiers did not come easily to Sherman, whose wartime concern for racial justice was limited at best, and who had displayed strong opposition to the idea of arming black soldiers against the Confederacy in the first place. Now, however, Sherman spoke on the black soldiers' behalf, specifically praising the Ninth Cavalry's troopers in Texas, who, he declared, "had certainly fulfilled the best expectations entertained by the friends of the Negro people."[64]

Two years later, in his comments before the ongoing hearings, Brigadier General E. O. C. Ord—then in command of the Department of Texas—appeared considerably less complimentary, describing those who tended to enlist in the black Regular regiments as representing "only the lowest class of colored men." Although he spoke harshly, it bears noting, however, that Ord did not explicitly support the dissolution of the black regiments, and his unfavorable remarks seem to have had to do with ongoing reports he was receiving at the time of conflicts between black soldiers and Mexican civilians on the Texas border rather than with his opinion of black soldiers' courage or military proficiency.

"The use of colored soldiers to cross the rivers after raiding Indians," Ord remarked, "is, in my opinion, impolitic, not because they have any want of bravery, but because their employment is much more offensive to the Mexican inhabitants than that of white soldiers."[65]

Still, word of Ord's comments spread from Washington to the West, provoking at least one white officer who had spent ten years in a black regiment—possibly Benjamin Grierson—to protest vigorously in the *Army and Navy Journal*. The black Regulars, he insisted, "endured cold, hunger, fatigue, and every hardship contingent to the duties . . . and there was not a single instance where one of them betrayed the trust reposed in him." Let the government investigate their performance, he challenged, and if the men were "weighed and found wanting," let them be discharged. If, on the contrary (and as the writer anticipated), black soldiers' records should be found comparable to those of white soldiers, "let them not have this rank injustice done them by doubting their fidelity" and making public statements about their incompetence.[66]

A month later the *Army and Navy Journal* published a second letter of support for the black troops from a correspondent who identified himself only as "A White Soldier" of twenty years' military service, and a Democrat. "No white soldier who is a man will refuse the black soldier justice because of his color," he wrote.

As one who has seen them fight at the battle of Nashville, who has seen them in Indian campaigns in Kansas standing all night at their horses' heads during a heavy storm, with the snow up to their knees; who has seen them in the hot months of July and August marching thirty miles a day on the "Staked Plains," with their heavy knapsacks, without a murmur; who has seen them put up with ill-treatment and injustice without complaint—I pronounce all the tales that have been told against them to be false. . . . [A]ny man who has served at the same posts with them, will tell you that they are sober, obedient, and trustworthy, and will fight as long as their officers will stand.[67]

In the course of these debates, and just over a year before Flipper's graduation from West Point, Congressman Henry B. Banning, an Ohio Democrat, introduced a new army reduction bill, to which he appended a section repealing the original 1866 Army Reorganization Act's stipulation that certain regiments be reserved for black enlistees. Banning asserted that the segregated regiments demeaned black soldiers, yet he went on to add that the army's black recruits were "of such a class that they can not be trusted or made of any benefit to themselves or the country." Banning, it seems, hoped to use desegregation as a device for restoring an exclusively white army. He expected that recruiting agents would select white men over black, and he further anticipated that black men who had considered military service would turn elsewhere for jobs, knowing that within integrated regiments they could hope for nothing better than subordinate status, discrimination, and white cruelty. Banning's bill passed in the now Democrat-controlled House, but not in the still Republican Senate.[68]

Some months later, increasingly distressed over these developments, a black Republican in Brownsville, Texas, wrote anxiously to Congressman Butler. In his letter, E. K. Davies argued that to abolish the black regiments and open the army up to supposedly color-blind enlistment meant that "the colored soldier would soon be a thing of the past." Davies urged Butler to take note, and to live up to his reputation as a "champion of the negro, who is willing to defend him and give him that justice which is his due." Impressed with Davies's argument, Butler forwarded the letter to Secretary of War James D. Cameron, son of Simon Cameron, who had held the same post for several months under President Lincoln. Cameron then sent the letter on to General Sherman, who, despite his earlier statements before the House Committee on Military Affairs (and the fact that black Regulars had saved his life), now dismissed any such concerns about the potential consequences of "color-blind" enlistment for black men's access to military service. Although he expressed certainty that "contact" between blacks and whites, in the army as elsewhere, would "obliterate prejudice of race," Sherman added that, in his opinion, "the experiment of converting" black men into soldiers had been no more than "partially successful," although by way of a backhanded compliment, Sherman attributed this to black Americans' inherently "kindly, peaceful" natures. But in the end, he declared, "the Army is not and should not be construed as a charitable institution." Sherman's primary concern, and the one that superseded all other considerations, was to maintain the size and strength of the army. Since the army was small and getting smaller all the time as a result of Congress's reductions, "we must get along with a minimum number" of soldiers, whose quality and potential for solid service "should be of the best." By this, he meant that the army's best soldiers were white.[69]

In his response to Sherman, Congressman Butler disagreed, sarcastically chalking up the general's opinion to his lack of direct experience commanding black soldiers during the Civil War, although a number of black regiments had been part of Sherman's vast army at least during the war's final year. It might be true, Butler noted, that black men tended to be "docile" and "temperate," even sometimes "lazy," but as their performance out west had proved, they were also "rugged," capable of living on spare rations and under harsh conditions and, when "well disciplined," of functioning as "good machines . . . in time of war." Sherman, in turn, insisted that while he supported black equality "in the Ranks as in Civil Life," he nevertheless believed that in contests with hostile Native people, whom he described as "the enemies of civilization," it was "men of muscle, endurance, will, [and] courage" who were needed—men who displayed "that wildness of nature that is liable unless properly directed to result in violence and crime." Given these requirements, Sherman concluded, somewhat curiously, that white men were better qualified.[70]

Like their postwar debates over the place of blacks in American society generally, the debate among whites over black men's overall status in the army—including their right to earn commissioned-officer status by completing a West Point education—had by no means been resolved by the time Henry Flipper graduated in the summer of 1877, although more than a decade had passed since the creation of the black Regular regiments and fourteen years since the formation of the USCT. Even as Flipper was giving lectures about his West Point experiences in the months before reporting for duty with the Tenth Cavalry on the frontier, the Civil War veteran Ambrose Burnside, once a general and now a senator representing his home state of Rhode Island, sponsored another bill, again ostensibly designed "to remove all restrictions now existing in regard to enlistments of the colored citizen in any arm of the United States army," but like Banning's bill, apt to have the result of removing black men from the army entirely. According to Burnside's bill, "hereafter the word color shall not be used to designate any soldier of the United States army," and at the same time "no distinction shall hereafter be made in the assignment of the soldier on account of color or previous descent."[71]

Like Banning's, Burnside's bill on its surface might appear progressive, particularly in relation to black men's quest for full citizenship through military service. Certainly it can be read positively, as a document of military desegregation, at least of the enlisted ranks, for it stated that as far as the black man was concerned, "all arms of the service, engineers, artillery, cavalry, infantry, [and] signal corps . . . shall be open to him." And Burnside himself claimed to believe that "integration was the only policy consistent with the doctrine of racial equality enshrined in Reconstruction legislation," not the least important of which was the Fourteenth Amendment, which had—in theory—guaranteed black Americans citizenship and equal protection under the law.[72]

Others who backed the bill also offered suggestions about ways in which the elimination of the segregated black regiments would improve the working conditions of the army's Regulars as a whole, not least its white officers. As the *New York Times* reported, sounding a now familiar theme, "For the reason that colored men are less susceptible to the evil effects of extreme heat, these regiments have been continually kept on duty along the Rio Grande River, from the Gulf of Mexico to the Pacific

Ocean, while other regiments have been transferred from one post to another at intervals of two or three years, and thus have been able to enjoy during at least a portion of their time the comforts and conveniences of civilization. . . . Many good [white] officers [of black regiments] have been compelled to resign for these reasons." The officers in question, the article continued, "do not desire the prohibition of colored men from the Army; on the contrary, they encourage their enlistment, but ask that they may be distributed equally throughout the service and not be confined to four regiments." By extension, desegregation of the army would lead to fairer deployment schedules for everyone, so that no regiments would be posted for too long in a region known for its particularly harsh climate.[73]

Still, like its predecessor, the Burnside bill must also be understood as a document whose ultimate consequence (if not necessarily its purpose) was likely to be what Banning had hoped for earlier: the complete exclusion of black American men from the U.S. army. This becomes even clearer when one reads the bill's second section, which authorized the president, as necessary, to fill the ranks of the four regiments currently designated as black regiments with enlisted men, "without reference or distinction of color." In other words, in cases where the regiments previously reserved for black soldiers did not have their full complement of enlisted men on the rolls, white soldiers could be enlisted in lieu of blacks. Those who strongly supported black men's right to military employment could hardly be expected to ignore the serious negative implications of this proposed policy.[74]

Ambrose Burnside's bill came before the Senate in the spring of 1878, just as Richard Henry Pratt's Indian former prisoners were making their way to Hampton Institute, Second Lieutenant Henry Flipper was taking up his responsibilities at Fort Sill in Indian Territory, and black Regulars were grappling with the Apache in Texas and New Mexico. As it turned out, the still Republican-controlled Senate voted to postpone discussion on the Burnside bill, and in the end, like Banning's bill, it never passed. But the debate over black men's proper place within the U.S. army was hardly over, and soon it would be intensified by the controversy surrounding the black cadet Johnson C. Whittaker, now struggling to complete his officer training at West Point without the comfort or benefit of Flipper's presence.

❋5❋

Insult and Injury

*[N]ever did a man walk the path of uprightness straighter than I did,
but the trap was cunningly laid and I was sacrificed, effective June
30, 1882.*

—Henry O. Flipper (1916)

JOHNSON WHITTAKER WAS BORN A SLAVE IN AUGUST 1858 IN CAM-
den, South Carolina, where his mother, Maria, served as a personal
attendant to Mary Chesnut, the famous elite Southern diarist.
After the Civil War, seven-year-old Whittaker, his mother, and his two
brothers remained in Camden and attempted to carve out a new life
for themselves in freedom. Like Henry Flipper's parents, Maria Whittaker was determined that her children would become educated, so she
sent her sons to a local school that had been set up by white Northern
missionaries. Young Whittaker studied there for five years. Later, he
went to the Camden public school before undergoing private tutoring
to prepare him for the recently integrated University of South Carolina's entrance examinations. These he passed when he was just shy of
sixteen, in July 1874.[1]

While studying at the University of South Carolina, Whittaker
came to the attention of Richard T. Greener, the first black graduate of

Harvard College and now a professor of mental and moral philosophy at the university. In 1876, Greener identified Whittaker as a strong candidate for an appointment to West Point, and on his recommendation, Congressman Solomon L. Hoge, who had also nominated James Webster Smith, nominated Whittaker to fill the vacancy created by Smith's dismissal. Late in August, Whittaker, who was now eighteen years old, five feet eight, and slight of build, arrived at the academy, where he soon took and passed the entrance examinations. For the next ten months, until Flipper's graduation, he and Flipper, West Point's only two black cadets, shared a room but did not, it appears, have a particularly close friendship.

Like the other black cadets who had preceded him, Whittaker experienced white resentment from the moment he arrived on campus. Early on, a white cadet from Alabama struck him in the face for no particular reason. Refusing to retaliate directly—perhaps under guidance from Flipper—Whittaker nevertheless informed school authorities what had happened. They responded, encouragingly, by court-martialing and then suspending the white cadet for six months, which meant that he had to repeat the school year. Whittaker, no doubt, was pleased with the initial results of having resisted fighting back with his fists. However, at least some white West Pointers seem to have interpreted Whittaker's restraint as cowardice (though they had also considered Smith's boldness an unacceptable form of aggression). Still, the rest of Whittaker's first year passed uneventfully, and although he was not at the top of his class academically, he was not at the bottom, either.[2]

After Flipper graduated in the summer of 1877, Whittaker briefly had the company of another promising black cadet, Charles A. Minnie of New York. But as Virginia's John Washington Williams had done in 1874, Minnie failed his midyear exams and was dismissed. Back in New York, Minnie reported to a journalist that "from the very moment he entered" the academy he had been "subjected constantly to a galling ostracism" by the white cadets, although he added—echoing Flipper's lenient attitude—that he had enjoyed relief from his peers' hostility in the form of the professors' and officers' "considerate and gentlemanly treatment," which "allowed no distinction of race or color to alter their bearing toward any student." Apparently believing that Minnie's criticism of the academy cadets might reflect poorly on his protégé, or have unpleasant consequences for him, Richard Greener wrote a letter of rebuttal to Minnie's accusations, asserting that Whittaker, unlike Minnie, had "won the respect of his teachers and fellow cadets" alike, and declaring, "Scholarship, gentlemanly conduct, and a punctilious regard for veracity will, in my humble judgment, enable any really meritorious colored youth to graduate from West Point."[3]

It is not clear how, in the end, Greener measured Whittaker's overall performance at the academy on the scale that he himself devised. Whittaker's fundamental academic abilities seem to have been sufficient, but he still ended up having to repeat his third year because of purported inadequacies in the classroom. Even with the advantage of taking classes a second time, Whittaker continued to struggle. Moreover, although he made friends with two of the academy's black servants and some black locals in the nearby town of Highland Falls, he had no one in his own position with whom to endure the white cadets' relentless hostility and harassment. In his Bible, Whittaker underlined passages expressing his loneliness.[4]

Then, in early April 1880, Whittaker's West Point experience took a dramatic turn: at the 6:00 a.m. roll call on the morning of April 6, Whittaker failed to appear. Responding to his absence, Major Alexander Piper sent the cadet officer of the day, George R. Burnett, to Whittaker's room. Getting no answer when he knocked on the door, Burnett entered. There he found the cadet lying to all appearances unconscious on the floor, wearing only his underclothes. Although Whittaker's head was resting on a pillow, his arms and legs were tied together with the same material that was used for cadets' belts, and his legs were also tied to his bed. Whittaker's body and face were covered with blood, and there was also blood all over the room, "on the center of the mattress, on the wall above the middle of the bed, and on the floor," as well as on

the door and on some material that was lying on the floor near Whittaker. Even the pillow under Whittaker's head was bloody, and near the
bed a blanket and comforter showed traces of blood as well. Also disturbing was the discovery of a blood-stained club, some burned pieces
of paper, a broken mirror, some clippings of hair that seemed to come
from Whittaker's head, a pocket knife with the blade open, a small pair
of scissors, and a bloodied handkerchief with the name tag removed.
Fearing that Whittaker was dead, Burnett—after asking two cadets to
stand guard—raced from the room to get help.[5]

When Burnett found Major Piper and told him what he had discovered, Piper rushed to the room, bringing an orderly with him. Check-
ing Whittaker's pulse, he was surprised to find it normal, and another
cadet informed Piper that he had just seen Whittaker's toe move. Obvi-
ously, Whittaker was not dead, but the extent of his injuries remained
unknown, and in an attempt to get a better look at them, Burnett
opened the tightly drawn curtains. He then cut the bindings on Whittaker's hands and legs. Whittaker remained motionless except for some
shivering, apparently caused by the coldness of the room. At this point
Major Piper sent his orderly for the academy's physician, Dr. Charles
Alexander. While he waited, Piper directed Burnett and several other
cadets who had gathered in the interim to join him in looking around
the room for clues about what had happened.[6]

When Dr. Alexander arrived about ten minutes later, he examined
Whittaker, who in Alexander's judgment was not even unconscious.
Alexander then attempted to elicit a response from Whittaker, whose
ear was bleeding, by shaking and pinching him and asking him questions. Although Whittaker mumbled vague responses, such as "Please
don't cut me," he did not seem to revive. To the doctor, though, a vague
flickering in one of Whittaker's eyelids and the appearance of discomfort when tapped hard on the chest suggested that the cadet was faking.
Meanwhile, Lieutenant Colonel Henry M. Lazelle, the commandant of
cadets at the academy, made his way to Whittaker's room. Lazelle was
the first official to hear Alexander's theory of Whittaker's deceit, upon

which the lieutenant colonel commanded Whittaker to "get up" and "be a man." At first Whittaker did not respond, but soon, thanks to additional shaking by Alexander, Whittaker opened his eyes and sat up.[7]

Shortly thereafter, Whittaker rose to his feet and limped across the room to his washbasin, where he began to scrub the blood from his face, even as Dr. Alexander attempted to examine and dress his wounds. At the same time, Whittaker began to speak about his ordeal: how he had been attacked in the middle of the night by three men, at least one of whom was wearing cadet gray; how he had been "seized by the throat and choked until [he] was almost suffocated" and "struck on the left temple and on the nose with something hard"; how he had been "completely overpowered" and thrown to the floor, his earlobes slashed by one of the men who claimed to want to "mark him like they do hogs down South," and cut large patches of hair from his head; and how he had struggled but been unable to resist, and then was tied up and left to suffer, but not before a pillow was placed under his head. According to Whittaker, his attackers had departed with the admonition that he remain silent about what had happened, and with words of assurance to one another that surely now Whittaker would abandon his studies at West Point. Too weak and frightened to cry for help, Whittaker had tried to free himself but, finding it impossible to do so, had lain on the floor until he either fell asleep or passed out.[8]

Whittaker's account was extensive, detailed and, as it turned out, unshakable. But it appears that Dr. Alexander and some others in the room had already made up their minds that he had fabricated the whole situation, and nothing in Whittaker's story then or later dissuaded them. When West Point Superintendent John M. Schofield, a Civil War veteran, arrived on the scene, he remained only long enough to have a look around, confirm that Whittaker was alive, and order Lazelle to initiate a full investigation. A number of cadets eagerly offered to help with the investigation, if only to prove that no white West Pointer was capable of committing such a horrible crime. Meanwhile, Dr. Alexander ordered Whittaker to the hospital, where he changed some dressings and asked

Whittaker to explain again what had happened. Whittaker repeated his story, and Alexander sent him away. A little later that morning, in conversation with yet another white officer, Whittaker added one crucial detail he had previously omitted: that he had received a threatening note the day before he was attacked. When asked to produce the note, he did so promptly. Then he went off to class while the investigation, which included a thorough examination of his room and all the evidence that had been found there, got underway.[9]

The investigation Lazelle oversaw over the next two days contained features that seem most irregular, including ordering that Whittaker's room be cleaned and reorganized immediately and all of his soiled and stained clothing be washed. In the end, Lazelle's report fingered Whittaker as the culprit. According to him, Whittaker had written the threatening note, staged the attack, inflicted his own wounds, cut off his hair, bound himself up, and bound his legs to the bed. He had then remained prone on his barracks room floor until it became necessary for him to feign unconsciousness after his absence at roll call drew notice. Clearly, Lazelle—who was hardly alone in his perspective—did not think it was possible for white cadets to have attacked Whittaker or, having attacked him, to lie about such deeds, although he was quite comfortable accusing the black cadet of deception. He recommended that Whittaker be given the opportunity to withdraw outright from the academy, or undergo either a court of inquiry—not unlike a grand jury investigation in the civil justice system—or a court-martial. Having read the report, Superintendent Schofield summoned Whittaker to his office and offered him the three choices. Whittaker requested that his story be heard by a court of inquiry. On April 8, Schofield issued the necessary orders, and on April 9 the court convened.[10]

In the days that followed, news of the incident at West Point traveled quickly beyond the bounds of the academy itself, in no small part because Superintendent Schofield agreed to a multitude of interviews about the case, in which he repeatedly expressed his suspicions about Whittaker's veracity. Newspapers like the *New York Times* and the *Wash-*

ington Post, as well as the military's own media organ, the *Army and Navy Journal*, picked up the story, which they followed for the many weeks to come. As a result, the Whittaker case "almost immediately became not simply the story of one cadet's plight but the account of West Point's treatment of [all] black cadets" and, by extension, of white Americans' treatment of black Americans more generally.[11]

As early as April 10, the *Army and Navy Journal* was weighing in on the case. At first, it posited two possible explanations for what had happened: either Whittaker had been attacked precisely as he claimed—and presumably on account of his race—by three men, at least one of whom was a fellow cadet; or he had fabricated the entire scenario to compensate for his academic inadequacies, in the hope that his wounds might land him in the academy hospital, prevent him from taking his exams, and buy him "another year of grace." Eventually the *Journal* published a third possible explanation: that Whittaker was essentially a coward who had "tamely submitted to an outrage which, in the case of any other cadet would be classed as an indignity," and then "quietly went to sleep and slept comfortably through reveille, and until awakened by the surgeon," at which point he found it necessary to devise a cover story.[12]

Other newspapers and some members of Congress, however, continued to believe that Whittaker was not only not a coward but was entirely innocent, the victim of a terrible, racial crime. These supporters argued that the academy was to blame on account of its failure to deal with its internal racism. The *Journal*, in turn, insisted that it was unfair to blame the white cadets—whom they, like Lazelle, considered upright and moral—for their ingrained racism, which was, after all, only a pale reflection of the racism found in the society at large. "[W]e think it unjust to hold the academy responsible for the existence of prejudice between the races that was implanted by parents and friends in the early years of life, which is far more deeply rooted in the public mind to-day than it is at West Point." The article even went so far as to cite some favorable comments about race relations at the academy from Henry Flipper's recently published autobiography, *The Colored Cadet at West*

"The West Point Outrage," a scene from the Whittaker court of inquiry. Originally published in *Harper's Weekly* in 1880. *Courtesy of the Library of Congress.*

Point. At the same time, the *Journal* also published an angry letter to the editor, signed by one "Ebbitt," who crudely likened Whittaker to Dred Scott as an unattractive "historical character" and suggested, paradoxically, that the case had been concocted to serve the agenda of members of Congress who supported the abolition of the Military Academy altogether.[13]

At the academy, Whittaker's court of inquiry dragged on. Also dragging on, it bears noting, was his painful isolation. Indeed, after the second day of the court of inquiry, it was determined that Whittaker should not even attend the sessions but should return to his classes, cutting him off from the proceedings and confining his knowledge of them to the newspapers or mentions of them in the halls. Even the *Army and Navy Journal* had to admit that Whittaker conducted himself during this stressful period with "nerve, coolness, self-possession, and defensive power that excited astonishment amongst all, and enthusiasm amongst those who still believe him innocent." Meanwhile, Whittaker communicated by letter with family and friends, especially Richard Greener, now dean of the law school at Howard University, who also came to visit. But in important, fundamental ways, Whittaker was alone.[14]

As for the case itself, as the weeks passed, it grew more and more convoluted, as different theories were brought into play about what had happened and about what the evidence presented at the court of inquiry meant. Over time, too, increasingly prominent figures in the army and the government became involved. Indeed, as early as April 14, only five days into the proceedings, no less a figure than the army's adjutant general, E. D. Townsend, arrived under orders from the secretary of war, Alexander Ramsey, to observe. Townsend promptly submitted to a newspaper interview, in which he expressed his own suspicions that Whittaker had indeed faked the attack.[15]

At the end of May 1880, the court of inquiry completed its business and issued its report, identifying Whittaker in no uncertain terms as guilty of having concocted the events under investigation. Superintendent Schofield immediately recommended that the black cadet be dismissed and perhaps also court-martialed. Surely Schofield yearned to bring an end to the incident and get the public spotlight off the academy as quickly as possible. But doing so was hardly simple. For one thing, many people who had found themselves wrapped up in the case still insisted that the court of inquiry's conclusions were questionable and that further discussion—about the events of April 6 and about the situation for black cadets at West Point generally—was required. These interested observers loudly demanded a new investigation, and some urgently called for Schofield's replacement as West Point's superintendent by someone more sympathetic to blacks' rights, such as Oliver Otis Howard. Meanwhile, Whittaker, who had been in the midst of his crucial year-end examinations when the court of inquiry issued its report, proceeded to fail his philosophy test.[16]

In this tense situation, an article entitled "Caste at West Point" appeared in the June 1880 issue of a highly influential popular journal, the *North American Review*. The article's author, Peter S. Michie, was a professor of natural and experimental philosophy at the academy, and much of his article was devoted to defending West Point against what he perceived to be the perennial assertions about its elitism and its function as an agency dedicated to producing military aristocrats. To the contrary, Michie argued, "[T]here is neither caste nor aristocracy now, and never has been, among the cadets. Men arrange themselves here, as elsewhere, by sympathy, by similarity of tastes, by ability, intelligence, and aptitude in their profession." Michie also devoted considerable attention to the fine moral record of the academy's nearly three thousand graduates to date (notably, he ignored the moral blemish represented by hundreds of cadets' demonstration of disloyalty to the nation during the Civil War). Wrote Michie, "The one sure, strong safeguard of the Military Academy is the degree in which its pupils hold sacred their word of honor. *They will not lie or steal.*" An army whose officers were without a strong moral core, Michie believed, was an army doomed to fail in any conflict. Fortunately for the U.S. army, West Point's graduates—at least the white ones—presumably suffered from no such character weakness.

Michie then turned to the question of black men's presence at the academy. Having just made a case for the lack of "caste" at the school, he nevertheless expressed doubts about whether, as he put it, "it was wise to endeavor to solve the problem of the social equality of the races at that time and at this place." Looking back over the years since James Webster Smith had first matriculated, Michie posited that things might have gone reasonably smoothly for the black cadets as a whole if they had only been more intelligent and—especially in the case of Smith—less "irascible" and "vindictive." Smith, Michie insisted, "came prepared to make trouble"; indeed, "the isolation that was his lot would have been the fate of any white cadet under similar circumstances," though one is hard-pressed to imagine how similar to Smith's a white cadet's circumstances could possibly have been. In any event, according to Michie, it was Smith's academic failures, not his race, that did him in. Turning to the other black cadets who had been appointed to the academy since Smith—including Flipper, the only one who had managed to graduate—Michie expressed the opinion that although they all seemed to have "excellent memories," to a man they had "displayed a marked deficiency in deductive reasoning."

As for the Whittaker case, Michie argued, quite stunningly, that rather than serving as an example of the academy's ongoing failure to embrace black cadets, it demonstrated how much *more* welcoming toward them the academy had in fact become over the past decade. After all, had not some of the white cadets expressed a measure of "human sympathy" toward Whittaker in the aftermath of his fabricated ordeal? More broadly, Michie insisted that none of the black cadets, including Whittaker, had ever been subjected to the "slightest indignity," nor had they been "hazed" or "deviled." To Michie, this was a detail of enormous importance, especially given that such good behavior on the part of white cadets toward black ones was really more than one had a "right to expect in this transition period," given the "almost universal prejudice" toward blacks that most white cadets had learned from their families and communities. Michie concluded, with an apparent attempt at magnanimity, "Let the authorities send here some young colored men who in ability are at least equal to the average white cadet, and possessed of manly qualities, and no matter how dark be the color of the skin, they will settle the question here as it must be settled in the country at large, on the basis of human intelligence and human sympathy."[17]

Michie wrote his article before the final decision in the Whittaker court of inquiry was handed down. In contrast, by the time his West Point colleague George L. Andrews, a professor of French, published his own article, "West Point and the Colored Cadets," in the November issue of the *International Review*, the court of inquiry's report had been published. In light of the report's conclusion that Whittaker had faked the attack, Andrews—who ironically had the same first and last name as the man who served with dedication as the black Twenty-fifth Infantry's colonel from 1871 to 1892—expressed even more vehemently than Michie his support for the academy, his faith in the fair treatment the black cadets to date had received, and his unwillingness to endorse any demand that white cadets should exceed the standards of race tolerance that their parents, friends, and communities manifested. At the same time, Andrews insisted, "Any assertion that either the authorities of the academy or the corps of cadets have intentionally pursued a course designed to get rid of colored cadets is wholly unwarranted. . . ."[18]

In his own annual report that fall, Superintendent Schofield addressed the Whittaker case along with the larger questions of whether blacks should be admitted to the academy and whether they could succeed either academically or socially there. Schofield declared that, to date, the black cadets' "social relations to their fellow-cadets" had been strained at best. Moreover, echoing Andrews and Michie, he asserted that "military discipline is not an effective means of promoting social intercourse or of overcoming social prejudice. On the contrary, the enforced association of the white cadets with their colored companions, to which they had never been accustomed before they came from home, appears to have destroyed any disposition which before existed to indulge in such an association." In order for black and white cadets to get along better at the academy, race relations across the nation would have to improve first.

Schofield went on to heap additional blame on the black cadets: the struggles of some, at least, had been the predictable consequence of their "bad personal character." He added, for good measure, that "to send to West Point for four years competition a young man who was born in slavery is to assume that half a generation has been sufficient to raise a colored man to the social, moral, and intellectual level which the average white man has reached in several hundred years. As well might the common farm horse be entered in a four miles race against the best blood inherited from a long line of English racers." That Whittaker's case had become a source of crude humor not just to Schofield but also far beyond the walls of the academy is indicated by the letter that Alice Grierson, wife of the Tenth Cavalry's colonel, wrote that fall to their son Charles, who had begun his studies at West Point the same year as Henry Flipper but had graduated after him: "Fanny Monroe gave a masquerade party last week," Alice wrote. "Lt Leavell said he wanted to person- ate Cadet Whittaker, and wanted to borrow your cadet uniform for the purpose. I loaned it to him, and he came in to show us how he looked, which was hideous. He had his face blackened, and then painted red in the most sav- age style."[19]

As discussion on the merits of his case contin- ued, Whittaker found him- self subject to orders issued on the last day of December 1880 by the nation's presi- dent, Rutherford B. Hayes,

Major General John M. Schofield, ca. 1865. *Courtesy of the Library of Congress.*

to come before a court-martial in connection with the April events. Although by now Whittaker must have expected the court-martial to produce the same verdict as his earlier court of inquiry, it did serve one key purpose: postponing his dismissal from the academy. The trial took place in New York City beginning on January 20, with the Fifth Infantry's General Nelson A. Miles presiding. The black Philadelphia newspaper, the *Christian Recorder*, was optimistic: "Miles," the paper declared, "believes in fair play for every man," and as a result, "the general opinion" was that the Whittaker case would be evaluated with impartiality. Two charges were brought against the defendant: "conduct unbecoming an officer and a gentleman" and "conduct prejudicial to good order and discipline."[20]

Although the testimony phase of the court-martial lasted four months, virtually no important new evidence or information was introduced, and public interest, perhaps predictably, gradually diminished. Then, on June 12, the *Washington Post* reported that the Whittaker court had "dissolved" and the judges had dispersed without immediately publicizing their verdict, which still required review by the army's judge advocate general (Brigadier General David G. Swaim), the secretary of war (Robert Todd Lincoln), and the newly inaugurated president (James A. Garfield). Subsequently, when the report of the court-martial became public, it revealed that Whittaker had indeed been found guilty on both counts, although it appears that six of the ten members of the court had signed a recommendation for clemency on the basis of Whittaker's "youth and inexperience," which would have eliminated the fine and the term of confinement required by his conviction but would not have revoked his discharge. Even more important: nine months later, in March 1882, President Chester Arthur (who took office following Garfield's assassination) disapproved the court's findings and sentence completely on the basis of procedural errors during the court-martial.[21]

In practice, though, none of these details made much difference: Whittaker's failure on his philosophy exam meant that he would be dismissed from the academy anyway, fulfilling the negative expectations Michie, Andrews, Schofield, and others had openly expressed. When news of the court's original decision first appeared, the *Washington Post* declared that it was Whittaker's character that had undone him, not his race. "Army officers are not prejudiced against Whittaker on account of the color of his skin," the paper declared. "Many, however, consider him ignorant and low in all his instincts." In contrast, however, the *Post* offered warm praise for Henry Flipper, who "gets along swimmingly with his brother officers, all of them white men, of the Tenth Cavalry." Flipper, the paper insisted, "is gentlemanly, intelligent and brave—qualities that are bound to command respect, be the color of their possessor's skin what it may." Ironically, within weeks of the *Post's* declaration of its support for the "gentlemanly, intelligent and brave" Tenth Cavalry's black second lieutenant, Flipper found himself under unusually severe confinement in a "sweltering six-and-one-half- by four-and-one-half-foot cell" in the guardhouse at Fort Davis, Texas, pending a court-martial of his own.[22]

Looking back over Flipper's brief span as a commissioned officer in the Tenth Cavalry, one finds no evidence to suggest that his military service would come to such a critical point so quickly, at least not on account of flaws in his performance as a soldier and an officer. His commanding officer Grierson noted that, since joining the regiment, Flipper had been "constantly on duty, serving as a company and staff officer with marked ability and success." He was, moreover, an honest man, whose "veracity and integrity" had "never been questioned" and whose "character and standing, as an officer and a gentleman," had been absolutely spotless. "I can testify to his efficiency and gallantry in the field," Grierson declared, pointing out that Flipper had "repeatedly been selected for special and important duties," which he had "discharged . . . faithfully and in a highly satisfactory manner." The fact that Flipper was the only black man to have completed officer training at West Point and achieved commissioned officer status in the U.S. army, Grierson acknowledged, meant that he served under particularly heavy pressure. And yet, Flipper had "steadily won his way by sterling worth and ability, by manly and soldierly bearing, to the confidence, respect and esteem of all with whom he has served or come in contact." Having learned of Flipper's arrest at Fort Davis, Grierson—who was himself then about three hundred miles away at Fort Concho—urged his superiors to offer Flipper a court of inquiry rather than consign him immediately to a court-martial, but he informed his wife that he thought the chances of his request being granted were slim.[23]

Flipper's military record with the Tenth Cavalry clearly bears out Grierson's confidence: during his first months of active duty, while at Fort Sill, Flipper had served for four months as acting commander of the regiment's G Troop during the troop captain's absence, and supervised road construction and the laying of telegraph lines in the area. During a stint at Texas's Fort Elliot, he worked as a surveyor and cartographer and also boldly led an investigation into illegal ammunitions

The guardhouse at Fort Davis where Lieutenant Flipper was held in August 1881. *Courtesy of the National Park Service: Fort Davis National Historic Site, Texas.*

sales that resulted in the arrest, court-martial, conviction, and three-year confinement of a white quartermaster sergeant, an outcome that surely caused resentment among some of his army officer colleagues, but not in Grierson. Returning to Fort Sill in 1879, Flipper devised and oversaw construction of a drainage system designed to eliminate the mosquito-breeding ponds of standing water that frequently plagued the fort, in order to improve the health of the soldiers posted there. This system, known as Flipper's Ditch, continues to be utilized today to control area floodwaters.[24]

Not all of Flipper's duties were related to his skills as an engineer: while posted at Fort Concho, Flipper also actively participated in the army's attempt to subdue the Apache leader Victorio, on one occasion riding almost a hundred miles in less than twenty-four hours—roughly twice the distance considered reasonable under the best of conditions—to convey important information to Grierson, then stationed at Eagle Springs. Flipper collapsed from exhaustion after he completed this task: "I had no bad effects from the hard ride till I reached the [commander's] tent," Flipper recalled years later. But "when I attempted to dismount, I found I was stiff and sore and fell from my horse to the ground" and proceeded to sleep "till the sun shining in my face woke me next morning." Then, on July 30, 1880, Flipper and his company of black Regulars engaged with Victorio's band for five hours, during which battle three of the soldiers serving with Flipper died. As it turned out, this was to be Flipper's only combat experience.[25]

Clearly, Flipper's record of excellent service in the Tenth Cavalry did not exempt him from criticism and accusation, however, and when he came before the judges at his Fort Davis court-martial in the fall of 1881, he faced two charges: embezzlement of federal funds and, like Whittaker, "conduct unbecoming an officer and a gentleman." Flipper had been the commissary of subsistence—the officer in charge of the fort's food supplies—since his arrival there the preceding fall, and according to the specifications in the case, between July 8 and August 13, 1881, he had falsified commissary records and mishandled accounts, resulting in a discrepancy of almost $4,000, which he seemed unable to explain satisfactorily. Testimony before a panel of eleven officers began on November 1 and lasted for about a month, during which time numerous local whites paid tributes to his fine character. "The more I saw of him, the better I liked him," declared J. B. Shields, a Fort Davis merchant. "I have always found him to be [a] straightforward man, of good character," testified another, Joseph Sender. "I have never seen anything in Lieutenant Flipper's conduct but what was becoming of a perfect gentleman," insisted W. S. Chamberlain, a watchmaker in town. At the same time, however, the prosecution brought forward a number of witnesses who presented contrary evidence, including their key witness Colonel William R. Shafter, now in command of the white First Infantry but previously—for more than a decade—the lieutenant colonel of the black Twenty-fourth.[26]

Since Shafter had taken command at Fort Davis in March 1881, there had been indications that his long-term willingness to command black troops did not necessarily reflect a comparable willingness to see black men themselves in command, at least not as commissioned officers. Or perhaps Shafter simply did not care for Henry Flipper. In any case, upon his arrival at Fort Davis, Shafter had acted quickly to curtail Flipper's responsibilities. In addition to his assignment as commissary of subsistence, Flipper had been serving for several months as acting

assistant quartermaster. "I had charge of the entire military reservation," he wrote later, "houses, water and fuel supply, transportation,
feed, clothing and equipment for troops and the food supply." Shafter,
however, replaced Flipper in this post with a white officer from his own
First Infantry. He also seems to have warned Flipper that his days as
commissary of subsistence were numbered.[27]

Reassigning army staff in this way was hardly unusual when a new
commander took charge, and Flipper's removal as assistant quartermaster may have been nothing more than the logical consequence of
Shafter's desire to select an officer of his own regiment for the position.
Moreover, at Flipper's court-martial Shafter insisted that he had found
the young black lieutenant, so far as he "could observe, always prompt
in attending to his duties," which Flipper had performed "intelligently
and to my entire satisfaction." Shafter maintained that his reasons for
replacing Flipper arose only from his belief that Flipper was a cavalry
officer who "ought to be assisting the other cavalry officers in performing their duties in the field" rather than doing administrative work at
the fort. But Flipper himself believed that the new post commander
was targeting him, especially after he received warnings from others in
and around the fort that he should do his best to stay on the famously
prickly Shafter's good side. "I had been cautioned," Flipper recalled
later, "that the commanding officer would improve any opportunity to
get me into trouble, and although I did not give much credit to it at the
time, it occurred to me very prominently when I found myself in difficulty. . . . [H]e had long been known to me by reputation and observation as a severe, stern man."[28]

Precisely how much Flipper failed in his quest to engender and sustain Shafter's goodwill, how much Shafter's "goodwill" was inflected
with deeply held racist notions, and how much Flipper simply bungled
his job as commissary of subsistence, can never be answered with certainty. The complicating features in Flipper's situation, and the court-
martial case itself, are too numerous, including the fact that another
of the prosecution's key witnesses was the white first lieutenant Louis

Wilhelmi, who not only was close to Shafter but also had been at West Point when Flipper was there; he had not, however, succeeded in graduating, for which he may have felt some personal resentment.[29]

Also complicating the situation, according to Flipper and others, was the interracial friction at the post that Flipper's friendship with a young white woman, Mollie Dwyer, seems to have stimulated. Dwyer was the unmarried sister-in-law of A Troop's Captain Nicholas Nolan (Nolan's wife, Annie Dwyer, was Mollie's older sister). Since the time that Mollie Dwyer and Flipper had met when he was on assignment with A Troop at Fort Sill in 1878, the two had been seen out riding together on many occasions. Indeed, for a time at Fort Sill, Flipper and Captain Nolan both had rooms in the officers' quarters, though there is no evidence that the relationship between the young black lieutenant and his captain's sister-in-law—who lived with Nolan and his wife—developed into an active, reciprocal romance during this period. Still, Flipper and Dwyer were clearly fond of each other. Things changed, however, once they were all at Fort Davis. A white officer and Civil War veteran with more substantial financial resources than Flipper—Lieutenant Charles E. Nordstrom—became interested in Dwyer, too. He even purchased "a luxurious riding buggy," apparently to lure Dwyer's attention away from Flipper, an affront that Flipper, understandably, resented. The rivalry between the two lieutenants appears to have become quite bitter and may well have fostered divisions among the other soldiers and officers posted there. One thing is certain: the Flipper-Dwyer-Nordstrom affair did not make Flipper's life at Fort Davis easier, nor did it help ensure his long-term success as an officer in the U.S. army.[30]

In the course of Flipper's court-martial, in the fall of 1881, Flipper insisted, with respect to the first charge against him, "I have never myself nor by another appropriated, converted, or applied to my own use a single dollar or a single penny of the money of the Government or permitted it to be done, or authorized any meddling with it whatever." That said, it seems clear, on the one hand, that Flipper—who had received no formal training for his administrative assignment—had indeed mishandled commissary money. At one point, rather than in the quartermaster's vault, he was storing some of the funds he had collected in a locked trunk in his quarters, to which Lucy Smith, a post servant, had access. He also left checks and cash lying about his room. On the other hand, most of the $4,000 originally believed missing was located, and the balance of a few hundred dollars, which Flipper in desperation temporarily tried to conceal by writing a check of his own on a non-existent account, was quickly covered by donations from members of the community who enthusiastically rallied to his support and some of whom were among the witnesses who later testified on his behalf.[31]

It is also clear that the officers (including Shafter) who might have provided Flipper with more guidance, training, and oversight in his position had failed to do so. Between May 28 and July 8, 1881, Shafter had, for unknown reasons, stopped performing regular reviews of Flipper's accounts, which allowed Flipper's errors and misjudgments to multiply. Unfortunately, rather than admitting that he had made errors, Flipper clumsily tried to cover his tracks, most likely out of a sense of panic exacerbated by his awareness that the eyes of the nation were upon him, especially in light of the recent events surrounding Whittaker. "I indulged," Flipper later wrote, "what proved to be a false hope that I would be able to work out my responsibility alone, and avoid giving him [Shafter] any knowledge of my embarrassment."[32]

But it was precisely Flipper's duplicity regarding the accounting problem that led to his downfall. For his part, Shafter seems to have been convinced that Flipper had been actively embezzling, rather than just being sloppy. But even if clumsiness and inexperience lay at the root of Flipper's bad accounting practices, Shafter felt strongly that Flipper's failure to come clean about his mistakes represented a failure of honor. As a result, his biographer Paul Carlson writes, Shafter was "unwilling to forgive his subaltern" and "struck back with all the considerable weight of his position as post commander."[33]

Flipper's court-martial at Fort Davis ended in early December 1881, almost exactly six months after Whittaker's court-martial had ended in

New York City. Unlike the Whittaker court-martial, however, Flipper's yielded a split verdict. That Flipper was found not guilty of embezzling federal funds implies that the judges recognized that he was careless rather than criminal. He was, however, found guilty of "conduct unbecoming an officer and a gentleman" on account of his behavior once he originally became aware of the discrepancies in the books that his blunders had produced. Like Whittaker's, Flipper's career with the U.S. army was over. Six months after the case closed, following a review by Judge Advocate General Swaim, Secretary of War Robert Lincoln, and President Arthur, Flipper was dismissed. And thus, by mid-June 1882, the U.S. army was once again without a single black commissioned officer, and West Point was once again without a single black cadet.[34]

Humiliated by their shared experiences with the army, both Flipper and Whittaker nevertheless went on to live impressively productive lives. Flipper's life in particular bore out the sort of confidence in him that Benjamin Grierson had expressed on account of his intelligence, competence, and integrity. From Fort Davis, Flipper moved briefly to El Paso, then took up work as a surveyor for a group of American mining companies in Mexico, where he became fluent in Spanish. He later worked as a cartographer before being hired as chief engineer for the Sonora Land Company of Chicago. In 1887 Flipper opened his own civil and mining engineer office in Nogales in the Arizona Territory, where he also edited a local newspaper. From 1890 to 1892 he worked as chief engineer for the Altar Land and Colonization Company in Nogales, in 1893 becoming a key witness in a land claims case in Nogales that pitted 700,000 acres' worth of white settlers' claims against those of a group of land speculators who were also lawyers; the judge ultimately found in favor of the settlers. As a result of this case and all of his previous work, Flipper was hired as a special agent for the U.S. Justice Department's Court of Private Land Claims and, according to the historian Quintard Taylor, for the next eight years "researched the Mexican archives, translated thousands of documents, surveyed land grants throughout southern Arizona, and prepared court materials. In the course of this work he translated and arranged, and the Justice Department published, a collection of Spanish and Mexican laws dating from the sixteenth century to 1853." In his final report about Flipper's work for the Justice Department, U.S. Attorney Matthew G. Reynolds offered nothing but praise. "During the seven years Mr. Flipper was connected with this office," Reynolds wrote, "his fidelity, integrity and magnificent ability were subjected to tests which few men ever encountered in life. How well they were met can be attested by the records of the Court of Private Land Claims and the Supreme Court of the United States."[35]

In 1901 Flipper took a job as an engineer for the Balvanera Mining Company in Mexico, which later became part of the Sierra Mining Company. Transferring to the company's El Paso office in 1912, Flipper remained an employee of Sierra until 1919, that year traveling to Washington, D.C., to become a translator and interpreter for the U.S. Senate's Committee on Foreign Relations. In 1921, he accepted a position as a special assistant to the Interior Department's Alaska Engineering Commission, and in 1923 he relocated to Caracas, Venezuela, as a consultant of the Pantepec Oil Company, over the next seven years aiding in developing Pantepec's oil-rich land holdings. Flipper's remarkable career finally ended after the stock market crash in 1929 severely damaged Pantepec's fortunes. He then spent a year in New York before returning in 1931 to the city of his youth, Atlanta, where—now retired—he moved in with his brother. Flipper died in Atlanta in May 1940, at the age of eighty-four.[36]

As for Johnson Whittaker, after his discharge from West Point, he initially took his case to the public, giving speeches in Buffalo, Baltimore, and Georgia about his West Point experiences. Subsequently, he moved to Charleston, South Carolina, where he accepted a job at the Avery Normal Institute, an all-black vocational and teacher-training school, and also took up the study of law. Whittaker was admitted to the South Carolina bar in 1885, and in 1887 he opened what quickly developed into a successful law practice in Sumter. Unlike Flipper, who remained single, Whittaker married in 1890 and had two children. In 1900, he moved his family to Orangeburg, South Carolina, gave up his law practice, and took a position teaching at the all-black Agricultural and Mechanical College—the same school, ironically, where James Webster Smith had served as commandant of cadets after his dismissal from West Point back in the 1870s. Eight years later, Whittaker moved his family again, this time to the new state of Oklahoma, where he taught at an all-black high school in Oklahoma City and ultimately became its principal. In 1925, the family returned to South Carolina. Whittaker died there in 1931.[37]

One way to understand the stories of Whittaker and Flipper in connection with West Point and the U.S. army is simply as chronicles of individual failure. But to read these stories—or those of other black American men, such as James Webster Smith and Michael Howard—purely as tales of individual failure is a mistake. For to do so ignores the fact that, just like the enlisted men in the USCT during the Civil War and early Reconstruction, and just like their counterparts in the postwar black regiments on the western frontier, Flipper, Whittaker, Howard, and Smith—their own personal flaws and weaknesses aside—were struggling to succeed as soldiers and as citizens under the extraordinary weight of the history and persistence of American racism.

Moreover, it cannot be denied that the timing of Flipper's and Whittaker's shared humiliation in the early 1880s raises important questions about the larger social and cultural context in which they—and the black Regulars generally—were operating, and how the dynamics of American race relations may have been spiraling downward in the second decade after Appomattox. Put another way, it is hard to avoid the conclusion that Flipper's and Whittaker's experiences reflect, at least in part, the renewal or intensification of white resistance to blacks' progress in the military, in conjunction with the ongoing deterioration in race relations nationally. It would seem that, by the beginning of the 1880s, black men's dedicated service on behalf of the national agenda had yielded only limited and tentative rewards, rather than the sort of richly construed and deeply meaningful citizenship that Frederick Douglass had envisioned for black soldiers in 1863 and that they, no doubt, envisioned for themselves. If Flipper's and Whittaker's cases are any guide, the social and political rewards that black men could hope for in return for their military service were diminishing, and the obstacles they, like black Americans generally, faced on the path to full and meaningful citizenship were intensifying.

As we have already seen, those who had hoped in the postwar period that the nation's justice system would steadily and consistently make the case for black Americans' full rights as citizens were destined to experience much disappointment and frustration. In addition to the events and issues discussed earlier, it bears noting that in 1873, even as Flipper was just beginning his career at West Point, the U.S. Supreme Court had declared, in what were collectively known as the *Slaughterhouse Cases*, that the crucial Fourteenth Amendment protected only those rights of citizenship "that owed their existence to the federal government," such things as "access to ports and navigable waterways" and "the ability to run for federal office, travel to the seat of government, and be protected on the high seas and abroad." All other rights of citizenship "remained under state control." Subsequently, in 1876, in the case *U.S.* v. *Cruikshank*, the justices overturned the convictions that a lower court had obtained against three whites in the 1873 Colfax, South Carolina, riot, added new language declaring that the Fourteenth Amendment "only empowered the federal government to prohibit violations of black rights by states," not by individuals, and reiterated that "the responsibility for punishing crimes by individuals rested where it always had—with local and state authorities." In 1878, in the case *Hall* v. *DeCuir*, which arose out of a claim by a black woman that she had been denied the right to sit in a Louisiana steamboat cabin reserved for whites, the Supreme Court declared segregation on public transportation legal. Then, in its 1882 decision in *United States* v. *Harris*, the Court voided the 1871 KKK Act. A year later, following its consideration of a series of racial discrimination cases that had arisen in Kansas, Tennessee, Missouri, and New

York—known collectively as the *Civil Rights Cases*—the Court determined that neither the Civil Rights Act of 1875 nor the Fourteenth Amendment could provide protection against discrimination by individuals. By the early 1880s, in short, as the U.S. army's officer corps was sealing its doors against black candidates, the Supreme Court was laying the foundation for Jim Crow.[38]

In the face of these and other disturbing developments, on New Year's Day 1883, a group of approximately fifty distinguished black leaders—including Frederick Douglass, his two sons who had served with the Fifty-fourth Massachusetts, and the USCT veteran and Medal of Honor winner Christian A. Fleetwood—gathered in the nation's capital to celebrate the twentieth anniversary of the Emancipation Proclamation. According to one contemporary account, the guests "represented a who's who of two generations of black politicians, civil servants, journalists, writers, professors, ministers," and, not least, black veterans. In the speech he gave at this event, Douglass "urged vigilance at the flame of black freedom and justice."[39]

The following September, just a short time before the Supreme Court handed down its decision in the *Civil Rights Cases*, a much larger gathering of black leaders took place at Liederkranz Hall in Louisville, Kentucky. Here, at the National Convention of Colored Men, more than two hundred men from twenty-seven states came together to discuss the political, social, and cultural situation facing black Americans and to consider the merits of blacks' ongoing loyalty to the Republican Party, the party of Abraham Lincoln. In the words of the *Los Angeles Times*—itself a testament to the success of the nation's postwar consolidation and expansion—the meeting was "a notable gathering of representative men of the race." Some observers described the gathering, which like its predecessor in January included many USCT veterans, less favorably: the Louisville convention, predicted the *New York Times* sourly on September 9, "bids fair to be a vent for jealousies and grievances."[40]

When he was asked why such a convention had been organized, Douglass, who served as chair and also gave the keynote speech, answered

simply, "because conventions in this free country are the usual instrumentalities through which great bodies of men make known their wants,
their wishes, and their purposes." Asked why black men deemed it necessary to come together on the basis of their race specifically, Douglass
pointed out, "We are, whether we will it or not, in some sense a separate
class from all other people of the country, and we have special interests
to subserve and special methods by which to subserve them." As he had
done in the nation's capital at the beginning of the year, Douglass urged
black Americans to continue to demand their rights as citizens in the
face of any and all emerging obstacles: "Now that we are free, we must,
like freemen, take the reins in our own hands and compel the world to
receive us as equals. . . . The negro's road downward is made easy, but
his struggle upward is obstructed from every quarter."[41]

The Louisville gathering, which lasted about four days and was
occasionally tumultuous, produced an official eleven-point statement
in which the delegates began by expressing appreciation for the abundant legislation that had been passed in the preceding twenty years on
black Americans' behalf. Signers of the statement noted, however, that
many of the new laws had quickly been reduced to meaninglessness,
especially in the South. There, "almost without exception," the conventioners pointed out, "the colored people are denied justice in the courts,
denied the fruits of their honest labor, defrauded of their political rights
at the ballot box, shut out from learning trades, cheated out of their civil
rights by innkeepers and common carrier companies, and left by the
States to an inadequate opportunity for education and general improvement." Notably, the conventioners did not directly address the situation
of blacks seeking U.S. army officer training, and indeed, that summer,
John Hanks Alexander of Helena, Arkansas—a freeborn man who had
attended Oberlin College before matriculating at West Point—had
succeeded in passing the academy's entrance exams. (In 1887, a decade
after Flipper, Alexander became only the second black man to graduate
from West Point, after which he served for seven years with the Ninth
Cavalry before dying in 1894 of natural causes.) But the delegates nev-

ertheless assailed the "distinction between white and colored troops in the army" as "un-American and ungrateful." White men, the delegates observed, "can enter any branch of the service, while colored men are confined to the cavalry and infantry services," a distinction that was "carried into the navy as well." Most likely because they believed that the desegregation of the army's regiments would lead directly to black men's exclusion from the service entirely, they did not express any negative sentiments about blacks' units being race-based.[42]

In their official statement, the delegates also condemned the collapse of the Freedman's Savings and Trust Company, which they termed "a marvel of our time." Established by the federal government in March 1865, the bank initially served as a depository for the savings of USCT soldiers but soon was opened to other black Americans as well. Its goal, in the words of the historian Carl Osthaus, was "to mold ex-slaves into middle-class citizens" by developing and encouraging among them "concepts of industry and thrift," as if such concepts were novelties for people who had lived lives of extreme deprivation for more than two centuries. The bank also offered a limited number of new employment opportunities for blacks, including both Christian Fleetwood and Frederick Douglass, the former as a clerk and the latter as the bank's president for a year. For a time, branches of the bank across the South did well, highlighting to the freedpeople and other observers "that progress was being made along the economic path 'up from slavery.'" But severe mismanagement (though not by Douglass, Fleetwood, or any of the other black officials of the bank), along with what Osthaus calls "the perversion of a philanthropic crusade into a speculative venture," from which "white speculators and real estate dealers" in Washington profited, led to the bank's collapse. The bank took with it almost three million dollars of the savings of its depositors—many of them still black veterans—only about half of which was ultimately repaid over the course of the next forty-odd years.[43]

The 1883 convention in Louisville decried the corruption that had led to the bank's collapse, which the delegates perceived as only one example of the many ways in which white Americans were continuing to obstruct black progress. In the end, the convention, writes the historian David Blight, "threw a bleak picture of African American conditions at the feet of the nation." Four years later, the frustrations of the men gathered in Louisville were reiterated when, in early August 1887, four thousand mostly black American civilians joined three hundred USCT veterans—led by those of the Fifty-fourth and Fifty-fifth Massachusetts Regiments—in what amounted to the first official black Civil War veterans reunion and "the largest known assembly of black former soldiers and sailors after the Civil War." In his welcoming speech for the two-day event, former second lieutenant James M. Trotter of the Fifty-fifth Massachusetts, one of the rare black men to have been granted an officer's commission during the war, reminded his fellow veterans that their history "was different from that of the rest of the army. You went forth to the war not knowing anything about the future," although "you knew that if you were captured you would be given no quarter." Trotter praised the courage and sacrifices of the men who had gathered on this occasion: "I see before me today," he declared, "men from all over . . . who were determined never to give up; men who were bound to fight until death."[44]

Similarly, General A. S. Hartwell, the white former commander of the Fifty-fifth Massachusetts, praised the veterans for their unique contributions to the nation's

Former Second Lieutenant James M. Trotter, in civilian dress, ca. 1880. *Courtesy of the Library of Congress.*

survival. "I know well," said Hartwell, "that when you enlisted in the war, you did what a white man could not do. You knew that the flag under which you fought . . . waved over enslaved millions of your own people. And yet you went to work." Later on that first day, James Trotter returned to introduce the black Sergeant William H. Carney, who "on the day of the terrible assault on Fort Wagner carried his country's flag triumphantly over the parapet amid the deadly storm of shot and shell." Still later, Trotter introduced Colonel W. H. Hart, the white former commander of the USCT's Thirty-sixth Connecticut Infantry, who expressed his enormous pride at having had the opportunity of "serving and commanding one of the best colored regiments ever mustered in [to] the service" of the U.S. army.[45]

Colonel Hart spoke of his pride, but he struck a different note as well, bringing his thoughts to a close by pointing out that "what the colored man wanted was justice, and that he was going to get it." The second day of the reunion was in fact dedicated to considering the conventioners' sense of black Americans' progress toward justice and full citizenship, as well as their ongoing responsibilities to the nation. By the end of that day, like the black men who had gathered in Louisville four years earlier, the black veterans in Boston produced a statement reflecting on "the present deplorable condition of the colored people in the South," who still accounted for more than 90 percent of the blacks in the United States as a whole. They cited black Americans' persistent "subjection to mob violence and deprivation of the right of suffrage." Like the delegates at Louisville, the former soldiers and their allies in Boston "declar[ed] it to be the duty of the Government to remedy these evils until the colored man shall have equal protection under the law with his white brethren." They also noted that, despite the military service of almost 200,000 black men in the army and navy during the Civil War, as yet no monument acknowledging their sacrifices—or, one could add, those of the black Regulars on the postwar frontier since Appomattox—had been constructed anywhere in the nation. Later that

year, the USCT veteran George Washington Williams sought to remedy this injustice when he introduced a bill in Congress for a monument
to USCT veterans like himself. The bill failed.[46]

As the men who had gathered in Boston in August 1887 prepared
to return to their homes, it was clear that the sacrifices of black soldiers
during the Civil War to save the nation, and of their counterparts on
the frontier in the late 1860s, 1870s, and 1880s to complete the nation's
postwar agenda, had yet to yield them their full rights as citizens. And the
situation was only getting worse. Just a year before the Boston reunion,
the *New York Age* had declared that "high handed tyranny in the administration of the law" remained a "favorite tenet" in the "creed of Southern white men in their dealings with colored men," and it urged black
men, "[S]tand up for your rights! Strike back! Yell when you are struck!
Show that you know how to give as well as to take blows!" Later that
year, the same paper noted that the U.S. Congress was, for the first time
in a quarter century, "without a colored congressman in either house."
Soon Mississippi would become the first Southern state to rewrite its
state constitution explicitly to exclude black men from voting.[47]

It bears noting that throughout the period under consideration,
efforts on the part of black Americans to lay claim to citizenship through
military service had been underway outside of the U.S. army as well,
including in the context of state and local militia. Black citizen-soldier
units had begun to form soon after the Civil War, and some were already
in existence in places like Ohio and Rhode Island by the time congressional legislation in July 1870 ensured their right to exist. Once the
federal law was passed, black militia forces took shape steadily in most
of the states of the former Confederacy, in part to provide defense to
black and white Republicans confronting white Democratic resurgence.
Predictably, white Democrats responded with vehemence, opposing the
creation of black militia units "as a challenge to white domination" and
doing everything in their power to undermine them. Still, black militia units persisted, even in the face of the federal government's 1877

removal from the South of its occupation troops. In 1878 there were still approximately 800 black citizen-soldiers in North Carolina. In 1882 there were 352 in Texas, and in 1885 there were 1,000 in Virginia. These militias gave their members opportunities for leadership and social status and an expansive example of blacks' assertion of citizenship.[48]

As it turned out, in connection with this movement, in December 1880, just as Whittaker's court of inquiry was concluding at West Point, none other than Christian Fleetwood had participated in the founding of what was called the Washington Cadet Corps. Although many of the black militia units created after the Civil War were led by white officers, some, including Fleetwood's Washington Cadet Corps, defied the traditions of the USCT and the postwar black Regulars and selected black men as officers. Starting with one company, Fleetwood, with the rank of captain, worked to increase the corps' size and strength, and before long it included four well-supplied companies of soldiers, all of whom paid for their own uniforms and equipment. The corps also had a twenty-five-piece brass band. In 1883, Fleetwood, as the men's commander, was awarded a large and impressive silver trophy—the gift of a wealthy local merchant—for the corps' performance in competition with other black citizen-soldier organizations in the District of Columbia.[49]

In 1887, the same year the black veterans met in Boston, the Washington Cadet Corps officially became the Sixth Battalion of the District of Columbia National Guard. (The Seventh and Eighth Battalions, also black, were added shortly thereafter.) At that point, Fleetwood received a commission from President Grover Cleveland as major of the Sixth Battalion. Some years later, Captain John Bigelow Jr. of the Tenth Cavalry—a white officer in that black regiment who was clearly familiar with the work, abilities, and accomplishments of the black Regulars—described Fleetwood's National Guard battalion, and Fleetwood himself, in highly positive terms. Bigelow wrote, "[H]is battalion impressed me very favorably by its proficiency in drill and the soldierly deportment of its officers and men individually. I am satisfied that Christian A. Fleet-

High School Cadet Corps at the M Street High School in Washington, D.C., 1895. *Courtesy of the Library of Congress.*

wood has the faculty of controlling men, and the talents and attainments necessary for making a good volunteer officer." Meanwhile, Fleetwood worked diligently and successfully to persuade local black schools to adopt a cadet system of military training and drill for male students, an example of his persistent faith in the principle that military service smoothed the path to citizenship and social equality. Unlike the corps, the high school cadets, who met weekly to train with Fleetwood as their instructor, were armed only with wooden guns.[50]

In January 1889, a large number of black Washingtonians signed a testimonial recognizing Fleetwood's "patriotic services to the Union during the late civil war" and his charitable and benevolent work in the community in the years since he had mustered out. The signers credited Fleetwood with the "high standing for proficiency achieved by the Colored Militia of the District of Columbia, both from a Military standpoint, and as reflecting credit upon the race." That same month, in a letter to a "Mr. Arnold," Frederick Douglass, now seventy-one years old, enthusiastically referred to Fleetwood as "our gallant friend and fellow citizen."[51]

It is true that, like the creation of the black Regular regiments in the U.S. army in 1866, the incorporation of Fleetwood's black Washington Cadet Corps into the previously all-white District of Columbia's National Guard in 1887 represented a positive development, a sign that in some circles, in some settings, black men's continuing contributions to the nation's work as soldiers had the potential to improve their social status, civil and political rights, and opportunities vis-à-vis white men. But this sign of progress, too, was undercut by other simultaneous and disheartening developments. As has already been pointed out, although sanctioned by federal law, postwar black militia units struggled in the face of white efforts to disband them, and the Washington Cadet Corps was no exception. Within a year after the corps became part of the D.C. National Guard, trouble surfaced. In 1888 the *Washington Bee*, a black newspaper, noted Fleetwood's failure to receive an invitation from the white commanding officer of the D.C. National Guard, the Civil War veteran General Albert Ordway, to the formal opening of the guard's new headquarters (indeed, none of the black officers in the guard received invitations). In response, Ordway explained that the event had been "a purely personal and social affair," not unlike a "private dinner," and that the members of the army, navy, and militia forces who had been invited were simply his friends. Although the *Bee* article quoted Fleetwood as refusing to comment negatively on the incident—Ordway was, after all, his superior officer—the newspaper nevertheless declared Ordway's behavior "a palpable insult" and urged "all colored officers" to "show that they resent the insult offered them by this man who is too small to be great." Subsequent articles in the *Bee* and other newspapers continued the discussion, in at least one case suggesting that more serious trouble between the races in the D.C. guard lay ahead. One white paper warned of what would happen if a black officer was in charge of white soldiers. "It would surprise no one if the white soldiers should come to a sudden and untactical halt and refuse to play until the colored ranking officer was superseded by a Caucasian. This is regarded by many as more than possible—it is highly probable."[52]

In the face of these developments, one black newspaper grumbled, "The negro is good enough when danger threatens the republic, but when there is quiet restored and the feasts commence, the negro militia can come as servants or some other [menials] but not as guests." In the weeks ahead, the *Bee* accused Ordway or someone in his inner circle of encouraging Congress, in stark contrast with its previous generosity, to suddenly slash its appropriation for the D.C. guard. Cutting the guard's budget, the *Bee* predicted, almost certainly meant eliminating the guard's black members. And indeed, within a couple of years, the *Bee*'s prophecy came true. In early March 1891, General Ordway issued orders eliminating the black battalions completely, citing the absence of congressional funding to support them. As Ordway put it, only these black battalions could be removed "without disturbing the regimental organizations of the Guard" as a whole.[53]

Some companies of militiamen within the three black battalions had been mustered out as early as 1889, the year prominent black Washingtonians signed their testimonial to Fleetwood praising him for his excellence as a commander and a citizen. Now the rest were to be dismissed. Ordered to turn in their uniforms and equipment, the black guardsmen gathered at the O Street Armory to return "every bit of property belonging to the United States which had been issued" to them. Then, having completed this painful duty, they assembled to hear Fleetwood solemnly read Ordway's order and then give a speech, in which he insisted that they adhere to the order "no matter with what regret." The men listened silently, their discipline unruffled. Some weeks later, Fleetwood—who as a faithful soldier had sworn himself to silence until the situation was resolved—finally spoke up in a letter to the editor of the *Washington Bee*. He noted that some black men had, in fact, already been readmitted to the guard, thanks to the "prompt, intelligent, and courageous action" of unnamed (presumably white) supporters who, in the wake of Ordway's orders, had expressed outrage at the men's dismissal. These supporters' advocacy had, it appears, persuaded President William Henry Harrison to countermand Ordway's order and reinstate at least some black militiamen. Still, Fleetwood no longer wanted to be a part of the D.C. guard, nor did he feel bound to "obey a man proven so unworthy of respect." He announced his resignation.[54]

⋇6⋇

Struggling for Citizenship
in the 1890s

First Sergt. George Jordan, retired, died for the want of proper atten-
tion. He lived alone and had no one to attend to his wants. The Doctor
made two applications for his admittance into Fort Robinson Hospital,
and was refused.

> —Report of Dr. J. H. Hartwell of Crawford, Nebraska,
> in 1904, commenting on the demise of George Jordan,
> thirty-year veteran of the Ninth Cavalry and recipient
> of the Congressional Medal of Honor

I N 1889, THE SAME YEAR THE FIRST COMPANIES OF CHRISTIAN FLEET-
wood's black militiamen were mustered out of the Washington, D.C.,
National Guard, a Paiute shaman in Nevada known as Wovoka began
preaching a doctrine of Native American renewal. Wovoka spoke about
a new world in which Native people would be reunited with their dead
and enjoy a future "free of pain, sickness, want, and death, free, above
all, of white people." Wovoka did not teach violence; rather, he urged
his followers to adhere to a moral code reminiscent of the Ten Com-
mandments, and to pray and sing and dance what came to be known as
the Ghost Dance, which he assured them would help bring the promised
new world into being. For many Native people who became believers,

Wovoka's teachings were initially a source of comfort. "He told them," the Sioux leader Black Elk later recalled, "that there was another world coming, just like a cloud. It would come in a whirlwind out of the west and would crush everything on this world, which was old and dying. In that other world there was plenty of meat, just like old times; and in that world all the dead Indians were alive, and all the bison that had ever been killed were roaming around again."[1]

In the fall of 1890, however, the revivalist movement that grew out of Wovoka's teachings gave way not to rebirth but to disaster. Returning home to South Dakota after their encounters with the shaman, Sioux emissaries such as Kicking Bear determined to give the prophet's teachings a more militant edge. They resented the federal government's continuing campaign to deprive them of their land, most recently by breaking up the Great Sioux reservation into six significantly smaller parcels and taking possession of the balance. "The flood of Wasichus [whites], dirty with bad deeds, gnawed away half of the island that was left to us," Black Elk recalled bitterly. In addition, the Sioux people were desperately hungry as a result of years of crop-killing droughts and unfulfilled promises of food rations from the government. As their frustration and fury increased, the remaining (and well-armed) leaders of the Native people on the Northern Plains—which had been relatively peaceful since the end of the Great Sioux War in 1876—reworked Wovoka's vision into one that needed to be realized through action. As a result, throughout much of 1890, Plains Indians engaged by the hundreds in what one historian has called "a badly perverted version of the Ghost Dance," groups frequently dancing themselves into what in the eyes of outsiders amounted to an irrational, hallucinogenic frenzy that seemed likely to produce widespread bloodshed.[2]

By the fall, white settlers on the Northern Plains, the U.S. army and government, and Bureau of Indian Affairs bureaucrats had become increasingly concerned about the potentially dangerous implications of the Ghost Dance phenomenon in the area, and with good reason. On November 15, Secretary of War Redfield Proctor ordered the army

Wovoka, a.k.a., Jack Wilson, 1918. Bureau of Catholic Indian Missions, image no. 11038. *Courtesy of Marquette University, Department of Special Collections and University Archives.*

to regain control in South Dakota, particularly in the area in and around the Pine Ridge Indian Agency, on the western end of the state's border with Nebraska. On November 22, in the *Army and Navy Journal*, a spokesman for General Nelson A. Miles, now in command of the U.S. army's Division of the Missouri, warned of the possibility of "one of the bloodiest Indian wars in the Northwest this winter the country has ever known." According to the spokesman, the army's goal should be to avoid war "by a display of troops that will demonstrate to the Indians the utter hopelessness of the success of an uprising." He added, "Of course, the Indians will be beaten in the end, but under the influence of the present religious craze there is great difficulty in making them understand anything."[3]

Sioux leader Black Elk, 1937. Walter Bernard "Ben" Hunt Collection, image no. 01287. *Courtesy of Marquette University, Department of Special Collections and University Archives.*

Observing from his vantage point at the Carlisle Indian Industrial School he had founded in Pennsylvania, Richard Henry Pratt described the developments on the Northern Plains as the predictable outcome of the Indians' having been compelled to live on reservations in "a condition of forced idleness." Still, he wrote hopefully to his former student Edgar Fire Thunder, "I am glad to hear that things are quiet at Pine Ridge. The newspapers have been saying a great deal against your people up there, but we have understood all along that it was lying white men and that there was no good reason to feel alarmed. I sincerely hope that all of our Carlisle students will keep entirely clear of the Messiah craze." Pratt went on to express confidence that Carlisle's graduates in the area would resist the temptation to join in the Ghost Dance: "Our boys and girls are not at all affected by what they see, except to be amused that some of their people are still so foolish."[4]

Despite Pratt's optimism, however, soon hundreds and then thousands of soldiers began to gather in the area of which Pine Ridge was "the storm center." This massive mobilization continued for several weeks, driving many more Sioux to seek safety at the regional Indian agencies. At the same time, the gathering of the army's forces drove others, including Kicking Bear, the Sioux leader Big Foot, and Sitting Bull—"still the mightiest of Sioux chiefs, still uncompromisingly opposed to the white man's ways"—to become more defiant. In December, General Miles ordered the arrest of Sitting Bull and Big Foot. However, during the attempted arrest on December 15, Sitting Bull was killed, ironically at the hands of other Sioux who were cooperating with the army as "Indian police." In an article headlined "Sitting Bull Gone to the Happy Hunting Grounds," the *Army and Navy Journal* gleefully reported, "Sitting Bull is dead. He died fighting the authority of the white men, as he has persistently done almost from infancy." Elsewhere in the same issue, the *Journal* declared that Sitting Bull's death now made him a "good Indian."[5]

The Sitting Bull fiasco was followed by an even greater one two weeks later when the army's attempt to arrest Big Foot descended into chaos and violence. At Wounded Knee Creek, some twenty miles from the Pine Ridge Agency, Colonel James W. Forsyth and the Seventh Cavalry caught up with Big Foot, who was desperately ill and was, in fact, trying to reach safety at the agency. Unaware of Big Foot's illness and concerned that the Sioux leader and his followers intended to resist capture, Forsyth ordered his 500 soldiers to disarm the Indians, numbering about 400 men, women, and children. But the Indians refused to surrender their guns immediately. Then, as tempers began to fray on both sides, a rifle went off—it is not clear whose. What followed was a brutal battle in which Native people and soldiers fought fiercely with one another at close range. When it was over, at least 150 Indians, including Big Foot, had been killed and 50 more wounded. In addition, 25 soldiers and officers were dead and almost 40 others hurt. Men, women, and children, Black Elk remembered years later, "were heaped and scattered all over the flat at the bottom of the little hill where the soldiers had their wagon-guns, and westward up the dry gulch all the way to the high ridge," a sight, he added, that caused him to wish that he, too, had been killed. The events at Wounded Knee, which permanently crushed Sioux resistance on the Northern Plains, also effectively subdued the remnants of Native peoples elsewhere in the United States, people who, as we have seen, for centuries and sometimes with furious desperation had resisted compulsory "civilization" and its military and nonmilitary agents.[6]

Within days, news of the disaster at Wounded Knee reached Richard Pratt at Carlisle. On January 7, having learned that at least seven Carlisle graduates had been involved in the uprising, Pratt nevertheless expressed satisfaction that "a pretty large proportion of the young men" from Carlisle who had returned to South Dakota in advance of the uprising "were enlisted as scouts and served the Government" during the campaign, "some of them being placed in a good deal of peril." Still, it is also clear that at least one former Carlisle student, known as Plenty Horses, not only participated in the Ghost Dance but also killed a federal officer during the campaign, explicitly as a way to reconnect with the community of his birth. Years later, Pratt still spoke defensively about the role of his former students in the events surrounding Wounded Knee. Recalling that, despite his West Point education, the Virginian Robert E. Lee had betrayed the federal government he had sworn an oath to serve, Pratt insisted, "Let us not find fault then with a few Indian children to whom we give the merest smattering of an education and then send back to their parents and reservations."[7]

General Miles was deeply dismayed by how the campaign had played out. Indeed, angry at what he believed to be Forsyth's incompetence, he had the colonel relieved of command. To his wife, Mary (who was William T. Sherman's niece), Miles commented, "I doubt if there is a Second Lieutenant who could not have made better disposition of 433 white soldiers and 40 Indian scouts, or who could not have disarmed 118 Indians encumbered with 250 women and children." Still, he arranged for a traditional grand review of the military forces that had been under his command, for January 21, 1891. Unlike the exhibition of the troops at the end of the Civil War, which had been graced by sunny, clear days, this impressive parade on the stark and open plains took place on a day that began with a "blinding, mid-winter snowstorm." "The scene was weird and in some respects desolate," Miles wrote later, but he recalled the review as "one of the most interesting in my experience. The vast prairie, with its rolling undulations, was covered with the white mantle of winter. That cheerless, frigid atmosphere, with its sleet, ice, and snow, covered all the apparent life of nature." To Miles, this review, like its predecessor in 1865, acknowledged the hard, if often unsavory, work of nation building that had been accomplished by the men who marched before him. Unlike the one in 1865, the 1891 review also symbolized the U.S. army's ushering of America's Native peoples into history. The scene, Miles believed, represented the burial "in oblivion, decay, and death" of "that once powerful, strong, defiant, and resolute race," the "doomed" American Indian. "And so," declared the Sioux leader Black Elk years later, as if echoing Miles, "it was all over."[8]

Led by General John R. Brooke, commander of the army's Depart-

"Consistency," an image from a post–Wounded Knee issue of *Puck* magazine (1891), satirizing the disparity between the United States' purported generosity to Africans, Asians, and Europeans and its destruction of Native Americans. *Courtesy of the Library of Congress*.

ment of the Platte, and his staff, the thousands of soldiers and others who paraded before General Miles on that bitterly cold day were all veterans of the campaign that had culminated in the terrible fight at Wounded Knee Creek. That battle—the "first," and indeed also the last, "great Indian fight to occur so near civilization and a telegraph office," according to one contemporary—and the campaign surrounding it had involved a military force representing approximately a quarter of the entire U.S. army, possibly as many as six thousand soldiers. Among those observing the review from the surrounding hills were scores of disheartened Sioux, who, Miles commented, must have been deeply impressed by what they saw, which served as "an indication to them of the advisability of remaining at peace in the future." The parade through the snow included wagon trains, pack trains, and the ambulance corps. As for the marchers, among them were the white soldiers of the First Infantry, under Colonel William Shafter, the man probably most responsible for ending Henry Flipper's career in army. Also marching were several other white infantry, artillery, and cavalry regiments. Significantly, unlike the Grand Review in 1865, this symbolically important, valedictory military parade included Native Americans, too: one observer noted the presence of "100 mounted Ogalala [sic] Indian scouts," who "in various ways . . . had rendered valuable service during the campaign," not unlike, one supposes, the "valuable service" provided by the Indian police who had helped bring about Sitting Bull's demise.[9]

And then there were the black Regulars: the men of the Ninth Cavalry's D, F, I, and K Troops, known by some as Henry's Brunettes, after the man who was then serving as their commander, Major Guy V. Henry. Born in 1839 the son of a U.S. army major stationed at Fort Smith in Indian Territory, Henry had graduated from West Point in 1861 and gone on to serve with distinction through the Civil War. After the war, Henry remained with the army and was sent out west. In 1881, he transferred from a white regiment to the black Ninth Cavalry, advancing his army rank from captain to major. In 1887, Henry and the Ninth had finally left the Southwest and established headquarters at Fort Robinson, Nebraska. In mid-November 1890, when summoned by Miles, Henry and the regiment's D Troop were about three hundred miles northwest of Pine Ridge at Fort McKinney in Wyoming. They hastened to the troubled area, where they met up with the regiment's K, F, and I Troops.[10]

At the end of December, after weeks of drilling to ensure their readiness, Major Henry and the Ninth Cavalry troopers had gone into action, participating in the mission to intercept and capture Big Foot and his followers. The first night they traveled fifty miles, a distance, Henry later noted, that normally might not seem far, "but on the back of a trotting horse on a cold winter's night . . . is not to be laughed at." Over the next few days, Henry and the black troopers scouted extensively, but they failed to encounter Big Foot and his band, who had moved farther east.[11]

Though Henry and his troopers were not present at the awful battle at Wounded Knee Creek—nor were any other black Regulars—mere hours after it was over they found themselves called to relieve the regiment's own wagon train, which was being besieged by Indians. Although the troopers were several days into their expedition to arrest Big Foot and were already very tired, "there was not a laggard," Henry recalled. Upon hearing their orders, the men's "tents went down like a flash; wagons were packed; every man sprang to his horse, and in less than forty minutes after the news had been received we were off." Once again the troopers marched through a cold, windy—and, on this occasion, moonless—night. "Muffled in their shaggy buffalo overcoats, and hooded by the grotesque fur caps used by our Western troops," Henry wrote, "the negro troopers looked like meaningless bundles that had been tied in some way to the backs of their horses." The men traveled with great speed and in silence: "Nothing could be heard," Henry continued, "but the clatter of hoofs and the clanking of the carbines as they chafed the metallic trappings of the saddle."[12]

The rescue of the wagon train was successful, but it did not occur without bloodshed: one black noncommissioned officer, Corporal William O. Wilson of Hagerstown, Maryland, earned the Congressional Medal of Honor for bravery, and another black Regular—Charles Haywood—died, along with his horse. Still, there was time neither to celebrate nor to mourn, for almost immediately Major Henry and his men received orders summoning them to go to the aid of the 7th Cavalry at a place known as Drexel Mission. There, in the wake of the fighting at Wounded Knee, the seemingly hapless Seventh had become trapped in a canyon surrounded by a sizable group of Sioux holdouts. Gathering what little remained of their own energy and their horses', the black troopers raced to the rescue of the white Seventh, surprising the attacking Indians and scattering them. The number of Sioux killed or wounded in this engagement is not known, but the black cavalrymen did not suffer a single casualty.

In the end, over the course of less than twenty-four hours, the troopers of the Ninth had traveled more than a hundred miles. Still, as Henry described it years later, "although one horse had died, there was not a sore-backed horse in the outfit," a "sore-backed horse" being a sure sign of a poor, negligent, or unkind rider. "Men and horses were fatigued," Henry recalled, "but all were in good condition." The rescue at Drexel Mission, the *Kansas City Times* declared, "made firm friends of the Seventh and the Ninth." And, the article continued, in the days and weeks ahead,

> [if] one of the colored troopers entered the Seventh's camp he was an honored guest. I have seen two of the white cavalrymen struggle with each other for the supremacy which would enable the winner to unsaddle and feed the horse of one of the rescuers who was called by duty into their quarters, while half a dozen others of General Forsyth's boys proffered whatever comforts were to be had. The color line was completely erased. When the Ninth in moving to its present location passed the Seventh the latter regiment strained its collective lungs in superhuman effort to express its appreciation and the brunettes returned the compliment with a will when the Seventh marched away to the railroad.

Apparently a cross-race fraternity that was difficult to accomplish either in theory or in practice in settings such as West Point or the National Guard was significantly more possible in the field.[13]

Through the cold of Miles's January 1891 grand review, Major Henry led the proud black cavalrymen under his command, himself "buried deep in a buffalo overcoat." Of those under review, the black Regulars caught the attention of a correspondent for the *Omaha Bee*, who described them as "centaurs." Bundled in their heavy, warm, winter gear, Henry's Brunettes seemed to this reporter like "Esquimaux rigged out for an active campaign, alike fearless of the elements and storms of shot and shell." (Notably, although his language was meant to be complimentary, the reporter did not go so far as to compare the black soldiers to white men.) Henry himself described the procession as "pathetically grand . . . the grandest demonstration that had ever been seen by the army in the West." That same month the *North American Review* published an article by Miles in which he summed up the feeling many on the Northern Plains shared that day: "The Indians are practically a doomed race, and none realize it better than themselves." Within the next few weeks, Sherman, who no doubt would have been pleased by Miles's statement, was dead, marking in a different way the end of the era of active nation building.[14]

Following Miles's grand review, the white regiments that had participated in the campaign against the Ghost Dancers dispersed to their regular posts. But Major Henry's Ninth Cavalry troopers remained on guard duty at Pine Ridge through most of that unusually cold and snowy winter, with limited supplies and only tall, conical Sibley tents, modeled on Native tepees, for shelter. At least one of the enlisted men, Private W. H. Prather, took to composing poems during this period about the campaign he and his comrades had just been through. In one of them, "The Indian Ghost Dance and War," Prather recalled the Ninth's involvement in the pursuit of Big Foot, modestly (or perhaps diplomatically) obscuring the record of its rescue of the Seventh Cavalry at Drexel Mission. In another untitled piece, he pondered with some frustration the Ninth's extended duty in South Dakota, now that all the white troops had departed. "The rest have gone home," Prather wrote,

> *To meet the blizzard's wintry blast*
> *The Ninth, the willing Ninth*
> *Is camped here till the last.*
>
> *We were the first to come,*
> *Will be the last to leave*
> *Why are we compelled to stay,*
> *Why this reward receive?*

In war barracks
Our recent comrades take their ease,
While we poor devils,
And the Sioux are left to freeze.

And cuss our luck,
And wait till some one pulls the string,
And starts Short Bull
With another ghost dance in the spring.

Cross-race fraternal feeling on the field notwithstanding, some black Regulars resented being left behind to fend with winter on the Plains while their white counterparts headed off to warmer quarters.[15]

Some white officers recognized and understood this resentment, particularly those, like Guy Henry, who were most impressed by the performance of the black soldiers under their command. As the weeks passed, Henry—who was dedicated to the men of the Ninth Cavalry in the same way Benjamin Grierson in particular, among the black Regular regiments' commanders over the years, had been dedicated to the men of the Tenth—remained determined to get relief for his men, many of whom fell sick under the harsh conditions. Charles Creek, who had enlisted in the Ninth sometime in the 1880s, described the regiment's suffering that winter with a touch of hyperbole: "It was so cold the spit froze when it left your mouth." At the very least, Henry sought permission to transfer the men to their home base at Fort Robinson, where there were proper barracks for protection. Permission, however, was not granted until late March, by which time the weather had already begun to warm.[16]

Even as he awaited orders to escort his black troopers back to Fort Robinson, Henry sought for them a much more significant and unprecedented reward for their service: an official acknowledgment that they had distinguished themselves in this most recent, and presumably final, major campaign against the Native people. Henry believed that the black Regulars deserved national, public recognition for what they had done in South Dakota and elsewhere. In a series of letters to men in superior positions, he made clear that, over the course of just a few days, the black Regulars of the Ninth Cavalry had not only done their duty, performing bravely and effectively against the Indians, but had also saved the lives of a contingent of white soldiers and officers. In return, he asked that the troopers of the Ninth, as representatives of the black Regulars generally, be rewarded with an assignment to prestigious Fort Myer, located just outside the nation's capital and a popular sightseeing spot for both local residents and visitors from across the nation and abroad. Henry sent his first request to General John Schofield, now the commanding general of the U.S. army in Washington, but previously the unsympathetic superintendent of West Point during the years Johnson Whittaker and Henry Flipper were cadets there. Suspecting that his own voice might not be loud enough to gain Schofield's assent, Henry also solicited the support of General Oliver Otis Howard, the former commissioner of the Freedmen's Bureau, longtime advocate of black Americans' rights, and ally and supporter of James Webster Smith during his time at West Point. Howard had briefly replaced Schofield as West Point superintendent in the wake of the Whittaker affair and was now in command of the military Division of the Atlantic in which Fort Myer was located. Henry solicited as well the endorsement of General Miles.[17]

Henry's request confronted bureaucratic obstacles; it also encountered public opposition, such as that expressed by the *New York Herald*, to the effect that "it would be 'detrimental to the best interests of the service' to station black troops on the outskirts of Washington, 'where the color line is so frequently the cause of discussion,'" not least in connection with military matters, as the experience of Fleetwood's black National Guardsmen had revealed. It should be noted, however, that Henry's efforts also enjoyed some public support. In February, the *Kansas City Times* predicted, "Nobody need be very much surprised if in the course of time . . . the Ninth Cavalry . . . is stationed at Fort Myer.

Never have the services of this regiment been acknowledged as they should have been, and there are forces now at work which may place at least one battalion of these Afro-American cavalrymen where they may be admired by residents of the national capital and paraded before the thousands who annually visit the city. The Ninth has a record which looks as though the regiment ought to receive some consideration."[18]

And indeed, although it took some time, the endorsements from Miles and Howard came through, and eventually Schofield yielded, too. On April 28, Secretary of War Proctor wrote the orders, directing Major Henry to assume command of Fort Myer and to choose one troop of the Ninth Cavalry for duty there. Henry chose K Troop, to which Schofield then assigned new white officers, and at the end of May, Henry and a contingent of sixty-nine black Regulars traveled east. At Fort Myer, K Troop became the first company of black soldiers to perform parade and other spectator-pleasing duties in the nation's capital in conjunction with white soldiers. Duty at Fort Myer consisted mainly of "drills, parades, practice and still more practice," outdoors in good weather, indoors when the weather was foul, often to large, curious crowds.[19]

Perhaps predictably, not all of the black Regulars from K Troop who were posted to Fort Myer lived up to Major Henry's expectations and hopes, or even their own aspirations. As it had for black soldiers since the days of the USCT and for the black cadets at West Point, public scrutiny increased the pressure under which they operated. One Ninth Cavalry trooper who seems to have struggled to perform adequately, especially in light of the apparent racial hostility of his troop commander, Captain M. B. Hughes, was Private George Battest. Battest got into trouble more than once, the first time almost immediately after K Troop's arrival in Washington, though his military service up to that point had been quite acceptable. In July 1891, however, Battest faced a court-martial on the charge of disregarding and failing to obey Hughes's commands while on drill. According to the specifications in the case, Battest addressed Hughes in a tone both "insolent and insubordinate" when Hughes tried to correct his drill performance.[20]

Battest, in turn, charged Hughes with failing to acknowledge that Battest's saber had come loose, and he insisted that his efforts to fix it had caused him to be somewhat distracted. Battest also claimed that Hughes, angry at being ignored, had threatened to cut Battest's "god damned black head" open with his own saber. Some witnesses agreed that Hughes had threatened Battest, although they did not remember the exact words he had used. Others stated that Battest was simply lying. Reflecting the volatility of the situation, Major Henry chose a vague middle ground. He testified that when Battest first approached him about Hughes's purported slur, he told Battest that he "allowed no officer to use such language to any soldier." After that, Henry said, Battest, for reasons of his own, had decided not to pursue the complaint. In the end, Battest was found guilty, fined twenty dollars, confined for two months, and returned to duty.

In December, however, Battest was court-martialed again, this time for what can only have been considered an even more egregious misdeed under the circumstances. Disobeying a superior officer was one thing; disgracing the uniform within sight of the nation's Capitol was something else entirely. Whether Battest's second offense confirms his bad character, or perhaps reflects his frustration with a life of racial subordination, or both, cannot be known. What is known is that in the middle of the afternoon on December 5, Battest was found by Major Henry, apparently drunk and "dismounted in the public highway, near the village of Roslyn, Va., with his breeches unbuttoned, urinating and exposing his person to passers by; this to the scandal and disgrace of the services of the U.S. uniform." On this occasion, Battest pleaded guilty, offering no statement in his own defense. He was dishonorably discharged.[21]

Battest's persistent struggles aside, over the course of their three years at Fort Myer, K Troop as a whole performed brilliantly. "I am very glad to hear such favorable reports concerning your command," General Miles wrote to Henry in December 1893, adding that he was hardly surprised. Undoubtedly their experience at Fort Myer brought black troopers great personal satisfaction, as they underwent a kind of daily grand review side by side with white soldiers for all the world to see. They were more than just showmen, too: troopers stationed at Fort Myer "were good saddle riders and complete masters of their horses. They practiced bareback on dead-level heats and jumped hurdles of varying heights that were designed to provide mastery and survival in the field." In August 1893, the black Regulars from Fort Myer even provided escort service to President Grover Cleveland during a "special parade." Still, it is clear that, although K Troop's duty at Fort Myer caused the contemporary *Army and Navy Journal* to announce "the death of prejudice against blacks" in the army, in fact, in the words of the historian Frank N. Schubert, "the arrival of K Troop on the south bank of the Potomac was the only concrete manifestation of the new military brotherhood." Another half century would pass before black soldiers and white soldiers experienced any true "military brotherhood" in the integrated regiments of the post–World War II period. Meanwhile, other aspects of full citizenship remained as stubbornly elusive for black Regulars as they were for black Americans generally. Indeed, in the final decade of the nineteenth century, the situation for blacks across America showed strong signs of continuing to deteriorate.[22]

In 1892, even as K Troop was drilling and performing at Fort Myer, the Louisiana-born Homer Plessy, only one of whose eight great-grand-parents was black, was thrown in jail for sitting in the whites-only car of a train. As is well known, the lawsuit Plessy subsequently brought to contest his removal from the car led to the 1896 U.S. Supreme Court decision *Plessy* v. *Ferguson*, which put the weight of the federal government firmly behind the principle of segregation. Even more frightening, on February 21 of the year Plessy was first arrested, the *New York Times* published a report about an event in Texarkana, Arkansas, in which "a mob apprehended a 32-year-old black man, Ed Coy, charged with the rape of a white woman, tied him to a stake, and burned him alive." Then, even as Coy asserted his innocence and begged for mercy, "his alleged victim herself somewhat hesitantly put the torch to his oil-soaked body."

Shockingly, even the *Times* sided with the lynchers, remarking that only by the "terrible death such as fire . . . can inflict" could other blacks "be deterred from the commission of like crimes." Ed Coy, write the historians Gary Nash and Julie Roy Jeffrey, "was one of over 1,400 black men lynched or burned alive during the 1890s."[23]

As had been true all along, black Americans in the early 1890s hardly remained passive in the face of such attacks on their civil, political, and human rights. The same year that Homer Plessy was thrown in jail and Ed Coy was burned alive in Arkansas, a former slave from Holly Springs, Mississippi, named Ida B. Wells—who was now a Memphis-based journalist, reformer, and impassioned advocate for full black citizenship—published her first meticulously researched and unnerving exposé of the nation's lynching crisis, *Southern Horrors: Lynch Law in All Its Phases*. "Somebody," Wells wrote in her preface, "must show that the Afro-American race is more sinned against than sinning, and it seems to have fallen upon me to do so." In her work, Wells discussed the Coy case along with many others. In addition, she struck at the foundation of the whole notion that the lynching of black American men by white Americans had anything substantial to do with black men's threats to white women's much vaunted "purity." "Nobody in this section of the country believes the old thread bare lie that Negro men rape white women," Wells famously declared. Instead, lynching, she insisted, was a technique designed to intimidate and destroy black Americans who were making progress, socially, financially, politically, or otherwise. In his endorsement of *Southern Horrors*, Frederick Douglass told Wells, "[T]hanks for your faithful paper on the lynch abomination now generally practiced against colored people in the south. There has been no word equal to it in convincing power. I have spoken, but my word is feeble in comparison."[24]

Three years after *Southern Horrors* appeared, Wells published a second report on the lynching crisis, this one entitled *A Red Record: Lynchings in the United States, 1892, 1893, 1894*. In it she provided still more grisly accounts as well as detailed statistics: in 1892 alone, she reported,

160 black Americans (5 women and 155 men) were lynched, 100 more than a decade earlier. In 1893, the number was about the same (159). In 1894, Wells counted a total of 134 lynchings (including 3 women) across eighteen different states, from Florida to Pennsylvania, and from Kansas to Texas, a slight improvement that may in fact be attributable at least in part to Wells's own relentless efforts to bring "lynch law" to light. Still, that "only" 134 lynchings of black Americans took place in 1894 hardly constitutes an irrefutable sign of progress, as Wells herself clearly knew. Indeed, in 1893, the year after she published *Southern Horrors*, Wells joined forces with Douglass to write and publish an eighty-one-page booklet that contained extensive information about lynching in America, as well as other material pertaining to the stalled progress of black Americans toward social and political equality with whites. At least ten thousand copies of the booklet were printed and handed out free of charge that year at the next great celebration of the nation's progress and its spread of civilization across the land, the World's Columbian Exposition.[25]

Originally scheduled for 1892, the four hundredth anniversary of Christopher Columbus's arrival in the "New World," the Columbian Exposition took place in Chicago, almost a thousand miles west of Philadelphia, where the Centennial Exposition had occurred in 1876, a detail that in and of itself signified the steady westward movement of American civilization on the continent. Also telling was the fact that Chicago's Jackson Park, where the fairgrounds were constructed, was named after the nation's most notorious enthusiast of Indian removal, President Andrew Jackson. The Columbian Exposition, which had a more international flavor than its predecessor, served as a declaration of the place on the world stage that the United States was preparing to assume now that the work of nation building on the continent was itself coming to a close. Indeed, it should come as no surprise that General Nelson Miles, fresh from Wounded Knee and now the nation's premier military figure, was invited to serve as grand marshal for the exposition's opening ceremonies. Miles had predicted that the exposition would be "the most important affair of the kind that has ever been held in the world." And for this reason, he had encouraged its planners to shine a bright light at the fair on the nation's military, suggesting the organization of "one grand encampment of the citizen soldiery of this country, where patriotism and the spirit of emulation would prompt each organization to attain the highest degree of excellence."[26]

At the time that building for the Columbian Exposition began, Jackson Park was hardly a model of advanced civilization. Less than a quarter of the park's more than a thousand acres of land had been "improved" by means of "cultivated lawns and constructed driveways"; the rest, consisting of sand dunes, marshes, and swamps, was still, in the eyes of at least some contemptuous observers—rather like most of the now twenty-year-old Yellowstone National Park—"in a state of nature." As a result, bringing the imagined fair into existence was an immense task, and immensely costly, involving not only taming the land but also constructing a monument to civilization and progress on its back. Over the course of two years, in the face of extreme weather conditions reminiscent of those the black Regulars routinely experienced on their tours of duty in the West, teams of laborers struggled to prepare the ground for the construction crews. Then, as the director-general and Civil War veteran Colonel George R. Davis wrote, "the greatest architects in America designed the structures, the most skilled artisans executed their designs, famous artists supplied the ornamentation, while an army of humbler workers ceaselessly toiled still over the soil itself." At long last, as if it had sprung magically from "the mud of a primeval prairie," what came to be known as the White City—so named because all of the large exhibition buildings were painted white—was ready.[27]

A dedication ceremony had taken place the preceding October, even before the Jackson Park fairgrounds were completed. The October ceremony was meant to draw attention to the upcoming events and, purportedly, to symbolize the dawning of "a millennium of universal liberty and the brotherhood of man." October 20, the first day of the three-day ceremony, witnessed a massive parade through downtown Chicago. All other traffic in the city was stopped in order to permit hundreds of thousands of local people to enjoy the spectacle: a train of colorful themed floats preceded by a procession of state governors.[28]

Impressive as this portion of the dedication ceremony was, the journalists Trumbull White and William Igleheart, who published the first history of the fair while it was still ongoing, described the following day as the true "dedication day." Preeminent among the celebratory events on October 21 was the magnificent military parade led by Grand Marshal General Miles, which began promptly at 9 a.m. Behind Miles, who rode on horseback, came a stream of white troopers from the Fifth Cavalry as well as white soldiers of the Illinois state militia, along with a long procession of fair organizers, officials, and their guests, with additional white military escorts. On the third day, October 22, the dedication of state exhibition buildings was complemented by more military displays in neighboring Washington Park. White soldiers performed

World's Columbian Exposition Parade, Chicago, October 1892. *Courtesy of the Library of Congress.*

maneuvers, such as those Miles had recommended back in 1891 for the occasion. Also part of the festivities leading up to the actual opening of the fair to the public was a huge international naval review that took place in New York harbor in April, designed to demonstrate the United States' position, and its growing security, in the international sphere. In preparation for this review, in addition to representatives of the U.S. navy, ships from many countries, including Great Britain, Russia, France, Germany, Italy, Portugal, and Scandinavia, gathered at Hampton Roads, Virginia, not far from Fortress Monroe—where Nelson Miles had begun his postwar army career watching over the imprisoned Jefferson Davis and where Benjamin Butler had welcomed the first "contraband" slave runaways to the protection of the U.S. army in 1861. There for many days the ships "manoeuvred, paraded and saluted" one another before heading north.[29]

Most who sailed their ships to Hampton Roads in April 1893 as part of the Columbian Exposition's opening festivities probably knew little or nothing about the life and educational work among freed blacks of the Civil War veteran Samuel Chapman Armstrong, who lay dying not far away—three years after having experienced a paralyzing stroke—at the school he had founded, Hampton Institute. Nor, when the gates to the White City opened on May 1—just around the time the nation's economy tumbled into a depression that later became known as the Panic of 1893 (an ironic echo of the Panic of 1873 that had preceded the Centennial Exposition in Philadelphia)—was the general public familiar with Richard Henry Pratt, who, in anticipation of the fair, had lobbied for a permanent exhibition there of his Carlisle Indian Industrial School, as well as the opportunity for representatives of the student body to march prominently in the October Chicago parade.[30]

The success of Pratt's lobbying efforts on behalf of his students should not be taken for granted: like those of the Centennial Exposition in 1876, organizers of the 1893 fair in Chicago carefully picked and chose what to include in this grand commemoration of national progress, and whom to involve in its planning, displays, and operations. To their credit, the Chicago exposition's organizers were somewhat more broadminded than their predecessors in Philadelphia had been. It is noteworthy, for example, that in 1893 a "Board of Lady Managers" not only provided funding for the exposition but also was given a hand in shaping the different state exhibits; the "Lady Managers" saw to the construction of a separate Woman's Building (which was not part of the original planning), designed by a woman architect, Boston's Sophia G. Hayden. The Woman's Building housed a collection of displays pertaining to American and international women's labor, organizations, and education, and their accomplishments in the literary and visual arts. Moreover, although it was organized primarily to flaunt American achievements, the Columbian Exposition included representative displays from many other nations, to further demonstrate the United States' place in the international realm. Mexico, Central America, and South America (which Director-General Davis patronizingly called "our foster children") had exhibits, as did many European countries and much of "The Orient." Even Haiti had a small building. Beleaguered by European imperialism, Africa, in contrast, was virtually without representation, at least in the main area of the fairgrounds.[31]

In any case, thanks to Pratt's efforts, hundreds of Indian students from Carlisle marched in the October 1892 parade preceding the fair and later, the following spring, in a similar parade in New York City in conjunction with the naval review. In both events, students (in New York, including about fifty girls) marched behind a "large and most elaborate silk banner" on which was "emblazoned in large letters, 'United States Indian Industrial School, Carlisle, Pennsylvania,' and conspicuously under that, 'Into Civilization and Citizenship.'" Once the fair had actually opened, five hundred boys and girls from the school returned to Chicago to participate in a permanent exhibit, a two-story replica of the school that was placed, thanks to Pratt's insistence, under the auspices of the fair's liberal arts department rather than its anthropology department. The presence of Carlisle's students and the Carlisle exhibit, Pratt later wrote, "showed how to make acceptable productive citizens out of

Indians" and "how the Indian could learn to march in line with America as a very part of it, head up, eyes front, where he could see his glorious future of manly competition in citizenship and be on an equality as an individual."[32]

That the Carlisle students enjoyed such favorable (if assimilationist) acknowledgment at the exposition is due in large part to Pratt's persistence in making the case for their successful "Americanization." However, it must be noted that, as had been true at Philadelphia in 1876, in the anthropology department's exhibits, other Native Americans were caricatured negatively. Indeed, one of the most admired statues at the fair harked back in deeply troubling ways to the events at Wounded Knee just three years earlier. Entitled *The Ghost Dance*, the statue depicted an Indian "in the wildest imaginable motion, carried away by fear and superstition, and more than half crazed by excitement." This figure, balanced on one foot, displayed a wide-open mouth and an expression of what one pleased viewer described as "brutal ignorance and fear." Perhaps more than the Carlisle students' evidence of successful assimilation into white culture, statues such as this, along with other displays, offered a glimpse into what Native America had been reduced to by the century's final decade in most white Americans' eyes.[33]

As for black Americans, the simple truth is that they were almost entirely invisible at the exposition, despite the efforts of many black activists who had repeatedly urged planners to include a range of exhibits demonstrating black progress since emancipation. Instead, as in 1876, blacks were virtually excluded from working at the fair, and their vast accomplishments and contributions to the nation's development and progress were not on display there. Particularly significant here is the fact that the exposition offered no representation of black soldiers' service on behalf of the nation's security and expansion over the past thirty years. Indeed, as one historian has pointed out, "[a]lthough a few applicants were accepted for positions as attendants to wheelchairs and rental carts and strollers," not a single black soldier was posted or on parade at the fair, none being accepted even for duty "among the several

World's Columbian Exposition Grounds, showing the "White City," 1893. *Courtesy of the Library of Congress.*

thousand candidates for the Columbian Guard, the Exposition's elite security force."[34]

The pamphlet Ida B. Wells and Frederick Douglass had prepared for the occasion focused on lynching and the progress (or lack thereof) of black Americans toward full citizenship, but its actual title was *The Reason Why the Colored American Is Not in the World's Columbian Exposition.* "It must be admitted," wrote Douglass in the pamphlet's introduction, that "the colored people of the United States have lost ground and have met with increased and galling resistance since the war of the rebellion." True, many of the beneficial laws that had been passed in the wake of Appomattox—and in light of black soldiers' contributions to the federal cause during the war—still stood. Nevertheless, Douglass continued, "the spirit and purpose of these have been in a measure defeated by state legislation and by judicial decisions." Black Americans were still "free," certainly, and by their own determination they continued to move forward, but their quest for equality was, if anything, facing more obstacles rather than fewer as the century drew to a close. "A ship rotting at anchor," Douglass explained, "meets with no resistance, but when she sets sail on the sea, she has to buffet opposing billows." Clearly, blacks' near-exclusion from the exposition epitomized this trend. One cannot help recognizing, too, the irony that, because there was no more appropriate place from which to distribute the pamphlet to fairgoers, it was handed out at the Haitian Pavilion, where Douglass was acting as commissioner. Douglass had served as U.S. ambassador to Haiti from 1889 to 1891, when he resigned after being accused of being too sympathetic to Haitian interests.[35]

The Haitian Pavilion certainly offered fairgoers a glimpse of the nonwhite world. Moreover, in response to considerable pressure from black Americans and their supporters—to the effect that the exposition should recognize in some formal manner black Americans' achievements and contributions—a single day (August 25, 1893) was, ultimately, designated "Colored American Day." On that day, approximately fifteen hundred black and eight hundred white Americans gathered at the fair to hear speeches and musical performances by black artists, including several classical violin pieces rendered by Frederick Douglass's grandson Joseph. Many black Americans, among them Ida B. Wells, at least initially opposed and boycotted this event, considering it a demeaning ghettoization of black achievement, an "attempt to relegate African Americans to a separate and inferior status that accentuated subordination." Others, such as Douglass, supported Colored American Day, although in many cases with mixed emotions. Douglass himself was named "president" of the day, and used the opportunity to give a bold keynote speech on race in America.[36]

Also a participant in the festivities on August 25 was the young black poet Paul Laurence Dunbar, described by one biographer as "America's first professional black literary man." Born in Dayton, Ohio, in 1872, Dunbar was the son of former slaves, Joshua and Matilda Dunbar. His father had served in the Union army's Fifty-fifth Massachusetts during the Civil War, a piece of family history of which Paul Dunbar was particularly proud and which he wove into his poetry more than once.

Indeed, on Colored American Day, Dunbar read an original poem inspired by the courage of men like his father and dedicated to "the gallant colored soldiers who [had] fought for Uncle Sam." Dunbar's "song heroic" recalled how the federal government at first spurned black men's willingness to enlist in the army during the Civil War, but eventually relented, when "the flag was drooping low" and victory had come to seem hopelessly elusive. In response to the nation's belated call, black men had nevertheless risen from "the darkness of their bondage" to take up arms with fervor, "like hounds unleashed and eager for the life blood of the prey." In battles extending "from the blazing breach of [Fort] Wagner to the plains of Olustee," and even to "the very mouth of hell," they had proceeded to sacrifice themselves without fear in order to defeat the enemy's forces and to annihilate slavery. Although the poem's immediate focus was on the USCT, its final stanzas alluded to the paradox of black men's military service, then and since, having failed to ensure their equality with white men. "They were comrades then and brothers," Dunbar noted, good enough to "stop a bullet," willing

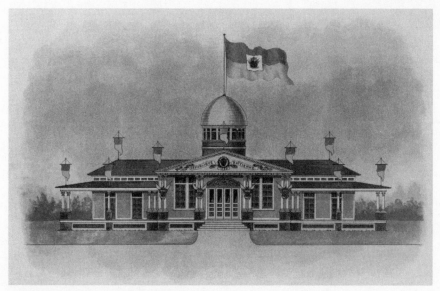

Haitian Pavilion at the Columbian Exposition, where Frederick Douglass served as "minister in charge." *Courtesy of the Library of Congress.*

to share white men's "nightly vigils" as well as their "daily toil," and as "brave and true" to the nation as any white man whose lifeblood, like their own, had been expended for its sake. Could they not be both citizens *and* soldiers now?[37]

For all its earnestness and power, Dunbar's poem celebrating the work of black soldiers in recent American history did not reach a wide audience that day. Rather, the vast majority of fairgoers turned instead for their taste of what the exposition offered as its representation of cultural diversity to the "Midway," so nicknamed because of its peripheral location on a narrow strip of land connecting Jackson Park with Washington Park. The Midway housed the fair's "Avenue of Nations," a collection of profit-making concessions that attracted visitors who enjoyed its "suggestive mimicry and departure from respectable decorum." (There may be some significance in the fact that the Woman's Building was situated adjacent to the Jackson Park end of the Midway.) The Midway was indeed the one area of the fair where the continent of Africa was on display, though only in the form of such things as a model of a street in Cairo and the "Dahomey Village," which housed about a hundred African men and women who regularly performed warlike dances and other staged rituals, sold "native" products, and demonstrated their crafts. (Fairgoers, the official history of the exposition noted, were requested to "refrain from questioning the natives of the village in regard to the past cannibal habits of themselves and their ancestors, as it was very annoying to them.") The Midway also boasted the "American Indian Village," complete with living Sioux, Pawnee, Blackfoot, and Cheyenne representatives.[38]

In the midst of the Columbian Exposition's celebration of the nation's progress and place in the world, and of its particular vision of what it meant to be both "American" and "civilized," the annual meeting of the American Historical Association (AHA), which had been founded in 1884, was also held in Chicago, although previously it had taken place only in cities on the East Coast. It was on this occasion that the historian Frederick Jackson Turner of the University of Wisconsin—who was born the year the Civil War erupted—first presented what has come to be known as his "frontier thesis," best articulated for the purposes of later generations of historians in his classic essay "The Significance of the Frontier in American History."

In his talk to the gathered members of the AHA, Turner responded to the 1890 U.S. census's declaration (published in 1892) that the national frontier was closed. Previously unsettled portions of the continent, the superintendent of this census had explained, were now home to so many and such widely spread pockets of settlement that the notion of a frontier line had become obsolete. Given that reality, Turner argued, discussion of an existing frontier was no longer meaningful. In light of this momentous development, he advanced his theory that the national progress so evident at the time of the frontier's closure—and, one could add, on display at the Columbian Exposition itself—could be understood only in relation to the existence, since European colonists had first arrived on the continent, of a vast expanse of open land. In turn, the advancing settlement of civilized people across this open land had fostered and ensured the creation of distinctly American institutions— especially democracy—as well as an American culture and a uniquely American character defined by, among other things, "coarseness and strength combined with acuteness and inquisitiveness," "individualism," and a "restless, nervous energy."[39]

Turner's interpretation of who precisely "the American people" were was a limited one, even in comparison with the racial worldviews demonstrated by men such as Richard Henry Pratt and Samuel Armstrong in their educational programs designed to "uplift" nonwhite Americans. Turner did not include Native Americans, whose stories he mostly erased in his enthusiastic discussion of the steady conquest of the continent's "wilderness" by the "stalwart" and "rugged" frontiersman. Turner did mention that dealing with the Indians had generated a degree of "political concern" since Europeans had arrived on the continent. Elsewhere he pointed out the importance of the Indian trails on top of which many railroad lines had been constructed. And on the subject of the warfare that had taken place for so many generations between frontier settlers and the Native people, Turner remarked that the frontier proved to be an excellent "military training school" for the former, but he ignored that it was also a massive burial ground for the latter.[40]

As for black Americans, Turner made no mention at all of the millions upon millions of enslaved people who had contributed so importantly to the nation's westward expansion by steadily transforming, over the course of almost three hundred years, what had been Indian lands or wilderness into white landowners' farms and plantations. Nor did he consider at any length the military—and certainly not the black Regulars—whose hard work and sacrifice had been an essential factor in the subjugation of the Native people, the spread of American culture, and the development of the supposedly distinctive "American" institutions he so generously praised. Even when he discussed his version of a "composite nationality" for the American people, Turner identified as contributors only the English, the Scots-Irish, the Germans, and the Pennsylvania Dutch, who over the course of the nation's history, he wrote, had "fused into a mixed race"—an interesting use of the term "race"—now definable as "American."[41]

As we have already seen, Turner was by no means the first thinker in the post–Civil War period to ponder the notion of what it meant to be an "American." Key military figures—especially those with experience with the USCT or the black postwar regiments on the frontier, such as Richard Henry Pratt, Samuel Armstrong, Guy V. Henry, Benjamin Grierson, and Nelson Miles—as well as the black Regulars themselves (not to mention their white Southern and Native "enemies") had all been doing so for decades. Nor was Turner even the first American to use the term "composite nationality," which Frederick Douglass had defined very differently in Boston back in 1869. But the context in which Douglass had spoken, Radical Reconstruction, was very different: a brief time of enormous optimism for many reform-minded Americans about the nation's future as a beacon of social justice—at least, social justice for those who accepted the fundamental premise that "savagery" must give way to "civilization."

It should be noted, too, that even Douglass in 1869 had not seen a place in America's future for the traditional ways of Native Americans; he did not see one in 1893, either. Indeed, in that same year, having been invited by Pratt (whom he had met some time before in Washington), Douglass visited Carlisle Indian Industrial School, where he delivered for the last time his familiar lecture on the topic "Self-Made Men" and encouraged the school's students to accept the ideals and practices of the nation's dominant culture. "Self-made men," Douglass explained, "are the men who, under peculiar difficulties and without the ordinary helps of favoring circumstances, have attained knowledge, usefulness, power and position. . . . They are the men who owe little or nothing to birth, relationship, friendly surroundings; to wealth inherited or to early approved means of education; who are what they are, without the aid of any of the favoring conditions by which other men usually rise in the world and achieve great results." Douglass urged his Carlisle audience to accept the model of self-made manhood (and, concomitantly, devoted and subordinate womanhood) that their white teachers offered. It was time, he declared, to leave savagery behind.[42]

When he spoke at Carlisle, Douglass added his voice to the chorus of Americans urging the remaining Native people to assimilate voluntarily and enthusiastically. There was, he believed, no other course to follow, as the experience of black Americans demonstrated. Black Americans had long since abandoned any remnants of their African heritage and had committed themselves to becoming people of "civilization." Indeed, black Americans, including black soldiers, had amply and repeatedly demonstrated that they were more than just people *of* civilization; they were in fact dedicated to building and preserving civilization on American soil. At the same time, no one believed more fervently than Douglass that blacks in the United States were entitled to all of American civilization's privileges, and few could have felt more acutely the frustrations that black veterans experienced as the century drew to a close, as they considered the limited rewards that their military service on behalf of the nation, and their unflinching quest for equality and the full rights of citizenship, had yielded.

One black veteran who had an opportunity to publicly express his disappointment in the final years of the century was Christian Fleetwood. Two years after Turner's articulation of his frontier thesis in conjunction with the Columbian Exposition and Douglass's speech at Carlisle, and four years after resigning from the D.C. National Guard in disgust over the racist practices of its white commander, Fleetwood appeared at the Cotton States and International Exposition in Atlanta, Georgia. The Cotton States Exposition, which lasted from mid-September to December 31, 1895, was segregated Atlanta's answer to the 1893 fair in Chicago. Ironically, perhaps in direct response to the exclusivity of the Chicago fair and almost certainly to demonstrate the South's progress in race relations since Appomattox, the fair in Atlanta included an entire "Negro Building." Built by black workers and designed to represent a broad range of black experience, it offered, among other things, exhibits of crafts produced by students enrolled in various black colleges and secondary schools, including Samuel Armstrong's Hampton Institute.[43]

Nevertheless, the Atlanta exposition hardly trumpeted unequivocally black Americans' progress toward equality with whites. It was here, after all, that Booker T. Washington—at the time Hampton Institute's most famous graduate and a dedicated protégé of Armstrong—gave his "Atlanta Compromise" speech on opening day (September 18), following his participation in a three-hour parade, in which both white and black militia troops marched, although not together. In his speech, Washington repeatedly urged black Americans to "cast their buckets down where they were," counseled them to "dignify and glorify common labor, and put brains and skill into the common occupations of life," and warned, "No race can prosper till it learns that there is as much dignity in tilling a field as in writing a poem. It is at the bottom of life we must begin, and not at the top." Washington's speech, writes the historian David Blight, "is most often remembered as the signa-ture statement" of his "accommodationist social philosophy," which his defenders have described as "a necessary strategy of educational and economic uplift in the segregated South," but his critics have deemed "a racial surrender to white supremacy and inequality." It is easy to criticize Washington from the perspective of the present for not taking a bolder stance on behalf of black progress toward a full and equal citizenship. But it is only fair to point out that he was attempting, to the best of his ability, to read the tea leaves with respect to the nation's tolerance for racial equality at the turn of the twentieth century. And some would say that he was doing so with painful accuracy.[44]

Two months after Booker T. Washington's oration, Fleetwood spoke at the Atlanta meeting of the National Negro Congress, held in conjunc-tion with the Cotton States Exposition then underway. Earlier, Major Reuben Romulus Mims, the commander of Alabama's black militia units, had called for the organization of a black National Guard association, an idea that Fleetwood, given his unhappy experiences in the nation's capital, surely endorsed. Perhaps it was even in support of Mims's vision that Fleet-wood gave his speech, entitled "The Negro as a Soldier." Fleetwood, it is clear, was also reading the tea leaves with respect to what black Americans—and especially black soldiers—could hope for as they pressed their claims to the full rights of citizenship in the years ahead. Among other things, he expressed sharp disappointment

Christian A. Fleetwood, ca. 1890, wearing his Congressional Medal of Honor. *Courtesy of the Library of Congress.*

Booker T. Washington, ca. 1890. *Courtesy of the Library of Congress.*

over the failure of black men's military service during the American Revolution, the War of 1812, and the Civil War to generate for them and their community greater respect from the rest of the nation, or more tangible, enduring rewards.[45]

Throughout the Revolution, Fleetwood declared, black soldiers "bore an honorable part. The history of the doings of the armies is their history, as in everything they took part and did their share . . . offering their lives [as] a willing sacrifice for the country." Building on this theme, Fleetwood cited a December 1814 testimonial from General Andrew Jackson regarding the performance of some black soldiers under his command during the War of 1812. "I knew that you loved the land of your nativity, and that, like ourselves, you had to defend all that is most dear to man," Jackson had written. "But you surpass my hopes." Still, Fleetwood pointed out, black veterans of that war had not only failed to receive recognition; they had also often been neglected once their service was no longer needed. Fleetwood relayed in particular the story of a black veteran who had earned Jackson's praise for rallying a group of faltering white troops during a battle and leading them to victory. In old age, however, this same decorated veteran was arrested after defending himself against a white assailant, and was "given nine and thirty lashes on his bare back," a brutal incident that may well have led to his death not long after.[46]

Turning to the Civil War—his war—Fleetwood described the process by which black men such as himself had ultimately gained access to federal army service, noting, "It took three years of war to place the enlisted Negro upon the same ground as the enlisted white man as to pay and emoluments; *perhaps* six years of war might have given him shoulder-straps, but the war ended without authorization of law for that step." Fleetwood went on to list a number of battles in which USCT soldiers had been engaged—Port Hudson, Milliken's Bend, Fort Wagner—all of which, he declared, "covered the actors with and reflected upon the race a blaze of glory." In their service in defense of the Union black soldiers had experienced "war indeed, upon its grandest scale, and in all its infinite variety." Like white soldiers, and indeed as the black Regulars on the frontier had done subsequently, they had endured "the tireless march under burning sun, chilling frosts and driven tempests, the lonely vigil of the picket under starless skies, the rush and roar of countless 'hosts to battle driven' in the mad charge and the victorious shout that pursued the fleeing foe." In the war for the Union, Fleetwood continued, "the Negro stood in the full glare of the greatest search light, part and parcel of the grandest armies ever mustered upon this continent." In the glare of that light, the black USCT soldier had proved himself, and his people, worthy.[47]

Second Lieutenant John Hanks Alexander. *Courtesy of the U.S. Military Academy at West Point.*

Second Lieutenant Charles Young. *Courtesy of the U.S. Military Academy at West Point.*

Perhaps in the interest of time, Fleetwood did not discuss the role the black Regulars had played over the last thirty years in suppressing the Native Americans, taming the land, and ensuring the westward spread of American civilization, but he certainly could have. Instead, he pointed out that in the wake of each of the wars in which black American men had served as soldiers, what had followed was not a fair reward for their military service but rather their "relegation to outer darkness" by means of the "absolute effacement of the remembrance of the gallant deeds" they had performed for the nation. "It is but a little thing to ask," he concluded, that black veterans' efforts be acknowledged, and rewarded. "*Be just*," Fleetwood urged his listeners; "but, oh, the shame of it for those who need [to] be asked!"[48]

By the time Fleetwood spoke, the Supreme Court had handed down its shameful decision in *Plessy* v. *Ferguson*. Moreover, the doors of West Point had been sealed tight once more against the enrollment of black cadets. After John Hanks Alexander graduated in 1887, only one other black American was able to do so for the next half a century: Charles Young, the son of a soldier who had served with the Fifth U.S. Colored Heavy Artillery during the Civil War, graduated in 1889 and went on to serve with both the Ninth and the Tenth Cavalry Regiments for almost thirty years. Black men continued to enlist in the U.S. army, however, several thousand of them volunteering for service in the Spanish-American War. In 1898, Fleetwood himself, now fifty-two years old, offered to command a regiment of black soldiers for the campaigns in Cuba and the Philippines. Fleetwood received enthusiastic endorsements of many white officers, including William Birney, who had enlisted him in the Fourth U.S. Colored Infantry Regiment back in 1863. "He was faithful and endowed with a remarkable aptitude for military matters," Birney declared. "His record was not only without a stain but distinguished for judgment and courage." Still, the War Department turned Fleetwood's offer down.[49]

Meanwhile, discharged and retired black Regulars found that the army had little to offer them beyond paid transportation back to the site of their enlistment; for the disabled, the possibility of a bed in a government-sponsored veterans home; and for those who could prove that they had been injured fighting Indians, "in a particular campaign in certain states and territories at a specific time," perhaps a small government pension. It did not feel like much, and certainly not like enough. As Reuben Waller, one of the Tenth Cavalry troopers who rescued George Forsyth's white command on Beecher's Island in 1868, put it many years later, "We were 'regular soldiers' and had to make the west safe for the soldiers of the Civil War to get homesteads in, and $72 per month pensions, while we poor 'regulars' got nothing." Recalled Arthur W. Winston, another Tenth Cavalry veteran, "I gave five of the best years of my life in the service. What class of soldiers suffered more hardships and fought a more cruel a foe than the boys of the Indian Wars?" A third recalled that he had "slept many a night on the cold frozen ground

Image of the Ninth and Tenth Cavalry Regiments fighting in Cuba in 1898. *Courtesy of the Library of Congress.*

covered with five foot of snow, without an overcoat, blanket or shelter tent, with half rations, chasing the redskins to help blaze a right of way for the settlers of the wild west." And, one must ask, for what?[50]

Certainly, writes the historian Arlen L. Fowler, service in the post–Civil War U.S. army "gave the black man a measure of human dignity and worth that few institutions in American society of that period could offer." Still, in 1937, *sixty* years after he had left the Tenth Cavalry's service, the veteran George W. Ford was bitter. Black Americans, including veterans like himself, continued to endure harsh legal discrimination as well as ghastly stereotyping in the popular media. "I am fully aware of the shortcomings of many of my people," he insisted, "but the great majority are peaceful and law abiding," and hardly deserving of such systematic ill treatment. "There are very many noble and high-minded white people," he went on, "who do not subscribe to the treatment to which we are subjected." The problem was that even the most benevolent whites seemed to "lack the courage and the interest to come out in the open and protest" against the injustices blacks still suffered.[51]

Had he been alive in 1937, Frederick Douglass, who died in 1895, would have been deeply grieved to learn that the quality of "citizenship" black Americans, even black veterans, then enjoyed was so little improved after forty years. In one of the last speeches of his life, delivered in January 1894 at the Metropolitan African Methodist Episcopal Church in the heart of the nation's capital, Douglass decried the race prejudice that seemed to obstruct every path to black advancement as the nineteenth century prepared to give way to the twentieth. "Can the negro be educated? Can the negro be induced to work for himself, without a master? Can the negro be a soldier?" Douglass asked then. "Time and events have answered these and all other like questions," and yet equality remained elusive. And why? Because white Americans persisted in defying the full implications of the "sublime and glorious truths" upon which the United States was founded, when the colonies first "summoned hoary forms of oppression and time honored tyranny to judgment." Back in 1776, the fledgling nation's mission had been to provide the world with a sterling example of "human brotherhood" and "the redemption of the world from the bondage of ages." All that was needed now, Douglass insisted wearily, was for white Americans to recommit to that original mission. "Apply these sublime and glorious truths to the situation now before you," Douglass urged. "Put away your race prejudice. Banish the idea that one class must rule over another. Recognize the fact that the rights of the humblest citizen are as worthy of protection as are those of the highest, and your problem will be solved . . . [and] your Republic will stand and flourish forever."[52]

Notes

Preface

1 *The Liberator*, July 24, 1863.

 The lines of poetry that appear before the preface are excerpted from an untitled poem by Anna Sykora, composed in July 2007. Although Ms. Sykora (who lives in Hanover, Germany, and happens to be my sister) dedicated her poem to U.S. Army General David H. Petraeus in the context of his bold efforts to reshape the war in Iraq, their truth seems timeless to me. Certainly that same truth is reflected in the story I tell here.

Chapter One. Wanted: Black Men for Federal Army Service

1 Diary of Christian A. Fleetwood, entry for July 7, 1863, in the Christian A. Fleetwood Papers, Library of Congress, Washington, D.C. (hereafter cited as Fleetwood Diary); Patricia L. Faust, ed., *Historical Times Illustrated Encyclopedia of the Civil War* (New York: Harper & Row, 1986), p. 61; *Liberator*, July 24, 1863. A small number of black men—approximately a hundred—did receive officers' commissions during the war. Among these, some were able to retain their commissions, but most others were edged out by white commanders who objected to their presence. See Joseph T. Glatthaar, *Forged in Battle: The Civil War Alliance of Black Soldiers and White Officers* (New York: Meridian, 1990), pp. 176–81, for a full discussion of this question. See also James M. McPherson, *The Negro's Civil War* (New York: Vintage Books, 1965), pp. 237–39.

 The epigraph for this chapter comes from the Fleetwood Diary, Nov. 9, 1863.

2 James F. Harrison, Biographical Sketch of Christian Fleetwood, in Fleetwood

Papers. See also Fleetwood Diary, July 21, 1862. Young Fleetwood's relatively unin-
hibited interactions with nearby white children recall antebellum slave children's
contact with white children in the American South, before they reached the age
when their primary responsibilities as producers—and reproducers—imposed harsh
constraints on their interracial socializing.

3 Harrison, Biographical Sketch of Christian Fleetwood; Robert E. Millette, "Lead-
ership and Shared Governance at HBCUs," *Lincoln Journal of Social and Political
Thought* 1 (Fall 2002): 1; Frank Bowles and Frank A. DeCosta, *Between Two Worlds:
A Profile of Negro Higher Education* (New York: McGraw-Hill, 1971), p. 12. Among
Lincoln University's most famous alumni is Thurgood Marshall. See the university's
website, www.lincoln.edu.

4 Fleetwood Diary, March 25 and July 5, 1862. If Fleetwood kept a diary before 1862,
it is no longer available.

5 Fleetwood Diary, May 5 and 11 and July 16, 1862; Aug. 17 and 18 and Dec. 31,
1863. So-called "free" blacks in Baltimore, as elsewhere, operated carefully within
the restrictions on mobility that local black codes imposed upon them. At the time
the Civil War began, almost all states required nonslaves to carry their "freedom
papers"—which any white person could demand and inspect at will—wherever they
went, and an individual black person caught without his or her papers in hand risked
imprisonment, or possibly even enslavement. For a thorough discussion of the limits of the freedom "free" blacks experienced in the antebellum period, see Ira Berlin,
Slaves without Masters: The Free Negro in the Antebellum South (New York: Vintage
Books, 1976).

   According to the historian James M. McPherson, out of the 180,000 black men
who served in the U.S. army over the course of the war, fewer than 100 received
officers' commissions, some of which were quickly revoked and none of which were
above the level of captain. McPherson, *Ordeal by Fire: The Civil War and Reconstruction* (New York: McGraw-Hill, 1992), p. 379.

6 McPherson, *The Negro's Civil War*, pp. 19–22. For a full discussion of "soft war"
versus "hard war" policies undertaken during the Civil War, see Mark Grimsley, *The
Hard Hand of War: Union Military Policy toward Southern Civilians, 1861–1865* (New
York: Cambridge University Press, 1995).

7 McPherson, *Ordeal by Fire*, p. 270; Glatthaar, *Forged in Battle*, pp. 6–8. See also
James G. Hollandsworth Jr., *The Louisiana Native Guards: The Black Military Experience during the Civil War* (Baton Rouge: Louisiana State University Press, 1995).

8 McPherson, *Ordeal by Fire*, p. 348; William E. Gienapp, ed., *The Civil War and
Reconstruction: A Documentary Collection* (New York: W. W. Norton, 2001), p. 165.

9 According to the secretary of war's 1865 annual report, the total number of black
enlisted men in the USCT was 178,975. See the *Annual Report of the Secretary of War
(1865)*, Serial Set no. 1249, p. 29. See also George Washington Williams, *A History
of the Negro Troops in the War of the Rebellion* (New York: Bergman Publishers, 1888),

p. 324; Glatthaar, *Forged in Battle*, pp. 10, 250–51; McPherson, *The Negro's Civil War*, p. 237; McPherson, *Ordeal by Fire*, p. 481.

10 Fleetwood Diary, Sept. 22, 1863.

11 Ibid., Sept. 29 and 30, Oct. 1, Dec. 9, 17, and 31, 1863; Jan. 29, Feb. 6, 7, and 10, and May 1, 1864.

12 McPherson, *Ordeal by Fire*, pp. 412, 414.

13 Fleetwood Diary, June 7, 15, and 16, 1864.

14 Glatthaar, *Forged in Battle*, p. 150. Unfortunately, Fleetwood's diary does not include any commentary about the Battle of the Crater—there is an unexplained gap from July 18 to Aug. 30, 1864. The Fourth USCT was a component of the Army of the James' XVIII Corps (third brigade, third division).

15 Glatthaar, *Forged in Battle*, pp. 150–51. For more on the battle, see also the *War of the Rebellion: The Official Records of the Union and Confederate Armies* (Washington, D.C.: Government Printing Office, 1881–1902), ser. 1, vol. 34, pt. 1, p. 28; ser. 1, vol. 42, pt. 1, pp. 20–21, 104, 109–10, 766–67, 772–73, 780–81, 798–801, and other entries. This source hereafter cited as *OR*.

16 *OR*, ser. 1, vol. 42, pt. 1, p. 849; ser. 1, vol. 42, pt. 3, p. 169; Fleetwood Diary, Sept. 27–30, 1864.

17 *OR*, ser. 1, vol. 42, pt. 3, pp. 163, 169.

18 Christian Fleetwood to F. C. Ainsworth, March 21, 1876, in Fleetwood Papers. See also the handwritten biographical sketch of Fleetwood ibid.

19 McPherson, *Ordeal by Fire*, p. 469; Fleetwood Diary, Dec. 16 and 29, 1864.

20 McPherson, *Ordeal by Fire*, p. 469; Unknown to Christian Fleetwood, April 9, 1865, Fleetwood Papers.

21 *New York Times*, May 24, 1865; Joshua Lawrence Chamberlain, *The Passing of the Armies* (New York: Bantam Books, 1993), pp. 249–50; *Harper's Weekly*, June 10, 1865, p. 358.

22 Faust, ed., *Historical Times Illustrated Encyclopedia of the Civil War*, p. 319; Allan Nevins, *The War for the Union*, vol. 4 (New York: Charles Scribner's Sons, 1971), p. 365; David S. Heidler and Jeanne T. Heidler, eds., *Encyclopedia of the American Civil War*, vol. 2 (Santa Barbara, Calif.: ABC-CLIO, 2000), p. 860; Ulysses S. Grant, *Personal Memoirs* (New York: Penguin Books, 1999), p. 629; William Tecumseh Sherman, *Memoirs* (New York: Penguin Books, 2000), p. 730. According to Allan Nevins, some spectators even "perched on lamp posts" to enjoy the parade (Nevins, *The War for the Union*, 4:365). The *New York Times*, which described the weather on the twenty-third as "magnificent," noted that in anticipation of the review, "Washington has been filled as it never was filled before; the hotel-keepers assert that the pressure upon their resources never was so great, and thousands of people have been nightly turned away to seek a place of rest where best they might" (*New York Times*, May 24, 1865).

23 Chamberlain, *The Passing of the Armies*, p. 276; Faust, ed., *Historical Times Illustrated*

Encyclopedia of the Civil War, p. 319; Nevins, *The War for the Union*, 4:366; Heidler and Heidler, eds., *Encyclopedia of the American Civil War*, 2:861; *New York Times*, May 25, 1865; Grant, *Personal Memoirs*, p. 629. Nevins gives the total number of soldiers gathered for the review as over 200,000 (Nevins, *The War for the Union*, 4:365). According to one observer, Sherman's troops were "some inches" taller on average than those of the Army of the Potomac (*Army and Navy Journal*, June 3, 1865).

24 *New York Times*, May 25, 1865; Heidler and Heidler, eds., *Encyclopedia of the American Civil War*, 2:861; Chamberlain, *The Passing of the Armies*, p. 277; Sherman, *Memoirs*, p. 731. Declared the *Times*, "The interest of to-day [the Twenty-fourth] has exceeded that of yesterday. The Army of the Potomac is our old acquaintance, but the Armies of Georgia and [the] Tennessee few people here had ever seen."

25 *The Personal Memoirs of P. H. Sheridan* (Cambridge, Mass.: Da Capo Press, 1992), p. 402; Peter R. DeMontravel, *A Hero to His Fighting Men: Nelson A. Miles, 1839–1925* (Kent, Ohio: Kent State University Press, 1998), p. 226; *Harper's Weekly*, June 10, 1865. See also Special Orders dated May 21, 1865, from the Headquarters of the Department of Virginia, in Nelson A. Miles Papers, U.S. Army Military History Institute, Carlisle, Pa.

26 Donald R. Shaffer, *After the Glory: The Struggles of Black Civil War Veterans* (Lawrence: University Press of Kansas, 2004), p. 185; "Extract from the Department Returns—Colored Troops for the Month of June 1865," in National Archives and Records Administration's Microfilm Series T823, "The Negro in the Military Service of the United States, 1639–1886," National Archives and Records Administration, Washington, D.C., roll no. 4 (hereafter cited as NARA Microfilm T823); Frank N. Schubert, ed., *On the Trail of the Buffalo Soldier: Biographies of African Americans in the U.S. Army, 1866–1917* (Wilmington, Del.: Scholarly Resources, 1995), pp. 36, 49–50; Bobby L. Lovett, "The Negro's Civil War in Tennessee, 1861–1865," *Journal of Negro History* 61 (Jan. 1976): 50. See also the materials pertaining to Samuel Cooper's pension case, in the Fort Davis Documents Files, Folder: Tenth Cavalry, Company C, Fort Davis National Historic Site, Fort Davis, Tex. See also Marvin E. Fletcher, "The Negro Volunteer in Reconstruction, 1865–1866," *Military Affairs* 32 (Dec. 1968): 126; and Monroe Lee Billington, *New Mexico's Buffalo Soldiers, 1866–1900* (Niwot: University Press of Colorado, 1991), p. 3.

27 *New York Times*, May 24, 1865; Sherman, *Memoirs*, p. 732.

28 Sherman, *Memoirs*, p. 732; Chamberlain, *The Passing of the Armies*, p. 279; Faust, ed., *Historical Times Illustrated Encyclopedia of the Civil War*, p. 319; *New York Times*, May 24, 1865.

29 McPherson, *Ordeal by Fire*, p. 471; David W. Blight, *Race and Reunion: The Civil War in American Memory* (Cambridge: Harvard University Press, Belknap Press, 2001), pp. 66–67.

30 Blight, *Race and Reunion*, pp. 69–70.

31 Fletcher, "The Negro Volunteer in Reconstruction," p. 126; E.S.W. to Editor, *Army and Navy Journal*, July 22, 1865.

32 *New York Times*, Aug. 28, 1865; Edwin M. Stanton to Major General John M. Palmer, April 18, 1865, in NARA Microfilm T823, roll no. 4.

33 *New York Times*, Aug. 28, 1865.

34 See "Extract from the Department Returns—Colored Regiments, June 1867," in NARA Microfilm T823, roll no. 4; James E. Sefton, *The United States Army and Reconstruction, 1865–1877* (Baton Rouge: Louisiana State University Press, 1967), p. 8; and Glatthaar, *Forged in Battle*, pp. 210, 214. According to the historian Drew Gilpin Faust, black soldiers, who "sought to win a place in the polity, as citizens and as men, through their willingness to give up their lives," were disproportionately represented among occupation troops in the South assigned to the gruesome duty of collecting and reburying the bodies of the Union dead. See Faust, *This Republic of Suffering: Death and the American Civil War* (New York: Alfred A. Knopf, 2008), pp. 48, 226–27.

35 According to the historian Marvin Fletcher, in mid-1865 there were 35,500 USCT soldiers in the Department of the Gulf, 18,732 in the Department of the Cumberland, and 27,109 in Texas. See Fletcher, "The Negro Volunteer in Reconstruction," p. 126. See also Sefton, *The United States Army and Reconstruction*, p. 27; and Glatthaar, *Forged in Battle*, pp. 214–15.

36 Paul H. Carlson, *"Pecos Bill": A Military Biography of William R. Shafter* (College Station: Texas A&M University Press, 1989), p. 28; William Shafter, General Orders No. 17, Sept. 22, 1865, in NARA Microfilm T823, roll no. 4.

37 Randolph B. Marcy to E. D. Townsend, May 16, 1865, in NARA Microfilm T823, roll no. 4.

38 Brevet Brigadier General O. H. Hart to Brevet Colonel P. Ord, March 5, 1866, in NARA Microfilm T823, roll no. 4; Fletcher, "The Negro Volunteer in Reconstruction," p. 126.

39 Resolution of the General Assembly of Kentucky, June 3, 1864, quoted in Morris J. MacGregor and Bernard C. Nalty, eds., *Blacks in the United States Armed Forces: Basic Documents*, vol. 3 (Wilmington, Del.: Scholarly Resources, 1977), p. 4.

40 O. A. Lochrane to Andrew Johnson, March 26, 1866, quoted in MacGregor and Nalty, eds., *Blacks in the United States Armed Forces*, p. 12; Ulysses S. Grant to George H. Thomas, March 28, 1866, quoted ibid., p. 13.

41 Ulysses S. Grant, Report to the Thirty-ninth Congress, Dec. 18, 1865, quoted in Gienapp, ed., *The Civil War and Reconstruction*, p. 322. See also Glatthaar, *Forged in Battle*, p. 214. The secretary of war's report for 1865 also expressed unwarranted optimism about the former Confederate states' willingness to submit to federal control, claiming in Nov. 1865 that the "disposition exhibited after the surrender of their armies in all the insurgent States to submit to the national authority" had

"dispensed with the necessity of keeping large armies on foot" (*Annual Report of the Secretary of War (1865)*, Serial Set no. 1249, p. 19).

42 Ulysses S. Grant to George H. Thomas, March 28, 1866, quoted in MacGregor and Nalty, eds., *Blacks in the United States Armed Forces*, pp. 13–14.

43 *New York Times*, May 3, 4, 10, 12, and 17, 1866. See also McPherson, *Ordeal by Fire*, p. 516.

44 Eric Foner, *Reconstruction: America's Unfinished Revolution, 1863–1877* (New York: Harper & Row, 1988), p. 262; *New York Times*, May 3, 4, 10, 12, and 17, 1866; McPherson, *Ordeal by Fire*, p. 516.

45 McPherson, *Ordeal by Fire*, p. 516; Foner, *Reconstruction*, pp. 262–64. See also James G. Hollandsworth Jr., *An Absolute Massacre: The New Orleans Race Riot of July 30, 1866* (Baton Rouge: Louisiana State University, 2001).

46 *New York Times*, July 31 and Aug. 1, 2, and 4, 1866; Foner, *Reconstruction*, p. 263; *The Personal Memoirs of P. H. Sheridan*, p. 416.

47 *Army and Navy Journal*, Aug. 11, 1866.

48 Fleetwood Diary, Dec. 25, 1863; Samuel A. Duncan to "To all whom it may concern," May 5, 1866, in Fleetwood Papers.

Chapter Two. Black Soldiers Go West

1 Undated, unidentified clipping (internal evidence suggests a date of Aug. 1867) in Christian A. Fleetwood Papers, Library of Congress, Washington, D.C. (hereafter cited as Fleetwood Papers). Unfortunately, according to the historian Donald R. Shaffer, the Colored Soldiers' and Sailors' League was "apparently short-lived, likely a victim of its own success." After the Fifteenth Amendment granting black men the right to vote was ratified in 1870, Shaffer writes, the league "disappears completely from the historical record." See Shaffer, "'I Would Rather Shake Hands with the Blackest Nigger in the Land': Northern Black Civil War Veterans and the Grand Army of the Republic," in Paul A. Cimbala and Randall M. Miller, eds., *Union Soldiers and the Northern Home Front: Wartime Experiences, Postwar Adjustments* (New York: Fordham University Press, 2002), p. 452.

The epigraph for this chapter comes from James H. Lane, quoted in Morris J. MacGregor and Bernard C. Nalty, eds., *Blacks in the United States Armed Forces: Basic Documents* vol. 3 (Wilmington, Del.: Scholarly Resources, 1977), p. 23.

A note on terminology: throughout the book, I adhere to the practice, maintained by a number of other historians, of referring to postwar black soldiers in the U.S. army by the more dignified term "black Regulars," rather than by the well-known nickname "Buffalo Soldiers." According to the historian Frank N. Schubert, "Although black regulars from the period of the frontier wars are now almost universally known as Buffalo Soldiers, the origins, significance, and prevalence of the phrase are not clear. There is general agreement that the Indians, either the Comanche or Cheyenne, first called the troopers 'Buffalo Soldiers,' sometime around 1870. Some historians . . . claimed that because the buffalo was so important to these tribes the term was probably meant as a sign of respect and that the soldiers so comprehended it. . . . However, since there is not contemporaneous evidence that the soldiers themselves actually used or even referred to this title, any claims concerning their views of the usage remain unproved suppositions." See Schubert, *Voices of the Buffalo Soldier: Records, Reports, and Recollections of Military Life and Service in the West* (Albuquerque: University of New Mexico Press, 2003), p. 48. See also William A. Dobak and Thomas D. Phillips, *The Black Regulars, 1866–1898* (Norman: University of Oklahoma Press, 2001), p. xvii.

2 Handwritten biographical sketch of Christian A. Fleetwood, in Fleetwood Papers.

3 Robert M. Utley, *Frontier Regulars: The United States Army and the Indian, 1866–1891* (New York: Macmillan, 1973), p. 12; *Army and Navy Journal*, June 10, 1865 (the letter from "H.C.M." published in this issue is dated May 28, 1865).

4 *Army and Navy Journal*, June 24, 1865. See also the March 31 and April 7, 14, and 28, 1866, issues.

5 Ulysses S. Grant to Henry Wilson, Jan. 12, 1866, quoted in MacGregor and Nalty, eds., *Blacks in the United States Armed Forces*, p. 15. See also James H. Lane, quoted ibid., p. 22.

6 James A. McDougall, quoted in MacGregor and Nalty, eds., *Blacks in the United States Armed Forces*, p. 17; Willard Saulsbury Sr., quoted ibid., pp. 20, 21.

7 Benjamin Wade, quoted in MacGregor and Nalty, eds., *Blacks in the United States Armed Forces*, pp. 19, 21.

8 Joseph T. Glatthaar, *Forged in Battle: The Civil War Alliance of Black Soldiers and White Officers* (New York: Meridian, 1991), pp. 7, 122, 176, 182; James H. Lane, quoted in MacGregor and Nalty, eds., *Blacks in the United States Armed Forces*, pp. 22, 23.

9 William H. Leckie, *The Buffalo Soldiers: A Narrative of the Negro Cavalry in the West* (Norman: University of Oklahoma Press, 1967), p. 6; Utley, *Frontier Regulars*, pp. 11–16; Frank N. Schubert, *Black Valor: Buffalo Soldiers and the Medal of Honor, 1870–1898* (Wilmington, Del.: Scholarly Resources, 1997), p. 5. See also the *Annual Report of the Secretary of War (1866)*, Serial Set no. 1285, p. 3.

Despite the consolidation of the four infantry regiments into two and the general trend toward cutting the army's strength as a whole—the overall strength of the army reached a low of about 27,000 in 1874—the number of enlisted men in the black regiments dropped below 2,000 only twice over the next three decades. After reaching a high of almost 6,000 in 1867, and then dropping down to about 4,200 in 1869 (the year of the consolidation), the average number of enlisted men in the black regiments between 1870 and 1896 was 2,333. See Frank N. Schubert, ed., *On the Trail of the Buffalo Soldier: Biographies of African Americans in the U.S. Army, 1866–1917* (Wilmington, Del.: Scholarly Resources, 1995), p. 509. See also Charles L. Kenner, *Buffalo Soldiers and Officers of the Ninth Cavalry, 1867–1898* (Norman: University of Oklahoma Press), p. 11; and Dobak and Phillips, *Black Regulars*, p. xi.

10 John H. Nankivell, *Buffalo Soldier Regiment: History of the Twenty-fifth United States Infantry, 1869–1926* (Lincoln: University of Nebraska Press, 2001), p. 18; Dobak and Phillips, *The Black Regulars*, p. 114. "In this way, too," added Carleton, "the negroes who serve in the army will become intelligent and be so much the better fitted to take their places as the political equals of white men, which they have become, under the constitution" (Nankivell, *Buffalo Soldier Regiment*, p. 18). See also the historical sketch of the Tenth Cavalry published in MacGregor and Nalty, eds., *Blacks in the United States Armed Forces*, p. 74.

11 Kenner, *Buffalo Soldiers and Officers of the Ninth Cavalry*, p. 41; Leckie, *The Buffalo Soldiers*, p. 8. See also Paul H. Carlson, *"Pecos Bill": A Military Biography of William R. Shafter* (College Station: Texas A&M University Press, 2003), p. 30.

12 See R. C. Rutherford to Benjamin H. Grierson, April 20, 1866, in Benjamin H. Grierson Papers, Fort Davis National Historic Site, Fort Davis, Tex. (hereafter cited as Grierson Papers, Fort Davis). See also William H. Leckie and Shirley A. Leckie, *Unlikely Warriors: General Benjamin Grierson and His Family* (Norman: University of Oklahoma Press, 1984), p. 299.

13 Leckie and Leckie, *Unlikely Warriors*, pp. 3, 5–8, 11.

14 Ibid., pp. 10–18.

15 Ibid., pp. 21–41.

16 Ibid., pp. 44–59.

17 Ibid., pp. 60–68.

18 Ibid., pp. 69–83; Grant, *Personal Memoirs*, pp. 266–67; Shirley Anne Leckie, *The Colonel's Lady on the Western Frontier: The Correspondence of Alice Kirk Grierson* (Lincoln: University of Nebraska Press, 1989), p. 4. James McPherson describes Grierson's Raid as "one of the most spectacular cavalry raids of the war . . . an exploit worthy of Forrest or Stuart at their best." See McPherson, *Ordeal by Fire: The Civil War and Reconstruction* (New York: McGraw-Hill, 1992), pp. 312–13.

19 Leckie and Leckie, *Unlikely Warriors*, pp. 124–38.

20 Kenner, *Buffalo Soldiers and Officers of the Ninth Cavalry*, pp. 30–47; Leckie, *The Buffalo Soldiers*, pp. 7, 251; Patricia L. Faust, ed., *Historical Times Illustrated Encyclopedia of the Civil War* (New York: Harper & Row, 1986), p. 349; Dobak and Phillips, *The Black Regulars*, p. 34.

21 Edward S. Cooper, *William Babcock Hazen: The Best Hated Man* (Madison, N.J.: Fairleigh Dickinson University Press, 2005), p. 168; Ezra J. Warner, *Generals in Blue: Lives of the Union Commanders* (Baton Rouge: Louisiana State University Press, 1964), pp. 225–26, 301–03, 338–39; Faust, ed., *Historical Times Illustrated Encyclopedia of the Civil War*, pp. 354–55, 462–63, 515–16; Dobak and Phillips, *The Black Regulars*, pp. 28–29.

22 Warner, *Generals in Blue*, pp. 322–24; Faust, ed., *Historical Times Illustrated Encyclopedia of the Civil War*, p. 492; Edwin M. Stanton to Nelson A. Miles, Aug. 2, 1866, in Nelson A. Miles Papers, Library of Congress, Washington, D.C. (hereafter cited as Miles Papers [LC]); Robert Wooster, *Nelson A. Miles and the Twilight of the Frontier Army* (Lincoln: University of Nebraska Press, 1993), pp. 46–47; Philip Sheridan to Nelson A. Miles, Sept. 23, 1866, in Miles Papers (LC). See also Winfield Scott Hancock to Nelson A. Miles, Oct. 15, 1866, ibid.

23 *Army and Navy Journal*, March 27, 1869; Warner, *Generals in Blue*, pp. 226, 323, 339. In Dec. 1870, Mackenzie transferred to command of the white Fourth Cavalry (Warner, *Generals in Blue*, p. 303). He was succeeded by Abner Doubleday, who was in turn succeeded by Joseph H. Potter, who then continued as colonel of the Twenty-fourth until 1886. Meanwhile, Joseph Mower died in January 1870, and command of the Twenty-fifth went to Joseph J. Reynolds—who stayed only a few months—then to John D. Stevenson, who remained only seventeen days. Finally, in Jan. 1871, George L. Andrews took command, and he stayed in the post until he finally retired from the army in 1892 (Dobak and Phillips, *The Black Regulars*, pp. 33–34).

24 William W. Holden to "the Senators and representatives in Congress," Jan. 20, 1869, in Nelson A. Miles Papers, U.S. Army Military History Institute, Carlisle, Pa. (hereafter cited as Miles Papers [USAMHI]). See also Nelson A. Miles, General Orders No. 9, Headquarters District of North Carolina, Oct. 14, 1868, and General Orders No. 3, Sept. 10, 1868, and Nelson A. Miles to James A. Garfield, precise date unknown, 1868, all in Miles Papers (USAMHI). And see Wooster, *Nelson A. Miles and the Twilight of the Frontier Army*, pp. 53–54.

25 Annual Report of Nelson A. Miles, Oct. 9, 1867, and Nelson A. Miles to R. C. Drum, Oct. 4, 1868, and related correspondence, all in Miles Papers (USAMHI). See also Peter R. DeMontravel, *A Hero to His Fighting Men: Nelson A. Miles, 1839–1925* (Kent, Ohio: Kent State University Press, 1998), pp. 54–57.

26 DeMontravel, *A Hero to His Fighting Men*, p. 63; *Personal Recollections & Observations of Nelson A. Miles*, 2 vols. (Lincoln: University of Nebraska Press, 1992), 1:51; Nelson A. Miles, *Serving the Republic: Memoirs of the Civil and Military Life of Nelson A. Miles* (Cranbury, N.J.: Scholar's Bookshelf, 2006), pp. 102–6.

27 Benjamin H. Grierson to "Dear Father," Sept. 28, 1866, in Grierson Papers, Fort Davis. See also Benjamin H. Grierson to Alice Grierson, Oct. 3, 1866, ibid.

28 Dobak and Phillips, *The Black Regulars*, pp. 3–4; Carlson, *"Pecos Bill,"* p. 38; Wooster, *Nelson A. Miles and the Twilight of the Frontier Army*, p. 47; Don Rickey, "The Negro Regulars: A Combat Record, 1866–1891" (unpublished paper, in the Ninth Cavalry Documents Files, Fort Davis Historic Site, Fort Davis, Tex.). According to the editor of Alice Grierson's correspondence, after her husband became commander of the Tenth Cavalry, this colonel's wife became a strong ally to the men under his command. Alice seems to have gladly taken on a "burden not usually assumed as

enthusiastically by other officers' wives: an unflagging commitment to furthering the welfare of the enlisted men in the regiment" (Leckie, ed., *The Colonel's Lady on the Western Frontier*, pp. 4–5).

29 Donald R. Shaffer, *After the Glory: The Struggles of Black Civil War Veterans* (Lawrence: University Press of Kansas, 2004), p. 29. See also the excerpt from E. D. Townsend's annual report for 1867, dated Oct. 20, 1867, in National Archives and Records Administration's Microfilm Series T823, "The Negro in the Military Service of the United States, 1639–1886," National Archives and Records Administration, Washington, D.C. (hereafter cited as NARA Microfilm T823), roll no. 4. On the recruitment of USCT veterans for the new black Regular regiments see *Annual Report of the Secretary of War (1866)*, Serial Set no. 1285, p. 3; *Army and Navy Journal*, Aug. 26, 1866. According to Dobak and Phillips, "About half of the black men who joined the regular army in the late 1860s had served during the Civil War. Of these, at least 533 transferred directly from USCT regiments that were mustering out in the fall of 1866" (Dobak and Phillips, *Black Regulars*, p. 24). See also ibid., p. 50, and Kenner, *Buffalo Soldiers and Officers of the Ninth Cavalry*, p. 11. On Pollard Cole, see Schubert, ed., *On the Trail of the Buffalo Soldier*, p. 95; and Harold Ray Sayre, *Warriors of Color* (Fort Davis, Tex.: Privately Published, 1995), pp. 139–43. On John Sample see Schubert, ed., *On the Trail of the Buffalo Soldier*, p. 368. Over the course of his twenty years in the military, Sample's character was consistently considered "good," "very good," or "excellent," which his elevation through the noncommissioned ranks corroborates. By 1885, when he left the army, Sample held the rank of sergeant major, the highest noncommissioned rank available and the same rank that Christian Fleetwood had achieved during the Civil War. On Fort Wagner see Glatthaar, *Forged in Battle*, pp. 135–40. And on James W. Bush see James W. Bush Pension File, App. no. 674386; Cert. no. 596465, in RG 15, Records of the Veterans Administration, National Archives and Records Administration, Washington, D.C.

30 Schubert, *Black Valor*, pp. 11–12; Wooster, *Nelson A. Miles and the Twilight of the Frontier Army*, p. 47.

31 Schubert, *Black Valor*, p. 12; Schubert, *Voices of the Buffalo Soldier*, p. 91. Dobak and Phillips insist, "Although the reorganization act of 1866 brought black soldiers into the regular army for the first time, it was not . . . designed to secure and protect the rights and liberties of black Americans" (*Black Regulars*, p. xv). That Congress had not created the new Regular black regiments with race uplift for black Americans as an explicit goal hardly means that the black men who enlisted in those regiments were devoid of their own expectations about the race (and personal) progress they might achieve.

32 Utley, *Frontier Regulars*, pp. 163–64.

33 Erwin N. Thompson, "The Negro Soldiers on the Frontier: A Fort Davis Case Study," *Journal of the West* 7 (April 1968): pp. 217–18; Kenner, *Buffalo Soldiers and*

Officers of the Ninth Cavalry, p. 159; Schubert, ed., *On the Trail of the Buffalo Soldier*, p. 400; Patrick A. Bowmaster, "Occupation—'Soldier': The Life of 1st Sgt. Emanuel Stance" (unpublished paper, Blacksburg, Va., May 1995), p. 1; Schubert, *Black Valor*, pp. 9–26. In conjunction with the XXV Corps, USCT troops on occupation duty had been stationed in Texas since 1865. According to David Work, they represented half of the federal army's presence in the state in 1865—more than thirty regiments—and "a considerable majority" by early 1866. Work writes that "African American soldiers heartily disliked the idea of going to Texas and complained about their new assignment," not only because they were compelled to confront the hostility of white Texans but also because, like so many white veterans, they simply "wanted to return home and start new lives with their families." See Work, "United States Colored Troops in Texas during Reconstruction, 1865–1867," *Southwestern Historical Quarterly* 109 (Jan. 2006): 338–42. I thank Michael Parrish for bringing this article to my attention.

34   Edward Hatch's Ninth Cavalry had soldiers at Fort Davis from July 1867 to April 1875; soldiers of the Forty-first Infantry (and its structural descendant the Twenty-fourth Infantry) were stationed there from March 1868 until April 1872, and from June to Nov. 1880; soldiers of the Twenty-fifth Infantry were at Fort Davis from July 1870 to July 1880; and Benjamin Grierson stationed troopers from his Tenth Cavalry there from May 1875 to April 1885. See unpublished document "Black Regiments at Fort Davis," in the Fort Davis Historic Site files, Fort Davis, Tex. White infantry and cavalry regiments also had companies stationed at Fort Davis on and off during the period from its revival in 1867 to its closure in 1891, but the majority of the soldiers there during this period were black. See also Lucy Miller Jacobson and Mildred Bloys Nored, *Jeff Davis County, Texas* (Fort Davis, Tex.: Fort Davis Historical Society, 1993), pp. 439–41; and Michael Welsh, *Fort Davis: Administrative History* (Santa Fe, N.M.: National Park Service, 1996), Ch. 1. Having bought land in the area surrounding the fort, Grierson retired to Fort Davis in 1890. For Grierson's first impression of the site, see Benjamin H. Grierson to Alice K. Grierson, May 29, 1878, in Grierson Papers, Fort Davis. For more on the fort generally see David J. Allen, "History of the Ninth U.S. Cavalry from 1866 to 1900" (unpublished paper in the Fort Davis Historic Site files, Fort Davis, Tex.), p. 6; and Thompson, "The Negro Soldiers on the Frontier," p. 218. Some key installations associated closely with Fort Davis were Forts Clark (1852) and Duncan (1849), 200 and 300 miles, respectively, to the southeast; Fort McKavett (1852), 300 miles almost directly east; Forts Stockton (1858), Concho (1867), and Griffin (1867), 90 miles, 300 miles, and 380 miles, respectively, to the northeast; and Fort Quitman (1858), 140 miles to the northwest. More distant but also closely associated with the Texas system were sites like Fort Sill, just over 500 miles to the northeast in Indian Territory (later Oklahoma), and Fort Bayard, about 350 miles to the northwest in New Mexico. According to James N. Leiker, Fort Davis consistently

had the largest number of black soldiers of all installations during this period, with some four hundred being stationed there in the early 1870s alone. "At their peak in 1873," Leiker writes, "more than sixteen hundred African American soldiers were stationed on the [Texas] border; by 1880, the aggregate number stood at less than seven hundred," and the "figure continued to decline until 1885, when the last black regiment left Texas, not to return for fourteen years." See Leiker, *Racial Borders: Black Soldiers along the Rio Grande* (College Station: Tex. A&M University Press, 2002), pp. 46, 64.

35 Warner, *Generals in Blue*, pp. 321–22; David S. Heidler and Jeanne T. Heidler, eds., *Encyclopedia of the American Civil War: A Political, Social, and Military History* (Santa Barbara, Calif.: ABC-CLIO, 2000), 3:1325; Kenner, *Buffalo Soldiers and Officers of the Ninth Cavalry*, p. 41.

36 A group of citizens from Indianola, Tex., to Brevet Brigadier General James Shaw Jr., in NARA Microfilm T823, roll no. 4.

37 Kenner, *Buffalo Soldiers and Officers of the Ninth Cavalry*, pp. 72–76.

38 Ibid., pp. 76–78. According to Kenner, the last of the fugitives had been rounded up by April 25 (ibid., p. 78).

39 Schubert, ed., *On the Trail of the Buffalo Soldier*, pp. 383, 471. See also Kenner, *Buffalo Soldiers and Officers of the Ninth Cavalry*, pp. 142–45.

40 *Roster of Non-Commissioned Officers of the Tenth Cavalry*, p. 17; Schubert, ed., *On the Trail of the Buffalo Soldier*, pp. 379–80; RG 153, Records of the Office of the Judge Advocate General, Army, Court Martial Cases, PP-2540, National Archives, Washington, D.C. (hereafter cited as NARA Court Martials, with the number of the case noted). See also the record of John Wiggins in Schubert, ed., *On the Trail of the Buffalo Soldier*, pp. 464–65; the record of Silas Jones in Sayre, *Warriors of Color*, pp. 327–29; and the File for Enlisted Men (Tenth Cavalry): Silas Jones, Fort Davis National Historic Site, Fort Davis, Tex. (hereafter cited as Silas Jones File, Fort Davis).

41 Kenner, *Buffalo Soldiers and Officers of the Ninth Cavalry*, pp. 78–79.

42 Dobak and Phillips, *The Black Regulars*, pp. 204–12. See also Schubert, *Black Valor*, pp. 12–15; and Kenner, *Buffalo Soldiers and Officers of the Ninth Cavalry*, p. 79.

43 Carlson, *"Pecos Bill,"* p. 56; Schubert, ed., *On the Trail of the Buffalo Soldier*, pp. 70, 193, 203. Black soldiers in postwar Texas, writes James Leiker, served in "a state almost unprecedented for its lawlessness and racial violence. With a population of less than one million, more than one thousand persons were murdered annually from 1865 to 1870, a fourth or more of these being black" (Leiker, *Racial Borders*, p. 34).

44 NARA Court Martials, PP-310, PP-775, PP-3052.

45 *New York Times*, Jan. 12, 1869; NARA Court Martials, PP-4517; Jacobson and Nored, *Jeff Davis County*, p. 386. See also the story of George Bentley in the George

Bentley File, Folders of Enlisted Men, Fort Davis National Historic Site, Fort Davis, Tex.

46 NARA Court Martials, PP-310.

47 Ibid., PP-775.

48 Ibid., PP-876 and PP-956.

49 Ibid., PP-1757.

50 Ibid., PP-2356. See also PP-4040.

51 Schubert, ed., *On the Trail of the Buffalo Soldier*, p. 4; Dobak and Phillipps, *The Black Regulars*, p. 194; NARA Court Martials, PP-2820, PP-4788, PP-956.

52 NARA Court Martials PP-4246, PP-1426, PP-2493, and PP-1400. See also NARA Court Martial PP-3132; Schubert, ed., *On the Trail of the Buffalo Soldier*, pp. 235, 359; and Dobak and Phillips, *Black Regulars*, p. 62. According to Dobak and Phillips, "The same factors that induced many black regulars to enlist probably also kept them from deserting. For some, the service clearly offered a better existence than they could find as civilians. Another probable reason for the low desertion rate, though, was that the color of a black man's skin made him conspicuous in the West. If he ran, he could easily be identified and caught."

53 NARA Court Martials, PP-4788.

54 Ibid., PP-4859.

55 *Army and Navy Journal*, Aug. 31 and Sept. 28, 1867. Notable outbreaks of smallpox occurred at Fort Davis in 1875, 1877, and 1880. See Jacobson and Nored, *Jeff Davis County*, p. 64; Sayre, *Warriors of Color*, pp. 29–32, 328; material on Jones in the Fort Davis Documents Files, Folder: Tenth Cavalry Enlisted Men; Thompson, "The Negro Soldiers on the Frontier," pp. 230–31; and Schubert, ed., *On the Trail of the Buffalo Soldier*, pp. 380, 492, 476.

56 Don Rickey Jr., *Forty Miles a Day on Beans and Hay: The Enlisted Soldier Fighting the Indian Wars* (Norman: University of Oklahoma Press, 1963), p. 116; Jacobson and Nored, *Jeff Davis County, Texas*, pp. 64–66.

57 Henry E. Alvord to Benjamin Grierson, Oct. 4, 1868, and Benjamin H. Grierson to Alice K. Grierson, April 2, 1869, both in the Grierson Papers, Fort Davis.

58 Sayre, *Warriors of Color*, pp. 163–71. See also the material on Ambrose Wiley in the Fort Davis Documents Files, Folder: 10th Cavalry, Company C.

59 Sayre, *Warriors of Color*, pp. 460–70; Schubert, ed., *On the Trail of the Buffalo Soldier*, pp. 26–27, 140, 321. See material on William Allen and George France in the Fort Davis Documents Files, Folder: 10th Cavalry Enlisted Men, Fort Davis National Historic Site, Fort Davis, Tex. See also Sayre, *Warriors of Color*, pp. 5, 22.

60 NARA Court Martials, RR-1258; Schubert, ed., *On the Trail of the Buffalo Soldier*, p. 63.

Chapter Three. Doing the Nation's Work on the Western Frontier

1 White resistance to federal control in the former Confederacy persisted, of course, for many years. See, for example, the *Army and Navy Journal*, Jan. 31, 1874.

   The epigraph for this chapter comes from John G. Neihardt, *Black Elk Speaks: Being the Life Story of a Holy Man of the Oglala Sioux* (Lincoln: University of Nebraska Press, 1961), p. 9.

2 See chap. 2. *Personal Recollections & Observations of General Nelson A. Miles*, 2 vols. (Lincoln: University of Nebraska Press, 1992), 2:590; and Henry Wilson, quoted in Morris J. MacGregor and Bernard C. Nalty, eds., *Blacks in the United States Armed Forces: Basic Documents*, vol. 3 (Wilmington, Del.: Scholarly Resources, 1977), p. 19.

3 According to Robert M. Utley, just fifteen years earlier, that number was closer to 360,000, in a U.S. population of more than 20 million. See Utley, *The Indian Frontier of the American West, 1846–1890* (Albuquerque: University of New Mexico Press, 1984), p. 4. The Treaty of Fort Laramie, Utley writes, which "laid the foundations for future reservations, as the Indians themselves may have sensed," also "marked off tribal boundaries, a provision designed to cool the warfare among tribes that posed a threat to white travelers" (p. 61).

4 Robert M. Utley, *Frontier Regulars: The United States Army and the Indian, 1866–1891* (New York: Macmillan, Inc., 1973), pp. 5, 166–67; Robert Wooster, *The Military and United States Indian Policy, 1865–1903* (New Haven: Yale University Press, 1988), p. 14; *Army and Navy Journal*, June 1, 1867.

5 *Army and Navy Journal*, June 2 and July 22 and 29, 1866.

6 Francis Paul Prucha, *The Great Father: The United States Government and the American Indians* (Lincoln: University of Nebraska Press, 1986), pp. 136–37; Alvin M. Josephy Jr., *The Civil War in the American West* (New York: Vintage Books, 1991), pp. 317–22. See also Thom Hatch, *The Blue, the Gray, & the Red: Indian Campaigns of the Civil War* (Mechanicsburg, Pa.: Stackpole Books, 2003), p. 22; and James M. McPherson, *Ordeal by Fire: The Civil War and Reconstruction* (New York: McGraw-Hill, 1992), p. 230.

7 Josephy, *The Civil War in the American West*, pp. 96, 98–121; Hatch, *The Blue, the Gray, & the Red*, pp. 47–58; Robert M. Utley, *Frontiersmen in Blue: The United States Army and the Indian, 1848–1865* (Lincoln: University of Nebraska Press, 1981), pp. 261–80; Utley, *The Indian Frontier of the American West*, pp. 78–81. Nelson Miles later called this conflict the Minnesota Massacre of 1862. See *Personal Recollections & Observations of General Nelson A. Miles*, 1:136.

8 Josephy, *The Civil War in the American West*, pp. 99–100; Prucha, *The Great Father*, p. 145; Utley, *Frontiersmen in Blue*, pp. 265–68.

9 Hatch, *The Blue, the Gray, & the Red*, pp. 187–92.

10 Ibid., pp. 192–202.

11 Utley, *The Indian Frontier of the American West*, pp. 92–93; Dee Brown, *Bury My Heart at Wounded Knee: An Indian History of the American West* (New York: Henry Holt, 2000), pp. 87, 91. According to Brown, "Most of the warriors were several miles to the east hunting buffalo for the camp" (p. 87).

12 Hatch, *The Blue, the Gray, & the Red*, pp. 202–12; Josephy, *The Civil War in the American West*, pp. 305–12; Prucha, *The Great Father*, p. 150; Utley, *Frontiersmen in Blue*, pp. 292–97. Miles later called this massacre "perhaps the foulest and most unjustifiable crime in the annals of America" (*Personal Recollections & Observations of General Nelson A. Miles*, 1:139).

13 *Army and Navy Journal*, Oct. 13, 1866, and Jan. 5, 1867. See also Utley, *Frontier Regulars*, p. 100; and Utley, *The Indian Frontier of the American West*, pp. 110–12.

14 Utley, *Frontier Regulars*, pp. 104–7, 111; Brown, *Bury My Heart at Wounded Knee*, p. 137; Robert Wooster, *The Military and United States Indian Policy, 1865–1903* (New Haven: Yale University Press, 1988), pp. 117–19; Utley, *The Indian Frontier of the American West*, p. 105; *Army and Navy Journal*, March 24, 1866, and Jan. 5, 1867.

15 Wooster, *The Military and United States Indian Policy*, pp. 120, 159. According to Robert Utley, in just the three years from 1867 to 1870, some 38 "actions" took place in western Texas, involving Native Americans and the soldiers stationed there (Utley, *Frontier Regulars*, p. 167). The *Roster of Non-Commissioned Officers of the Tenth U.S. Cavalry* lists more than 80 engagements between soldiers of the Tenth Cavalry and hostile Native Americans between 1866 and 1891 (pp. 35–44). One Internet source identifies 133 different military actions "in which regular army troops of African American soldiers participated from 1866–1893." See http://www.coax.net/people/lwf/WF_AABTL.HTM.

16 *Army and Navy Journal*, May 18 and Oct. 19, 1867; Frank N. Schubert, ed., *On the Trail of the Buffalo Soldier: Biographies of African Americans in the U.S. Army, 1866–1917* (Wilmington, Del.: Scholarly Resources, 1995), pp. 246, 345–46, 431, 486; William H. Leckie, *The Buffalo Soldiers: A Narrative of the Negro Cavalry in the West* (Norman: University of Oklahoma Press, 1984), pp. 34, 84–85.

17 *Army and Navy Journal*, July 6, 1867; William H. Leckie and Shirley A. Leckie, *Unlikely Warriors: General Benjamin Grierson and His Family* (Norman: University of Oklahoma Press, 1984), pp. 149–50; Quintard Taylor, *In Search of the Racial Frontier: African Americans in the American West, 1528–1990* (New York: W.W. Norton, 1998), p. 170; Schubert, ed., *On the Trail of the Buffalo Soldier*, p. 89; Leckie, *The Buffalo Soldiers*, p. 22. See also George B. Jenness, in *Collections of the Kansas State Historical Society* 9 (1905–06): 443–52, included in Peter Cozzens, ed., *Eyewitnesses to the Indian Wars, 1865–1890*, 5 vols. (Mechanicsburg, Pa.: Stackpole Books, 2001–05), 3:61–62.

18 Utley, *Frontier Regulars*, pp. 147–48. See also Leckie, *The Buffalo Soldiers*, p. 34; and George A. Forsyth, in an 1895 article for *Harper's New Monthly Magazine*, included in Cozzens, ed., *Eyewitnesses to the Indian Wars*, 3:129–30.

19 Sherman referred to the two reservations in western Indian Territory created by the Medicine Lodge Treaties of 1867 (one for the Kiowa, Comanche, and Kiowa-Apache, and the other for the Cheyenne and Arapaho), as well as the Great Sioux reservation encompassing most of South Dakota, established by the Fort Laramie treaty of 1868. See William Tecumseh Sherman, *Memoirs* (New York: Penguin Books, 2000), p. 782; Utley, *Frontier Regulars*, pp. 133–35; and Utley, *The Indian Frontier of the American West*, p. 46.

20 Leckie and Leckie, *Unlikely Warriors*, p. 154; Forsyth, *Harper's New Monthly Magazine* article, cited in Cozzens, ed., *Eyewitnesses to the Indian Wars*, 3:128; Utley, *Frontier Regulars*, pp. 142–48. See also Leckie, *The Buffalo Soldiers*, pp. 34–36.

21 Forsyth, *Harper's New Monthly Magazine* article, cited in Cozzens, ed., *Eyewitnesses to the Indian Wars*, 3:143–44; Utley, *Frontier Regulars*, p. 148.

22 Carpenter subsequently earned the Congressional Medal of Honor for his courage and calm on this occasion. See William A. Dobak and Thomas D. Phillips, *The Black Regulars, 1866–1898* (Norman: University of Oklahoma Press, 2001), p. 31. See also James Peate, in a 1930 publication of the Beecher Island Battle Memorial Association, included in Cozzens, ed., *Eyewitnesses to the Indian Wars*, 3:233.

23 Fletcher Vilott, in an 1896 interview published in the *National Tribune*, included in Cozzens, ed., *Eyewitnesses to the Indian Wars*, 3:167; Reuben Waller, letter to the Editor of *Winners of the West*, Aug. 1925. Waller, one of the Tenth Cavalry's original members, went on to serve ten years with the regiment, for a time as Lieutenant Carpenter's orderly, before he settled into civilian life in Kansas in 1877. Also present on Beecher's Island was the trumpeter James H. Thomas of Virginia, who had enlisted in the Tenth in June 1867 and remained with it until he retired, as "chief trumpeter," in 1897. See Schubert, ed., *On the Trail of the Buffalo Soldier*, pp. 421, 447. See also the letters to the editor written by Waller in the July 1924 and Oct. 1924 issues of *Winners of the West*; and *Roster of Non-Commissioned Officers of the Tenth U.S. Cavalry* (Bryan, Tex.: J. M. Carroll, 1983), p. 29.

24 Leckie, *The Buffalo Soldiers*, p. 36; Sigmund Schlesinger, in a 1930 publication of the Beecher Island Battle Memorial Association, included in Cozzens, ed., *Eyewitnesses to the Indian Wars*, 3:204; Forsyth, quoted in Dobak and Phillips, *The Black Regulars*, p. 248. See also the *Army and Navy Journal* article on the event, Oct. 3, 1868.

25 Henry Carpenter to the *Christian Recorder*, Feb. 1, 1868.

26 John W. Blassingame and John R. McKivigan, eds., *The Frederick Douglass Papers*, ser. 1, *Speeches, Debates, and Interviews*, vol. 4, *1864–1890* (New Haven: Yale University Press, 1991), pp. 245–47.

27 Ibid., pp. 251–256.

28 Schubert, *Black Valor*, p. 18; Leckie, *The Buffalo Soldiers*, pp. 89–90; Charles L. Kenner, *Buffalo Soldiers and Officers of the Ninth Cavalry, 1867–1898* (Norman: University of Oklahoma Press, 1997), p. 54; Erwin N. Thompson, "The Negro Soldiers on the Frontier: A Fort Davis Case Study," *Journal of the West* 7 (April 1968): 221.

29 Leckie, *The Buffalo Soldiers*, pp. 81, 88.

30 As the historian Erwin Thompson has written of the roadwork black Regulars performed around Fort Davis, "In the twisting canyons that led to the fort, they constructed rock-walled roadbeds that still stand, now weed-covered monuments that testify to back-breaking labor and a high degree of proficiency." Thompson, "The Negro Soldiers on the Frontier," p. 219. See also Monroe Lee Billington and Roger D. Hardaway, eds., *African Americans on the Western Frontier* (Niwot: University Press of Colorado, 1998), pp. 58–59.

31 Paul H. Carlson, *"Pecos Bill": A Military Biography of William R. Shafter* (College Station: Texas A&M University Press, 1989), pp. 61, 75; John H. Nankivell, *Buffalo Soldier Regiment: History of the Twenty-fifth United States Infantry, 1869–1926* (Lincoln: University of Nebraska Press, 2001), p. 22.

32 Post surgeon Daniel Wiesel, quoted in Thompson, "The Negro Soldiers on the Frontier," p. 221.

33 David J. Allen, "History of the Ninth U.S. Cavalry from 1866 to 1900" (unpublished manuscript in the Fort Davis Documents Files, Fort Davis National Historic Site, Fort Davis, Tex.), p. 8; Patrick A. Bowmaster, "Occupation—'Soldier': The Life of 1st Sgt. Emanuel Stance of the 9th U.S. Cavalry 'Buffalo Soldiers' " (unpublished manuscript in the Fort Davis Files, Fort Davis National Historic Site, Fort Davis, Tex.), pp. 5–7; Kenner, *Buffalo Soldiers and Officers of the Ninth Cavalry*, pp. 160–62; Schubert, *Black Valor*, p. 21; Schubert, ed., *On the Trail of the Buffalo Soldier*, p. 400.

      Stance's story is an unusually complicated one, for he was both talented and troubled, a strict disciplinarian and a man with a fierce temper and perhaps also a drinking problem, who rose and fell through the ranks repeatedly over more than two decades in the army. Between 1866 and 1887, he was advanced and then demoted multiple times. Then, on the morning of Christmas Day 1887, he was found dead on a road not far from where his regiment was stationed. Stance was believed to have been killed by bullets fired by a fellow trooper. See Kenner, *Buffalo Soldiers and Officers of the Ninth Cavalry*, p. 159; Schubert, ed., *On the Trail of the Buffalo Soldier*, p. 400; Bowmaster, "Occupation—'Soldier,' " p. 1; and Schubert, *Black Valor*, pp. 9–26.

34 See Harold Ray Sayre, *Warriors of Color* (Fort Davis, Tex.: privately published, 1995), pp. 81–132; Schubert, ed., *On the Trail of the Buffalo Soldier*, p. 84. See also material on John F. Casey in the Fort Davis Documents Files, Folder: 10th Cavalry Enlisted Men, Fort Davis National Historic Site, Fort Davis, Tex. (hereafter cited as Casey File, Fort Davis).

35 Sayre, *Warriors of Color*, pp. 81–132; Schubert, ed., *On the Trail of the Buffalo Soldier*, p. 84; Casey File, Fort Davis.

36 Ibid.

37 Leckie, *The Buffalo Soldiers*, p. 57; Utley, *Frontier Regulars*, p. 209.

38 Leckie, *The Buffalo Soldiers*, p. 58. See also the *Roster of Non-Commissioned Officers of the Tenth U.S. Cavalry*, pp. 19–21.

39 Utley, *Frontier Regulars*, pp. 115–16, 207; Leckie, *The Buffalo Soldiers*, pp. 58–59.

40 Leckie, *The Buffalo Soldiers*, p. 59. The troopers included Robert Kurney of Virginia, who served in the army (both in the Tenth and in the Twenty-fifth Infantry) from 1867 to at least 1897, rising to the rank of sergeant. See the *Roster of Non-Commissioned Officers of the Tenth U.S. Cavalry*, pp. 19–20; and Schubert, ed., *On the Trail of the Buffalo Soldier*, p. 255.

41 Leckie, *The Buffalo Soldiers*, 59–61; Utley, *The Indian Frontier of the American West*, pp. 146–47; *Roster of Non-Commissioned Officers of the Tenth U.S. Cavalry*, pp. 19–21.

42 Leckie, *The Buffalo Soldiers*, p. 63; William T. Sherman to Benjamin H. Grierson, June 28, 1871, in Benjamin H. Grierson Papers, Fort Davis National Historic Site, Fort Davis, Tex. (hereafter cited as Grierson Papers, Fort Davis). For another account of this event, see Leckie and Leckie, *Unlikely Warriors*, pp. 186–88.

43 Kenner, *Buffalo Soldiers and Officers of the Ninth Cavalry*, p. 60; Utley, *Frontier Regulars*, pp. 212–13.

44 See Sayre, *Warriors of Color*, pp. 81–132; Schubert, ed., *On the Trail of the Buffalo Soldier*, p. 84; Casey File, Fort Davis.

45 See Sayre, *Warriors of Color*, pp. 81–132; Schubert, ed., *On the Trail of the Buffalo Soldier*, p. 84; Casey File, Fort Davis. Similarly, William Henry Bush, a veteran of C Troop, Ninth Cavalry, recalled his service from 1878 to 1883, largely in New Mexico territory, in his 1915 pension application: "My company was continuously on scouting service which subjected us to great exposure, such as sleeping in rains and snows in the mountains unprotected from the elements, sometimes no sleep for two days, sometimes subsisting on the most meager diet, sometimes marches of ninety miles across the prairies of New Mexico and Texas in hot scorching sun, sometimes marching through blinding sand storms and beating rains, sometimes wearing wet apparel for days." See Schubert, ed., *On the Trail of the Buffalo Soldier*, p. 72.

46 See Sayre, *Warriors of Color*, pp. 81–132; Schubert, ed., *On the Trail of the Buffalo Soldier*, p. 84; and Casey File, Fort Davis.

47 Ibid. Casey's pension was approved, and in later years he took up work as a barber.

48 See Nicholas Nolan to the Assistant Adjutant General, Dept. of Texas, Aug. 20, 1877, in the National Archives and Records Administration Microfilm of the Records of the War Department, U.S. Army Commands, Fort Concho, Tex., Reports of Scouts, 1872–1881. I am grateful to Mary Williams, historian at Fort Davis National Historic Site, Fort Davis, Tex., for lending me her personal copies of this microfilm (hereafter cited as NARA [Williams] microfilm, Fort Davis). See also the *Roster of Non-Commissioned Officers of the Tenth U.S. Cavalry*, pp. 22–23.

49 See letter to Benjamin Grierson from an unidentified source, dated Aug. 28, 1877, in Grierson Papers, Fort Davis. A letter from Alice to Benjamin Grierson, dated

Aug. 7, 1877, adds to this grisly picture: "Capt. Nolan gave me his report to read as published in the San Antonio Herald," she wrote. "What I wrote you in regard to the men drinking their own, and the horses urine is published in the report, also that a liberal amount of sugar was issued to them to make it palatable!!" (quoted in Shirley Anne Leckie, ed., *The Colonel's Lady on the Western Frontier: The Correspondence of Alice Kirk Grierson* [Lincoln: University of Nebraska Press, 1989], p. 108). See also J. H. T. King, "A Brief Account of the Sufferings . . . ," Fort Davis, Tex.: Charles Krull, post printer, 1877, included in Cozzens, ed., *Eyewitnesses to the Indian Wars*, 3:588–89.

50 Nicholas Nolan to Robert G. Smither, Aug. 4, 1877, in NARA (Williams) microfilm, Fort Davis. This letter provides a detailed report of the events of the disastrous scouting expedition, albeit from Nolan's perspective. See also Leckie, *The Buffalo Soldiers*, pp. 157–62; Paul H. Carlson, *The Buffalo Soldier Tragedy of 1877* (College Station: Tex. A&M University Press, 2003); Utley, *Frontier Regulars*, pp. 241–44; Dobak and Phillips, *The Black Regulars*, p. 253; Leckie and Leckie, *Unlikely Warriors*, pp. 241–45; *Army and Navy Journal*, Aug. 11 and Sept. 15, 1877; and the account by the black Regular sergeant George W. Ford in the April 1924 issue of *Winners of the West*.

51 Among the black Regulars who were present for duty with John Casey during the Victorio campaign was William H. Givens of Kentucky, who had enlisted in the Tenth in Aug. 1869 and who remained in the army (first in the Tenth and then in the Ninth Cavalry) until 1901, rising through the noncommissioned ranks while serving not only on the western frontier but also, during the Spanish-American War, in Cuba, where he earned a citation for distinguished service. See Schubert, ed., *On the Trail of the Buffalo Soldier*, pp. 164–65; and *Roster of Non-Commissioned Officers of the Tenth U.S. Cavalry*, pp. 27–28. For more on the Victorio campaign, see Thompson, "The Negro Soldiers on the Frontier," p. 222; Schubert, *Black Valor*, pp. 48–58; Charles B. Gatewood, article for *The Great Divide* (April 1894), cited in Cozzens, ed., *Eyewitness to the Indian Wars*, 1:213; and Billington, *New Mexico's Buffalo Soldiers*, pp. 47–56, 87–97.

52 Gatewood, article for *The Great Divide*, p. 214; Leckie, *The Buffalo Soldiers*, p. 112; Benjamin H. Grierson to Alice Kirk Grierson, April 12 and 16, 1880, Grierson Papers, Fort Davis.

53 Benjamin H. Grierson to Alice Kirk Grierson, April 16 and 17, 1880, Grierson Papers, Fort Davis.

54 See Charles Grierson to Alice Kirk Grierson, April 17, 1880, in Grierson Papers, Fort Davis; and Thompson, "The Negro Soldiers on the Frontier," pp. 222–23.

55 Thompson, "The Negro Soldiers on the Frontier," pp. 223–24; Benjamin H. Grierson to Alice Kirk Grierson, Aug. 2, 1880, Grierson Papers, Fort Davis.

56 Sayre, *Warriors of Color*, pp. 108–9.

57 Benjamin H. Grierson to Alice Kirk Grierson, Aug. 22, 1880, Grierson Papers, Fort

Davis; Thompson, "The Negro Soldiers on the Frontier," pp. 223–24; Leckie and Leckie, *Unlikely Warriors*, pp. 259–67. Also present during this campaign was Private John Wiggins. See the *Roster of Non-Commissioned Officers of the Tenth U.S. Cavalry*, pp. 21–22; and Schubert, ed., *On the Trail of the Buffalo Soldier*, pp. 464–65.

58 Utley, *Frontier Regulars*, pp. 369–71. And he adds, "It may well be doubted that even an ideal reservation could have contained a people so warlike and contemptuous of restraint" (ibid.).

59 Utley, *Frontier Regulars*, pp. 371–75.

60 Henry W. Daly, "The Capture of Geronimo," quoted in Cozzens, ed., *Eyewitnesses to the Indian Wars*, 1:448; Utley, *Frontier Regulars*, pp. 379–80.

61 Wrote the veteran Charles P. Elliott of the Fourth Cavalry, in 1948: among the Apache, "tiswin drunks were responsible for many fights amongst themselves, but they were so secretive in making and hiding their liquor that it was only after the resultant fight that the fact of tiswin came to our knowledge. It was never my good fortune to get possession of any of this liquor, but I was told that it was made usually by the very old women from corn and was a sort of 'sour mash'" (Elliott, article for *Military Affairs* [Summer 1948], quoted in Cozzens, ed., *Eyewitnesses to the Indian Wars*, 1:412). For more on the Geronimo campaign, see James S. Pettit, article for the *Journal of the Military Service Institution of the United States* (Sept. 1886), quoted ibid., p. 532; and Utley, *Frontier Regulars*, pp. 381–85.

62 See Sayre, *Warriors of Color*, pp. 51–61, 81–132; Schubert, ed., *On the Trail of the Buffalo Soldier*, p. 84; and Casey File, Fort Davis. Also participating with the Tenth in the Geronimo campaign was Maryland's Washington Brown, an original member of Nelson Miles's Fortieth Infantry, who transferred to the Tenth in April 1885 and remained with the regiment for another dozen years. See the *Roster of Non-Commissioned Officers of the Tenth U.S. Cavalry*, pp. 23–24; and Schubert, ed., *On the Trail of the Buffalo Soldier*, p. 63.

63 See Miles's own account of the Geronimo campaign in *Personal Recollections & Observations of General Nelson A. Miles*, 2:494ff.

64 Clarence Chrisman, article for *Winners of the West* (March–July 1927), quoted in Cozzens, ed., *Eyewitnesses to the Indian Wars*, 1:545. See also Utley, *Frontier Regulars*, pp. 385–89; Leckie, *The Buffalo Soldiers*, p. 245. There is considerable irony in the fact that back in New York, in late Oct. of this same year, the Statue of Liberty was dedicated on Bedloe's Island. See Brown, *Bury My Heart at Wounded Knee*, p. 391.

65 *Personal Recollections & Observations of General Nelson A. Miles*, 2:517; Schubert, ed., *On the Trail of the Buffalo Soldier*, pp. 28, 84, 220, 419. See also the cases of Isaac Jackson, Joseph Cammel, and Charles Lincoln Terry, in *Warriors of Color*, pp. 258–326, 428–55. See also the material on Joseph Cammel in the Fort Davis Documents Files, Folder: 10th Cavalry Enlisted Men, Fort Davis Historic Site, Fort Davis, Tex.

66 After Ford left the army in 1877, he went on to marry, have eight children, and

work at a series of national cemeteries over the next half century, taking a short break from his cemetery work to serve with the Twenty-third Kansas Volunteers in the Spanish-American War. See Schubert, ed., *On the Trail of the Buffalo Soldier*, pp. 146–48.

67 Ibid., pp. 67, 69, 376; Don Rickey Jr., *Forty Miles a Day on Beans and Hay: The Enlisted Soldier Fighting the Indian Wars* (Norman: University of Oklahoma Press, 1963), p. 310. Congress began awarding these certificates in March 1874. I do not know what proportion of them were earned by black Regulars.

68 Schubert, ed., *On the Trail of the Buffalo Soldier*, p. 515. According to Schubert, in the period from 1866 to 1891, black Regulars "received fewer than 4 percent" of the medals of honor awarded, though they made up "20 percent of the cavalry force and 12 percent of the infantry" (Schubert, *Black Valor*, p. 164).

69 Schubert, ed., *On the Trail of the Buffalo Soldier*, pp. 323, 448; Kenner, *Voices of the Buffalo Soldier*, pp. 45–46, 70ff; Schubert, *Black Valor*, pp. 18, 27–40. I believe these scouts remained, for official purposes, members of the Twenty-fourth Infantry. Of the Seminole Scouts, James Leiker writes, "Historians can only speculate on the reactions of eastern recruits to seeing fellow blacks who rode about in Indian regalia and spoke an unfamiliar language. Despite their cultural distinctiveness, the black Seminoles constituted anything but a closed ethnic group. Descriptive records reveal a membership that included Texas freedmen, runaway slaves, blacks born in Mexico, mulattoes of German and Irish ancestry, former black servants of white officers, and even buffalo soldiers who rode with the scouts after their expiration of enlistment." See Leiker, *Racial Borders: Black Soldiers along the Rio Grande* (College Station: Texas A&M Press, 2002), p. 32.

70 Schubert, ed., *On the Trail of the Buffalo Soldier*, pp. 49, 57, 119, 171, 291; Leckie, *The Buffalo Soldiers*, p. 178; Schubert, *Black Valor*, pp. 45–46. See also the cases of Henry Johnson, George Jordan, Thomas Shaw, August Walley, Moses William, and Brent Woods, in Kenner, *Buffalo Soldiers and Officers of the Ninth Cavalry*, pp. 66–68; Schubert, *Black Valor*, pp. 61–67; and Schubert, ed., *On the Trail of the Buffalo Soldier*, pp. 249, 377, 448, 473, 483.

71 Leiker, *Racial Borders*, pp. 6–7, 15–16, 25.

72 Quoted in Nankivell, *Buffalo Soldier Regiment*, pp. 35–36; Nelson A. Miles to the Adjutant General of the U.S. Army, March 1, 1887, in Grierson Papers, Fort Davis.

73 See historical sketch of the Tenth Cavalry (1902) in MacGregor and Nalty, eds., *Blacks in the United States Armed Forces*, 3:53, 59. Another white Tenth Cavalry officer represented in this sketch recalled, "I organized one of the troops in 1867, and commanded it more or less for several years. I was never afraid to match it against any other troop in the service, as to cleanliness, discipline or otherwise. It was always a source of much pride to me" (p. 72). Wrote a third, "I found the colored man to be as good a soldier as the white man of his own class. . . . I am sufficiently

familiar with the histories of dark-skinned people to know that the white or Saxon races have not a monopoly on bravery. . . . Most depends on discipline, which the colored man possesses by nature" (pp. 77–78).

74 Sayre, *Warriors of Color*, p. 55.

Chapter Four. National Progress, Race Thinking, and Taking On West Point

1 *Personal Recollections & Observations of General Nelson A. Miles* (Lincoln: University of Nebraska Press, 1992), 2:320. Notes the historian Eric Foner, "While the South struggled with the problems of recovery, a new agricultural empire arose on the Middle Border (Minnesota, the Dakotas, Nebraska, and Kansas), whose population grew from 300,000 in 1860 to well over 2 million twenty years later." See Eric Foner, *Reconstruction: America's Unfinished Revolution, 1863–1877* (New York: Harper & Row, 1988), p. 463.

   The epigraph for this chapter comes from an article on Michael Howard in the *New York Times*, June 4, 1870.

2 *Army and Navy Journal*, May 15, 1869; *New York Times*, May 11, 1869.

3 Chris J. Magoc, *Yellowstone: The Creation and Selling of an American Landscape, 1870–1903* (Albuquerque: University of New Mexico Press, 1999), p. 23; Robert M. Utley, *Frontier Regulars: The United States Army and the Indian, 1866–1891* (New York: Macmillan, 1973), p. 242; *Personal Recollections & Observations of General Nelson A. Miles*, 1:151–52 and 2:320. According to Brown, "In the summer of 1883, when the Northern Pacific Railroad celebrated the driving of the last spike in its transcontinental track, one of the officials in charge of ceremonies decided it would be fitting for an Indian chief to be present to make a speech of welcome to the Great Father and other notables. Sitting Bull was the choice . . . and a young Army officer who understood the Sioux language was assigned to work with the chief in preparation of a speech." When it was time to give his speech, however, Sitting Bull chose to speak words other than those that had been prepared for him. "I hate all white people," he said. "You are thieves and liars. You have taken away our land and made us outcasts." Virtually no one but the interpreter who had helped Sitting Bull with the original speech knew what he was saying. See Dee Brown, *Bury My Heart at Wounded Knee: An Indian History of the American West* (New York: Henry Holt, 2000), p. 426.

4 Magoc, *Yellowstone*, pp. 2, 5. According to Magoc, the first white man to explore the region was a trapper-explorer named John Colter. See also Paul Schullery and Lee Whittlesey, *Myth and History in the Creation of Yellowstone National Park* (Lincoln: University of Nebraska Press, 2003), p. 6.

5 Magoc, *Yellowstone*, pp. 2, 4–5, 16–18, 63, 135, 141. See also *The National Parks: Shaping the System* (Washington, D.C.: U.S. Department of the Interior, 2005), p. 13; and *Army and Navy Journal*, Dec. 11, 1875. According to Magoc, "indigenous peoples

shaped the landscape of the Yellowstone plateau and the surrounding region from prehistoric time through the arrival of Euro-Americans. . . . Early explorers and officials encountered widespread evidence of Indian presence within the park, including numerous trails beaten down by the Bannocks, Arapahoes, and Shoshones . . . conically shaped lodges likely built by the Crows, various ancient archaeological sites, and freshly burned landscapes" (Magoc, *Yellowstone*, p. 141). The U.S. cavalry managed the park until the creation of the National Park Service in 1916 (p. 63).

For a discussion of "genteel" Americans' growing interest, over the course of the nineteenth century, in "scenic tourism," see, among others, Paul E. Johnson, *Sam Patch, the Famous Jumper* (New York: Hill and Wang, 2003). For a nineteenth-century tourist's view of Yellowstone in particular, see Henry T. Finck, *The Pacific Coast Scenic Tour* (New York: Charles Scribner's Sons, 1890).

6 Utley, *Frontier Regulars*, p. 232. See also Robert Wooster, *Nelson A. Miles and the Twilight of the Frontier Army* (Lincoln: University of Nebraska Press, 1993), p. 69. "World's fairs," the historian Robert W. Rydell has written, both reflect and declare the ideas and values of a given nation's "political, financial, corporate, and intellectual leaders" and present these ideas and values "as the proper interpretation of social and political reality." In American history, Rydell continues, world's fairs like the Centennial Exposition also functioned as "arenas for asserting the moral authority of the United States government." See Rydell, *All the World's a Fair: Visions of Empire at American International Expositions, 1876–1916* (Chicago: University of Chicago Press, 1984), pp. 10–13. See the *Army and Navy Journal*'s article about the opening of the fair, May 13, 1876; J. S. Ingram, *The Centennial Exposition, Described and Illustrated* (Philadelphia: Hubbard Bros., 1876), pp. 18, 89; Foner, *Reconstruction*, p. 564; and Trumbull White and William Igleheart, *The World's Columbian Exposition, Chicago, 1893* (Boston: Standard Silverware Co., 1893), p. 34.

7 Rydell, *All the World's a Fair*, pp. 15, 17; *Army and Navy Journal*, Nov. 13, 1875, and May 13, 1876; Ingram, *The Centennial Exposition*, pp. 76, 80. According to the *Army and Navy Journal* of May 13, 1876, General Winfield Scott Hancock was also on hand for the opening.

8 Ingram, *The Centennial Exposition*, pp. 119, 146; Rydell, *All the World's a Fair*, p. 22. For discussions of the War Department's exhibits see *Army and Navy Journal*, May 27, June 10 and 17, and July 1, 1876.

9 Foner, *Reconstruction*, p. 565; Ingram, *The Centennial Exposition*, p. 368; Patricia L. Faust, ed., *Historical Times Illustrated Encyclopedia of the Civil War* (New York: HarperPerennial, 1991), p. 545.

10 Rydell, *All the World's a Fair*, pp. 27–29; Foner, *Reconstruction*, p. 565.

11 Rydell, *All the World's a Fair*, pp. 22–27; Ingram, *The Centennial Exposition*, p. 151; Foner, *Reconstruction*, p. 565; Jerome A. Greene, *Yellowstone Command: Colonel Nelson A. Miles and the Great Sioux War, 1876–1877* (Lincoln: University of Nebraska Press, 1991), pp. xiii, 10; Wooster, *The Military and United States Indian Policy,*

p. 161. See also the *Army and Navy Journal*'s July 8, 1876, report of the Little Big-horn fight; and Wooster, *The Military and United States Indian Policy*, p. 166.

12 Utley, *Frontier Regulars*, pp. 278–84; Greene, *Yellowstone Command*, p. 10; John G. Neihardt, *Black Elk Speaks: Being the Life Story of a Holy Man of the Oglala Sioux* (Lincoln: University of Nebraska Press, 1961), p. 150. See also Robert A. Clark, ed., *The Killing of Chief Crazy Horse* (Lincoln: University of Nebraska Press, 1976); and Richard G. Hardoff, ed., *The Death of Crazy Horse: A Tragic Episode in Lakota History* (Lincoln: University of Nebraska Press, 1998).

13 Greene, *Yellowstone Command*, p. 224; Utley, *Frontier Regulars*, pp. 284–88, 315. See also Helen Addison Howard, *Saga of Chief Joseph* (Lincoln: University of Nebraska Press, 1978), pp. 326–35; Brown, *Bury My Heart at Wounded Knee*, p. 417; and *Army and Navy Journal*, July 23, 1881.

14 Magoc, *Yellowstone*, pp. 32, 54, 155; *New York Times*, Sept. 9, 1883; *Army and Navy Journal*, Sept. 15, 1883; Brown, *Bury My Heart at Wounded Knee*, 391; Neihardt, *Black Elk Speaks*, p. 217. In Sept. 1883, General Sherman wrote to his wife, Mary, from Santa Fe, "The truth is that the modern Railroad has so revolutionized this western world that Indian wars & complications are not probable, even if possible." See William T. Sherman to Mary Sherman, Sept. 16, 1883, in Nelson A. Miles Family Papers, Library of Congress, Washington, D.C.

According to the historian Louis S. Warren, as early as 1868 railroad companies began advertising buffalo hunts "as an inducement to western tourism." See Warren, *Buffalo Bill's America: William Cody and the Wild West Show* (New York: Alfred A. Knopf, 2005), p. 129. According to Utley, in 1872–73 alone, over a million buffalo hides were sent east to market (Utley, *Frontier Regulars*, p. 213). Moreover, "many policy makers regarded the extinction of the buffalo as the key to the Indian problem." See Utley in Richard Henry Pratt, *Battlefield and Classroom: An Autobiography* (Norman: University of Oklahoma Press, 2003), p. 63, n. 5. Dee Brown writes that, "[o]f the 3,700,000 buffalo destroyed from 1872 through 1874, only 150,000 were killed by Indians," and that, "[w]hen a group of concerned Texans asked General Sheridan if something should not be done to stop the white hunters' wholesale slaughter, he replied: 'Let them kill, skin, and sell until the buffalo is exterminated, as it is the only way to bring lasting peace and allow civilization to advance.'" See Brown, *Bury My Heart at Wounded Knee*, p. 265. Of the destruction of the buffalo, Nelson Miles wrote, "This might seem like cruelty and wasteful extravagance, but the buffalo, like the Indian, stood in the way of civilization and in the path of progress, and the decree had gone forth that they must both give way." See *Personal Recollections & Observations of General Nelson A. Miles*, 1:134–35.

15 Foner, *Reconstruction*, p. 198; James M. McPherson, *Ordeal by Fire: The Civil War and Reconstruction* (New York: McGraw-Hill, 1992), p. 509.

16 McPherson, *Ordeal by Fire*, p. 499, 509.

17 Ibid., pp. 538, 582; Foner, *Reconstruction*, pp. 425–28. See also *Army and Navy Jour-*

nal, June 1, 1867, regarding a riot in Mobile, Alabama (additional riots took place in this period in Pulaski, Tennessee; Opelousas, Louisiana; Camilla, Georgia; Meridian, Mississippi; Eutaw, Alabama; and elsewhere); and ibid., Oct. 17, 1868.

18 On April 11, 1868, for example, the *Army and Navy Journal* reported on General Meade's various measures designed to suppress the KKK's "violence and atrocity" in Camilla, Georgia. See also Foner, *Reconstruction,* pp. 454–59.

19 Foner, *Reconstruction,* pp. 437, 571–72.

20 *Army and Navy Journal,* Dec. 5, 1868.

21 McPherson, *Ordeal by Fire,* p. 506.

22 James M. McPherson, "The Second American Revolution," cited in Michael Perman, ed., *Major Problems in the Civil War and Reconstruction,* 2nd ed. (Boston: Houghton Mifflin, 1998), pp. 439–41; McPherson, *Ordeal by Fire,* p. 569.

23 From Frederick Douglass, *Life and Times of Frederick Douglass* (Boston: De Wolfe, Fiske and Co., 1892), cited in William E. Gienapp, ed., *The Civil War and Reconstruction: A Documentary Collection,* (New York: W.W. Norton, 2001), p. 417.

24 Robert Francis Engs, *Educating the Disfranchised and Disinherited: Samuel Chapman Armstrong and Hampton Institute, 1839–1893* (Knoxville: University of Tennessee Press, 1999), p. xii; L. P. Jackson, "The Origin of Hampton Institute," *Journal of Negro History* 10 (April 1925): p. 133; Donal F. Lindsey, *Indians at Hampton Institute, 1877–1923* (Urbana: University of Iliinois Press, 1995), pp. 1–4, 6–9.

25 Engs, *Educating the Disfranchised and Disinherited,* pp. xi, xiii; Lindsey, *Indians at Hampton Institute,* pp. 5, 71; Jackson, "The Origin of Hampton Institute," p. 143.

26 Lindsey, *Indians at Hampton Institute,* pp. 1, 5, 7, 9; Jackson, "The Origin of Hampton Institute," pp. 146, 148. See also Charles H. Thompson, "Editorial Comment: The Educational and Administrative Reorganization of Hampton Institute," *Journal of Negro Education* 9 (April 1940): 139, 141.

27 Lindsey, *Indians at Hampton Institute,* pp. 20–21. See also Brad D. Lookingbill, *War Dance at Fort Marion: Plains Indian War Prisoners* (Norman: University of Oklahoma Press, 2006), p. 4; Utley, *The Indian Frontier of the American West,* p. 218. Over this period of time, Indian students represented about one in six of all Hampton students (Lindsey, *Indians at Hampton Institute,* p. 33).

28 Utley, *Frontier Regulars,* pp. 233–34; Archibald Hanna, "The Richard Henry Pratt Papers," p. 39, and "Negroes and Indians," address of Richard H. Pratt before the Pennsylvania Commandery, Military Order of Foreign Wars, Jan. 14, 1913, both in box 16a, Carlisle Barracks Collection, U.S. Army Military History Institute, Carlisle, Pa. (hereafter cited as Carlisle Barracks Collection, USAMHI); Lindsey, *Indians at Hampton Institute,* p. 23. See also Pratt's own account of his journey east with the captives in the 23rd Annual Report of the Board of Indian Commissioners (1891), box 16a, Carlisle Barracks Collection, USAMHI.

29 Hanna, "The Richard Henry Pratt Papers," p. 39; Richard Henry Pratt, *Battlefield and Classroom: An Autobiography* (Norman: University of Oklahoma Press, 2003),

pp. xxii, 7; Lindsey, *Indians at Hampton Institute*, p. 26; Francis Paul Prucha, *The Great Father: The United States Government and the American Indians* (Lincoln: University of Nebraska Press, 1986), p. 236.

30 Pratt, *Battlefield and Classroom*, p. 100; Hanna, "The Richard Henry Pratt Papers," p. 39; Richard Henry Pratt to Joseph B. Foraker, Jan. 8, 1907, in Richard Henry Pratt Papers, Beinecke Library, Yale University, New Haven, Conn. (hereafter cited as Pratt Papers, Yale University).

31 Richard Henry Pratt to Montgomery C. Meigs, April 7, 1891, in Pratt Papers, Yale University; "Negroes and Indians," Address of Richard H. Pratt before the Pennsylvania Commandery, Military Order of Foreign Wars, Jan. 14, 1913, in box 16a, Carlisle Barracks Collection, USAMHI. See also the excerpts from the Proceedings of the Lake Mohonk Conferences, 1901–04, and the excerpt from Frances E. Willard, *Glimpses of Fifty Years*, both ibid. For the Douglass speech, see John W. Blassingame and John R. McKivigan, eds., *The Frederick Douglass Papers*, ser. 1, *Speeches, Debates, and Interviews*, vol. 4, *1864–1890* (New Haven: Yale University Press, 1991), p. 206.

32 "Our Twelfth Year: The Third Graduating Exercises of the School," in the school paper, *The Red Man*, June 1891, in box 16a, Carlisle Barracks Collection, USAMHI. See also *Army and Navy Journal*, April 8, 1876.

33 Lookingbill, *War Dance at Fort Marion*, pp. 68–69. See also Pratt's own account, in the 23rd Annual Report of the Board of Indian Commissioners (1891), box 16a, Carlisle Barracks Collection, USAMHI; and Hanna, "The Richard Henry Pratt Papers," p. 39.

34 Pratt suggests that all of his Indian charges initially wished to remain in the East: in his 1891 annual report he recalled that, upon being granted their release, "[t]hey all said, 'Give us our women and children. We would rather stay here than go back to our reservations, where there are so many Indians as bad or worse than we were.'" Permission to remain was denied to most of them (Pratt, 23rd Annual Report, in box 16a, Carlisle Barracks Collection, USAMHI). See also *Army and Navy Journal*, Nov. 23 and Dec. 2, 1878, and Oct. 11, 1879; Helen Ludlow and Elaine Goodale, "Captain Pratt and His Work," in box 16a, Carlisle Barracks Collection, USAMHI; Utley, *Frontier Regulars*, p. 233; and Hanna, "The Richard Henry Pratt Papers," p. 40. According to Ludlow and Goodale, the men arrived at Hampton in the middle of the night. "No one who witnessed that midnight Indian raid on Hampton Institute will ever forget it. The camp was ready for the raiders with coffee and words of welcome. The next night old chief Lone Wolf told the large audience gathered to hear him: 'We have started on God's road now, because God's road is the same for the red man as for the white man'" (Ludlow and Goodale, "Captain Pratt and His Work," box 16a, Carlisle Barracks Collection, USAMHI). See also *Army and Navy Journal*, May 4, 1878.

35 Lindsey, *Indians at Hampton Institute*, p. 94. Adds Lindsey, "Armstrong called his Indian program the first instance of black philanthropy" (ibid., p. 95).

36 Ibid., pp. 100, 111.

37 Ibid., pp. 159–61. Involvement in these sorts of paramilitary activities in connection with the school's Native American students may well have motivated some black Hampton students, such as Horace W. Bivins, to enlist in the frontier army. Having been a student at Hampton, Bivins, a native of Virginia, in 1887 enlisted in the Tenth Cavalry, with which he went on to serve for almost fifty years, until 1932. One Feb. 1899 magazine article described Bivins, who had by then served on the frontier as well as in Cuba and the Philippines, as "a sober, sensible, industrious Negro, who, in his daily life, evinces that kind of race pride that is beautifully commendable and who would have all men thoroughly convinced that the Negro can learn, if given the opportunity, all the arts and cunning performed by any race of men," though one wonders whether the author of that comment also meant to suggest that Bivins knew his "place" in the pecking order of the races. See Frank N. Schubert, ed., *On the Trail of the Buffalo Soldier: Biographies of African Americans in the U.S. Army, 1866–1917* (Wilmington, Del.: Scholarly Resources, 1995), pp. 39–40. See also Don Rickey, "The Negro Regulars: A Combat Record, 1866–1891" (unpublished paper, in the Ninth Cavalry Files, Fort Davis National Historic Site, Fort Davis, Tex.).

38 Historian David Wallace Adams, quoted in Lookingbill, *War Dance at Fort Marion*, p. 5; Pratt, *Battlefield and Classroom*, p. 213; L. A. Abbott to National Commander, Order of the Indian Wars, May 20, 1907, in Order of the Indian Wars Collection, box 1, USAMHI; *Carlisle Indian Industrial School Annual, 1918*, p. 2, in box 16a, Carlisle Barracks Collection, USAMHI. Carlisle Barracks still stands and is operational, though the Indian Industrial School closed in 1918. The barracks now houses the U.S. Army War College. Just outside the post's secure entrance is a small, deeply moving graveyard full of headstones marking the sites of the remains of Native American children who died at the school. See also Robert W. Larson, *Red Cloud: Warrior-Statesman of the Lakota Sioux* (Norman: University of Oklahoma Press, 1997), p. 227; Utley, *The Indian Frontier of the American West*, p. 245; Prucha, *The Great Father*, p. 234. According to Hanna, by the end of the Carlisle school's first year, Pratt had recruited two hundred students (Hanna, "The Richard Henry Pratt Papers," pp. 40–41). According to Robert Utley, "During his twenty-four-year tenure the school educated, in all, 4,903 Indian boys and girls from seventy-seven tribes" (Pratt, *Battlefield and Classroom*, p. xxi).

39 See Peter S. Michie, "Caste at West Point," *North American Review* 130 (June 1880): 609; *New York Times*, May 28 and June 4, 1870; Charles L. Kenner, *Buffalo Soldiers and Officers of the Ninth Cavalry, 1867–1898* (Norman: University of Oklahoma Press, 1999), p. 159; and *Army and Navy Journal*, June 4, 1870.

40 Quintard Taylor, ed., *The Colored Cadet at West Point: Autobiography of Lieutenant Henry Ossian Flipper, U.S.A.* (Lincoln: University of Nebraska Press, 1998), p. xiv; John C. Waugh, *The Class of 1846: From West Point to Appomattox* (New York: Ballantine Books, 1994), p. 513. According to Waugh, the 304 West Point graduates who endorsed the Confederacy represented 20 percent of all those who had graduated from the academy.

41 Taylor, ed., *The Colored Cadet at West Point*, p. xiv; *New York Times*, May 28 and June 4, 1870. Ely S. Parker, a Seneca Indian, is a known exception to the Civil War officer corps' "whiteness"; he did not attend West Point.

42 *New York Times*, May 28, 1870.

43 Ibid., June 4, 1870.

44 Taylor, ed., *The Colored Cadet at West Point*, p. 21; *Army and Navy Journal*, July 23, 1870. See also John F. Marszalek, *Assault at West Point: The Court-Martial of Johnson Whittaker* (privately published, 1984), p. 21.

45 See James Webster Smith to the Editor of the *New National Era*, July 30, 1874, cited in Taylor, ed., *The Colored Cadet at West Point*, p. 290; William S. McFeely, *Grant: A Biography* (New York: W.W. Norton, 1981), p. 375.

46 *Army and Navy Journal*, July 23, 1870. See also Marszalek, *Assault at West Point*, p. 21; and Israel Smith to James Webster Smith, July 3, 1870, cited in Taylor, ed., *The Colored Cadet at West Point*, p. 316. See Edward S. Cooper, *William Worth Belknap: An American Disgrace* (Madison, N.J.: Fairleigh Dickinson University Press, 2003), pp. 132–45, for a full discussion of the Smith case.

47 *Army and Navy Journal*, June 23, 1870. General Howard's interest in James Webster Smith may also have been enhanced by his memories of the social ostracism he himself had experienced as a student at the academy two decades earlier, as a result of what one biographer has described as Howard's "failure to observe the rank structure" and his willingness to befriend "lesser sorts," which led some cadets to treat him with disdain. See John A. Carpenter, *Sword and Olive Branch: Oliver Otis Howard* (Pittsburgh: University of Pittsburgh Press, 1964), p. 7; and *Autobiography of Oliver Otis Howard, Major General, United States Army*, 2 vols. (New York: Baker and Taylor Co., 1907), 1:50–51. For the story of Howard's life and Civil War career see, among others, Carpenter, *Sword and Olive Branch*; William S. McFeely, *Yankee Stepfather: General O. O. Howard and the Freedmen* (New Haven: Yale University Press, 1968); and Howard, *Autobiography of Oliver Otis Howard*.

48 Eli Perkins to the Editor of the *Daily Graphic*, undated, cited in Taylor, ed., *The Colored Cadet at West Point*, p. 313; McFeely, *Grant*, pp. 375–76; excerpt from an 1874 New York *Sun* article, reprinted in Taylor, ed., *The Colored Cadet at West Point*, p. 310. See also Marszalek, *Assault at West Point*, p. 22.

49 Richard Newman, "Harvard's Forgotten First Black Student," *Journal of Blacks in Higher Education* 38 (Winter, 2002–03): 92; Garry L. Reeder, "The History of

Blacks at Yale University," ibid., *26* (Winter 1999–2000):125; *Army and Navy Journal*, Feb. 25, 1871.

50 McFeely, *Grant*, pp. 376–78; *Army and Navy Journal*, July 11, 1874.

51 James Webster Smith to the Editor of the *New National Era*, July 27, 1874, cited in Taylor, ed., *The Colored Cadet at West Point*, p. 290. The rest of Smith's letters to the newspaper are reprinted on pp. 289–308. See also Marszalek, *Assault at West Point*, p. 23. In Sept. 1997, U.S. Representative John Spratt of South Carolina presided over a ceremony at South Carolina State University in which the secretary of the army posthumously awarded James Webster Smith a second lieutenant's commission, which is the commission he would have earned had he graduated from West Point. See http://www.house.gov/spratt/newsroom/97_98.

52 Article cited in Taylor, ed., *The Colored Cadet at West Point*, pp. 162–64.

53 James Webster Smith to the Editor of the *New National Era*, Aug. 19, 1874, cited in Taylor, ed., *The Colored Cadet at West Point*, p. 299. See also p. xv.

54 Taylor, ed., *The Colored Cadet at West Point*, pp. viii–x, 7–11; Theodore D. Harris, ed., *Black Frontiersman: The Memoirs of Henry O. Flipper* (Fort Worth: Texas Christian University Press, 1997), pp. 3–4.

55 Taylor, ed., *The Colored Cadet at West Point*, p. xi.

56 Ibid., pp. xi–xiii, xvi, 12–16, 20, 130. Flipper dedicated *The Colored Cadet at West Point*, published in 1878, to the American Missionary Society College's faculty and president.

57 Taylor, ed., *The Colored Cadet at West Point*, pp. xiii, xv, 28, 42.

58 Ibid., pp. xvi, 30. See also *Army and Navy Journal*, June 5, 1875. According to the author of this article, Smith, in contrast to Flipper, was "a dull scholar."

59 Taylor, ed., *The Colored Cadet at West Point*, pp. xvii, 61, 120. For a thorough discussion of Victorian notions of manhood, see Amy S. Greenberg, *Manifest Manhood and the Antebellum American Empire* (New York: Cambridge University Press, 2005).

60 Taylor, ed., *The Colored Cadet at West Point*, pp. xviii, 13, 120–21, 134, 151.

61 Ibid., pp. xvi, xx, 106–7, 114–15, 119, 139, 140, 172. See also *Army and Navy Journal*, June 23, 1877. Butler's nominee had been proven to be underage and therefore ineligible. Marszalek, *Assault at West Point*, p. 18. Of the twenty-seven black men nominated for appointment at West Point between 1870 and 1887, only three graduated and went on to become U.S. army officers.

62 *Army and Navy Journal*, June 23, 1877. Certainly Flipper himself believed that his persistence and refusal to fight back had earned him the praise he now enjoyed. "I know I have so lived," he wrote, "that they could find in me no fault different from those at least common to themselves, and have thus forced upon their consciences a just and merited recognition whether or not they are disposed to follow conscience and openly accept my claim to their brotherly love." See Taylor, ed., *The Colored Cadet at West Point*, pp. xxi–xxii, 107, 244, 258–59; and the *Christian Recorder*, June

14, 1877. Two decades from now, the *Christian Recorder* predicted, "if not sooner, the young white gentlemen of West Point will read of the fastidiousness of their predecessors with incredulous wonder."

63 See William A. Dobak and Thomas D. Phillips, *The Black Regulars, 1866–1898* (Norman: University of Oklahoma Press, 2001), p. 69; Utley, *Frontier Regulars*, pp. 61–62.

64 Michael Fellman, *Citizen Sherman: A Life of William Tecumseh Sherman* (New York: Random House, 1995), p. 156; Sherman, quoted in Dobak and Phillips, *Black Regulars*, p. 70.

65 *Army and Navy Journal*, June 7, 1876; Dobak and Phillips, *Black Regulars*, p. 70; See also E. O. C. Ord to R. C Drum, Oct. 1, 1877, in Morris J. MacGregor and Bernard C. Nalty, eds., *Blacks in the United States Armed Forces*, vol. 3 (Wilmington, Del.: Scholarly Resources, 1977), p. 122.

66 *Army and Navy Journal*, March 11, 1876.

67 Ibid., April 15, 1876.

68 *New York Times*, Aug. 20, 1877; Dobak and Phillips, *Black Regulars*, pp. 71–72.

69 E. K. Davies to Benjamin F. Butler, Dec. 7, 1876, in MacGregor and Nalty, eds., *Blacks in the United States Armed Forces*, pp. 116–17; William T. Sherman to Benjamin Butler, Feb. 6, 1877, ibid., p. 119. The army had been reduced from 54,000 in 1866, to 37,000 in 1869, to 30,000 in 1870, and to 27,000 in 1874.

70 Benjamin F. Butler to William T. Sherman, Feb. 15, 1877, in MacGregor and Nalty, eds., *Blacks in the United States Armed Forces*, p. 120; Sherman to Butler, Feb. 21, 1877, ibid., p. 121.

71 S. 178, 45th Cong., 1st sess., Oct. 31, 1877, cited in National Archives and Records Administration's Microfilm Series T823, "The Negro in the Military Service of the United States, 1639–1886," National Archives and Records Administration, Washington, D.C. (hereafter cited as NARA Microfilm T823), Roll no. 5.

72 Ibid. See also Dobak and Phillips, *Black Regulars*, p. 74. The debate over the black Regular regiments continued for some time: in 1880, General Sherman wrote that, in his judgment, "the requirement that all the enlisted men of the Ninth and Tenth Cavalry and of the Twenty-fourth and Twenty-fifth Infantry shall be colored men, whilst the Officers are white, is not consistent with the amendment to the constitution above referred to. All men should be enlisted who are qualified, and assigned to regiments, regardless of color or previous condition. Such has been the law and usage in the Navy for years, and the Army would soon grow accustomed to it." See 1880 Annual Report of William T. Sherman, in the NARA Microfilm Series T823, roll no. 5. As Sherman's report indicates, the U.S. navy had accepted black enlistees for service since before the Civil War, and although they served side by side with white enlistees, they typically filled more menial posts and could not become commissioned officers. The first African American graduated from the U.S. Naval

Academy at Annapolis, Maryland, in 1949. See Joseph P. Reidy, "Black Men in Navy Blue during the Civil War," *Prologue* 33 (Fall 2001): 1–6.

73 *New York Times*, Aug. 20, 1877.

74 S. 178, 45th Cong., 1st sess., Oct. 31, 1877, cited in NARA microfilm T823, Roll no. 5.

Chapter Five. Insult and Injury

1 John F. Marszalek, *Assault at West Point: The Court-Martial of Johnson Whittaker* (privately published, 1984), pp. 27–36.

  The epigraph for this chapter comes from Theodore D. Harris, ed., *Black Frontiersman: The Memoirs of Henry O. Flipper* (Fort Worth: Texas Christian University Press, 1997), p. 37. The chapter title comes from the historian Edward S. Cooper. "What blacks wanted" in the postwar period, Cooper writes, was "social, political, and economic justice. What they received was insult and injury." See Cooper, *William Worth Belknap: An American Disgrace* (Madison, N.J.: Fairleigh Dickinson University Press, 2003), p. 134.

2 Marszalek, *Assault at West Point*, p. 39.

3 *Army and Navy Journal*, Feb. 2 and 9, 1878.

4 Marszalek, *Assault at West Point*, pp. 41, 43.

5 Ibid., pp. 1–2, 44–46. See also *Army and Navy Journal*, April 10, 1880.

6 Marszalek, *Assault at West Point*, pp. 46–48.

7 Ibid., pp. 49–50.

8 See Whittaker's report of the attack, *Army and Navy Journal*, April 10, 1880. See also Marszalek, *Assault at West Point*, pp. 50–52.

9 Marszalek, *Assault at West Point*, pp. 52–55.

10 Ibid., pp. 53, 57–60.

11 Ibid., pp. 62–64.

12 *Army and Navy Journal*, April 10 and 17, 1880.

13 Quintard Taylor, ed., *The Colored Cadet at West Point* (Lincoln: University of Nebraska Press, 1998); *Army and Navy Journal*, April 17, 1880.

14 *Army and Navy Journal*, May 22, 1880; Marszalek, *Assault at West Point*, pp. 61, 64, 72–73.

15 Marszalek, *Assault at West Point*, pp. 85, 87.

16 *Army and Navy Journal*, June 5 and 19, 1880; Marszalek, *Assault at West Point*, pp. 132–35. See also Howard's own recollections of these events in *Autobiography of Oliver Otis Howard, Major General, United States Army*, 2 vols. (New York: Baker and Taylor Co., 1907), 2:485–86.

17 Peter S. Michie, "Caste at West Point," *North American Review* 130 (June 1880): 604–13.

18 George L. Andrews, "West Point and the Colored Cadets," *International Review* (Nov. 1880): 477–98. The instructor at West Point was George Leonard Andrews; the Twenty-fifth Infantry's commander was George Lippitt Andrews.

19 See the 1880 Annual Report of General John Schofield to the Secretary of War, in Morris J. MacGregor and Bernard C. Nalty, eds., *Blacks in the United States Armed Forces: Basic Documents*, vol. 3 (Wilmington, Del.: Scholarly Resources, 1977), pp. 139–42. See also Taylor, ed., *The Colored Cadet at West Point*, p. xv; Alice Kirk Grierson to Charles Grierson, Oct. 24, 1880, in the Benjamin H. Grierson Papers, Fort Davis National Historic Site, Fort Davis, Tex. (hereafter cited as Grierson Papers, Fort Davis); and William H. Leckie and Shirley A. Leckie, *Unlikely Warriors: General Benjamin Grierson and His Family* (Norman: University of Oklahoma Press, 1984), p. 211. In his 1880 annual report, General Sherman wrote, "Prejudice is alleged against colored cadets. Prejudice of race is the most difficult thing to contend against of any in this world. There is no more such prejudice at West Point than in the community at large, and the practice of equality at West Point is in advance of the rest of the country." See the 1880 Annual Report of William T. Sherman, in the National Archives and Records Administration's Microfilm Series T823, "The Negro in the Military Service of the United States, 1639–1886," National Archives and Records Administration, Washington, D.C. (hereafter cited as NARA Microfilm T823), roll no. 5.

20 *Christian Recorder*, Jan. 13, 1881.

21 *Washington Post*, June 12, 1881; Marszalek, *Assault at West Point*, pp. 152–67, 238–39, 246–49.

22 *Army and Navy Journal*, April 2, 1881; *Washington Post*, June 12 and 18, 1881, and March 23, 1882; *New York Times*, March 22, 1882.

　　　Regarding Flipper's arrest see Taylor, ed., *The Colored Cadet at West Point*, p. xxix; *New York Times*, Aug. 25, 1881; and the *Army and Navy Journal*, Aug. 21, 1881. According to the historian Barry C. Johnson, "It was not unlawful to confine an officer in the guardhouse, but it was exceedingly unusual. The customary forms of arrest were 'open'—under which an officer had the limits of the post—and 'close,' which confined him to his quarters. A more stringent measure was the placing of a sentinel at the quarters; but the actual removal of an officer so that he was under direct charge of the guard was seldom necessary. The punishment for breach of arrest was dismissal, and few officers were so desperate as to need the kind of forcible restraint that was inflicted upon Flipper." See Johnson, *Flipper's Dismissal: The Ruin of Lt. Henry O. Flipper, U.S.A.* (London: privately printed, 1980), p. 38.

23 Benjamin H. Grierson to "Whom it May Concern," Nov. 1, 1881, cited in "Papers Relating to the Army Career of Henry Ossian Flipper" (unpublished bound volumes, Fort Davis National Historic Site, Fort Davis, Tex.), vol. 6, exhibit no. 109; Benjamin H. Grierson to Alice K. Grierson, Aug. 6, 1880, in Grierson Papers, Fort Davis.

24 Taylor, ed., *The Colored Cadet at West Point*, pp. xxii–xxiii; Harris, ed., *Black Frontiersman*, p. 5; "Flipper's Ditch" was designated a National Historic Landmark in 1977 (ibid., p. 5). It was while he was at Fort Sill that Flipper wrote his first autobiography. See Taylor, ed., *The Colored Cadet at West Point*, p. 247.

25 Taylor, ed., *The Colored Cadet at West Point*, pp. xxvi; Harris, ed., *Black Frontiersman*, p. 34; James N. Leiker, *Racial Borders: Black Soldiers along the Rio Grande* (College Station: Texas A&M University Press, 2002), p. 46.

26 For the testimony of the character witnesses, see "Papers Relating to the Army Career of Henry Ossian Flipper," 3:433, 464, 477. Predictably, interrogators challenged the value of Sender's testimony on the basis that Sender's Jewishness undermined the value of the oath he had taken before testifying (p. 463). Barry Johnson asserts that W. S. Chamberlain was probably Flipper's "most intimate friend" at Fort Davis (Johnson, *Flipper's Dismissal*, p. 17).

  During the war Shafter had organized and then commanded—apparently with "patience, vigilance, intelligence, and skill"—the Seventeenth U.S. Colored Infantry. Having mustered out of the volunteer army in Nov. 1866, Shafter had only to wait until Jan. 1867 to receive his next summons to duty. Shafter, it seems, "had thought 'considerable' of his black troops" during the Civil War, and he accepted the appointment immediately. See Paul H. Carlson, *"Pecos Bill": A Military Biography of William R. Shafter* (College Station: Texas A&M University Press, 1989), pp. xi, 28–32, 36–37, 114.

27 Taylor, ed., *The Colored Cadet at West Point*, pp. xxviii–xxxii; Carlson, *"Pecos Bill,"* p. 120; Harris, ed., *Black Frontiersman*, pp. 35, 37.

28 According to Barry C. Johnson, "Flipper's relief as quartermaster was a mere matter of military routine," not Shafter's racial prejudice. (Johnson, *Flipper's Dismissal*, p. 11). See also "Papers Relating to the Army Career of Henry Ossian Flipper," 1:54 and 3:506; Carlson, *"Pecos Bill,"* p. 122; Harris, ed., *Black Frontiersman*, pp. 37, 79.

29 Carlson, *"Pecos Bill,"* p. 122. See also "Papers Relating to the Army Career of Henry Ossian Flipper," 2:300–304.

30 Carlson, *"Pecos Bill,"* p. 122; Taylor, ed., *The Colored Cadet at West Point*, p. xxiii, xxvii–xxviii. Mollie Dwyer later married Nordstrom, a native of Maine (ibid.).

31 Harris, ed., *Black Frontiersman*, p. 76; Taylor, ed., *The Colored Cadet at West Point*, p. xxviii, xxxi; *New York Times*, Oct. 30, 1881.

32 Taylor, ed., *The Colored Cadet at West Point*, p. xxviii; Harris, ed., *Black Frontiersman*, p. 80. See also *Army and Navy Journal*, Aug. 27, 1881; and *New York Times*, Oct. 30, 1881.

33 Carlson, *"Pecos Bill,"* p. 125.

34 Taylor, ed., *The Colored Cadet at West Point*, pp. xxxii–xxxiii. See also Leiker, *Racial Borders*, p. 81. I tend to agree instead with the black newspaper the *Christian Recorder*, which observed in Oct. 1881 that Flipper himself believed that he had been "the victim of a set up job by certain white officers who wish[ed] him out of the way."

The article continued, "We have little doubt that he is being persecuted instead of prosecuted. It seems that the intense hatred of the Negro, which is so universally present among the pauper snobs (cadets, we should say) at West Point, follows them into the army as officers, and though they are glad enough to accept commands in colored regiments, yet they would not stop at any dishonorable means to destroy the character of a colored officer." The article went on to quote from a letter written by Flipper concerning his case: "I am confident," Flipper wrote, "that I can win the case. My friends are numerous here, as I have made friends everywhere, my own Colonel is like a father to me, and my Captain and I have written him fully of the whole affair. I would prefer to keep silent and not parade my wrongs before the people. When the time comes I am confident I can vindicate myself" (*Christian Recorder*, Oct. 13, 1881).

35 See Taylor, ed., *The Colored Cadet at West Point*, pp. xxxiv–xliii; Harris, ed., *Black Frontiersman*, 7–16. At least for the first several years after his discharge, Flipper remained in cordial contact with his former colonel, Benjamin Grierson, and his family. See Shirley Anne Leckie, ed., *The Colonel's Lady on the Western Frontier: The Correspondence of Alice Kirk Grierson* (Lincoln: University of Nebraska Press, 1989), p. 163.

36 See Taylor, ed., *The Colored Cadet at West Point*, pp. xxxiv–xliii; Harris, ed., *Black Frontiersman*, 7–16.

37 Marszalek, *Assault at West Point*, pp. 254–73.

38 Eric Foner, *Reconstruction: America's Unfinished Revolution, 1863–1877* (New York: Harper & Row, 1988), pp. 529–31; James M. McPherson, *Ordeal by Fire: The Civil War and Reconstruction* (New York: McGraw-Hill, 1992), p. 514n. The Court's decision in *Cruikshank* was reinforced by a similar decision, that same year, in the case *U.S. v. Reese* (p. 585). See also Joseph R. Palmore, "The Not-So-Strange Career of Interstate Jim Crow: Race, Transportation, and the Dormant Commerce Clause, 1878–1946," *Virginia Law Review* 83 (Nov. 1997): 1774; Gary B. Nash and Julie Roy Jeffrey, eds., *The American People: Creating a Nation and a Society* (New York: Harper & Row, 1986), p. 582; David W. Blight, *Race and Reunion: The Civil War in American Memory* (Cambridge: Harvard University Press, Belknap Press, 2001), p. 309. The *Civil Rights Cases* of 1883 are also sometimes referred to by the name of the first of the four cases, *U.S. v. Stanley*.

39 Blight, *Race and Reunion*, p. 301.

40 *New York Times*, Sept. 9, 1883; *Los Angeles Times*, Sept. 25, 1883.

41 *New York Times*, Sept. 9, 1883. For accounts of the convention, see also ibid., Sept. 25, 26, and 28, 1883; *Washington Post*, Sept. 5, 26, and 28, 1883; *Los Angeles Times*, Sept. 25, 1883; and *Boston Daily Globe*, Sept. 28, 1883.

42 On John Hanks Alexander, see Charles L. Kenner, *Buffalo Soldiers and Officers of the Ninth Cavalry, 1867–1898* (Norman: University of Oklahoma Press, 1999), p. 293; Frank N. Schubert, ed., *On the Trail of the Buffalo Soldier: Biographies of African*

Americans in the U.S. Army, 1866–1917 (Wilmington, Del.: Scholarly Resources, 1995), pp. 3–4. By the time Alexander arrived at West Point, Wesley Merritt, who had served as lieutenant colonel of the black Ninth Cavalry from 1866 to 1876, was the academy's superintendent, in which position he served from 1882 to 1887. Merritt's presence in the top post at the academy can only have served to improve the climate for black cadets. On Charles Young, who graduated from West Point in 1889, see below, chap. 6.

43 *Boston Daily Globe*, Sept. 28, 1883; *New York Times*, Sept. 28, 1883; Carl R. Osthaus, *Freedmen, Philanthropy, and Fraud: A History of the Freedman's Savings Bank* (Urbana: University of Illinois Press, 1976), pp. 1, 101, 206, 215.

44 Blight, *Race and Reunion*, p. 308; Donald R. Shaffer, *After the Glory: The Struggles of Black Civil War Veterans* (Lawrence: University Press of Kansas, 2004), p. 161. See also Donald R. Shaffer, "'I Would Rather Shake Hands with the Blackest Nigger in the Land': Northern Black Civil War Veterans and the Grand Army of the Republic," in Paul A. Cimbala and Randall M. Miller, eds., *Union Soldiers and the Northern Home Front: Wartime Experiences, Postwar Adjustments* (New York: Fordham University Press, 2002), p. 451; and *Boston Daily Globe*, Aug. 2, 1887. Trotter was one of the very few black men to have achieved commissioned officer status during the Civil War. See Joseph T. Glatthaar, *Forged in Battle: The Civil War Alliance of Black Soldiers and White Officers* (New York: Meridian, 1991), p. 262.

45 *Boston Daily Globe*, Aug. 2, 1887.

46 Ibid., Aug. 2 and 3, 1887. Williams, who had enlisted in the USCT under an assumed name at age fourteen, had also attended the 1883 convention in Louisville. In 1888, he published the first history of black military service in the United States. See George Washington Williams, *A History of the Negro Troops in the War of the Rebellion, 1861–1865* (New York: Harper & Brothers, 1888). See also John Hope Franklin, *George Washington Williams: A Biography* (Chicago: University of Chicago Press, 1985).

47 *New York Age*, May 29, July 17, and Nov. 13 and 20, 1886; *New York Times*, Aug. 3, 1887. The Mississippi legislation disenfranchising black men came in 1890. See Blight, *Race and Reunion*, pp. 194–97, 271.

48 Beth Taylor Muskat, "Mobile's Black Militia: Major R. R. Mims and Gilmer's Rifles," *Alabama Review* 57 (July 2004): 184; Alwyn Barr, "The Black Militia of the New South: Texas as a Case Study," *Journal of Negro History* 63 (July 1978): 209, 215.

49 Handwritten biographical sketch of Christian A. Fleetwood, in Christian A. Fleetwood Papers, Library of Congress, Washington, D.C. (hereafter cited as the Fleetwood Papers).

50 Anonymous published article, "The History of the Cadet Corps," in Fleetwood Papers. There was also a second black battalion, under the command of Major Frederick Revells. See James F. Harrison, typed biographical sketch of Christian

Fleetwood, in Fleetwood Papers. See also the handwritten biographical sketch of Fleetwood, and John Bigelow Jr. to Whom it May Concern, April 30, 1898, both in the above papers. Added Bigelow, "As to [Fleetwood's] past services, it is only necessary to state that he is a legal and rightful wearer of the medal of honor."

51 Handwritten testimonial to Christian A. Fleetwood, Jan. 11, 1889, and Frederick Douglass to "My Dear Mr. Arnold," Jan. 27, 1989, both in Fleetwood Papers.

52 Barr, "Black Militia of the New South," p. 215; Muskat, "Mobile's Black Militia," p. 184; undated article from *Washington Bee* entitled "The Color Line in the Militia," in Fleetwood Papers.

53 Undated article from an unidentified paper, entitled "The District Malitia [*sic*]," in Fleetwood Papers. "Genl. Ordway," the article continued, "is a republican and all he is to-day was through the instrumentality of the colored people of this district." See also *New York Times*, March 12, 1891; and undated article from *Washington Bee* entitled "The Colored Troops Disbanded," in Fleetwood Papers. On March 14, the *Washington Post* commented that the reasons Ordway gave for disbanding the black battalions were "too weak and flimsy for a battle-scarred veteran to indulge in." Scratching the surface of the *Post*'s apparent sympathy for the black guardsmen, however, quickly reveals less appealing sentiments: "It is not the purpose of *The Post* to discuss the merits of the colored soldiers," the article continued, "as compared with their white comrades. There is one thing certain: there is no way of getting rid of the colored citizens of the District unless they voluntarily decide to move away. They are here. They are as full-fledged citizens as citizens can be full-fledged under the strange laws that govern the District. They are property-holders. Like our white people, some of them are good citizens and some of them are very bad citizens. Even admitting that they are not up to the Brigadier-General standard, intellectually—to go further and admit that they are not a desirable class of citizens—it seems to *The Post* that any policy that will subject them to a discipline which strengthens and enlightens them is not a bad thing" (*Washington Post*, March 14, 1891). See also the article from an unidentified paper, dated March 11, 1891, entitled "Mad at Gen. Ordway," in Fleetwood Papers.

54 Article from an unidentified paper, dated March 11, 1891, entitled "Mad at Gen. Ordway," in Fleetwood Papers. See also *New York Times*, March 12, 1891; untitled, undated article from an unidentified newspaper, beginning "Pursuant to the order," ibid.; and Christian A. Fleetwood to the Editor, *Washington Bee*, April 16, 1891.

Chapter Six. Struggling for Citizenship in the 1890s

1 Robert M. Utley, *Frontier Regulars: The United States Army and the Indian, 1866–1891* (New York: Macmillan, 1973), p. 402; John G. Neihardt, *Black Elk Speaks: Being the*

Life Story of a Holy Man of the Oglala Sioux (Lincoln: University of Nebraska Press, 1961), p. 237.

The epigraph for this chapter comes from Frank N. Schubert, ed., *On the Trail of the Buffalo Soldier: Biographies of African Americans in the U.S. Army, 1866–1917* (Wilmington, Del.: Scholarly Resources, 1995), p. 249.

2 Neihardt, *Black Elk Speaks*, p. 235; Robert W. Larson, *Red Cloud: Warrior-Statesman of the Lakota Sioux* (Norman: University of Oklahoma Press, 1997), pp. 263, 272; Utley, *Frontier Regulars*, p. 403.

3 Utley, *Frontier Regulars*, p. 403; *Army and Navy Journal*, Nov. 22, 1890.

4 Richard Henry Pratt to James B. Watson, Nov. 28, 1890, and to Edgar Fire Thunder, Dec. 2, 1890, in Richard Henry Pratt Papers, Yale University, New Haven, Conn. See also Richard Henry Pratt to Samuel Little Hawk, Dec. 8, 1890, in the same collection.

5 *Army and Navy Journal*, Nov. 22, 1890; Utley, *Frontier Regulars*, p. 404. According to the historian Francis Paul Prucha, beginning in 1878, Congress authorized $30,000 to pay for roughly 430 Indian police on the reservations. By 1880, the number of police authorized had doubled. These police, writes Prucha, "were immediately useful to the [Indian] agents as an extension of their authority." See Prucha, *The Great Father: The United States Government and the American Indians* (Lincoln: University of Nebraska Press, 1986), p. 196.

6 Utley, *Frontier Regulars*, pp. 405–7; Neihardt, *Black Elk Speaks*, p. 266. Added Black Elk, "I thought there might be a day, and we should have revenge." That day never came. According to Robert M. Utley, "Wounded Knee was the last major armed encounter between Indians and whites in North America. A few scattered clashes occurred later, but Wounded Knee was the last of great consequence." See Utley, *The Indian Frontier of the American West, 1846–1890* (Albuquerque: University of New Mexico Press, 1984), p. 257.

7 Richard Henry Pratt to J. W. Leeds, Jan. 7, 1891; and Richard Henry Pratt to a Mr. Gregg, Jan. 26, 1891, both in the Pratt Papers, Yale University. See also Richard Henry Pratt, *Battlefield and Classroom: An Autobiography* (Norman: University of Oklahoma Press, 2003), p. xxiv; Utley, *The Indian Frontier of the American West*, p. 245; and Richard Henry Pratt, "How to Deal with the Indians: The Potency of Environment," box 16a, Carlisle Barracks Collection, U.S. Army Military History Institute, Carlisle, Pa. (USAMHI). Date of speech unknown; probably early twentieth century.

8 *Army and Navy Journal*, Jan. 10, 1891; Virginia Weisel Johnson, *The Unregimented General: A Biography of Nelson A. Miles* (Cambridge, Mass.: Riverside Press, 1962), p. 289; Charles L. Kenner, *Buffalo Soldiers and Officers of the Ninth Cavalry, 1867–1898* (Norman: University of Oklahoma Press, 1999), p. 128; Charles D. Rhodes, "Diary Notes of the Brule-Sioux Indian Campaign, SD, 1890–91," Folder S-18, box 8,

Order of the Indian Wars Collection, U.S. Army Military History Institute, Carlisle, Pa. (hereafter cited as Order of the Indian Wars Collection, USAMHI); Nelson A. Miles, *Serving the Republic: Memoirs of the Civil War and Military Life of Nelson A. Miles* (New York: Harper & Brothers, 1911), p. 246; Peter R. DeMontravel, *A Hero to His Fighting Men: Nelson A. Miles, 1839–1925* (Kent, Ohio: Kent State University Press, 1998), p. 210; Neihardt, *Black Elk Speaks*, p. 276. See also Miles's 1891 annual report, in which he wrote in detail about the events leading up to and including Wounded Knee, in Brian C. Pohanka, ed., *Nelson A. Miles: A Documentary Biography of His Military Career, 1861–1903* (Glendale, Calif.: Arthur H. Clark Co., 1985), pp. 189–224.

Major Guy Henry recalled the morning a bit differently: "The morning," he wrote a few years later, "broke with a pelting flurry of a combination of snow and dirt. A veil of dark clouds hung suspended above the hills, which surrounded the campground like a coliseum, and a piercing breeze swept from the north." See Guy V. Henry, "A Sioux Indian Episode," article for *Harper's Weekly*, Dec. 26, 1896, in the Guy V. Henry Papers, U.S. Army Military History Institute, Carlisle, Pa.

9 Henry, "A Sioux Indian Episode." According to Guy Henry, the watching Indians "looked on from a distance in amazement and distrust, fearing that our arrangements might mean an attack instead of a peaceful march in review previous to the return of the troops to their posts." See also Guy H. Preston to "Dear Colonel," April 5, 1931, in the Order of the Indian Wars Collection, USAMHI; Frank N. Schubert, *Voices of the Buffalo Soldier: Records, Reports, and Recollections of Military Life and Service in the West* (Albuquerque: University of New Mexico Press, 2003), p. 163; *Army and Navy Journal*, Nov. 22, 1890; Utley, *Frontier Regulars*, pp. 408–9; Miles, *Serving the Republic*, pp. 246–47; and Rhodes, "Diary Notes."

10 Henry, "A Sioux Indian Episode"; Obituary for Henry, in the *Christian Herald and Signs of Our Times*, Nov. 8, 1899, in Henry Papers, USAMHI; "On Their Battle Banners," *New York World*, Sept. 30, 1939, in Henry Papers, USAMHI; Utley, *Frontier Regulars*, p. 409; Kenner, *Buffalo Soldiers and Officers of the Ninth Cavalry*, p. 125. "Our cavalry has for soldiers negroes," wrote one observer, a correspondent for the *Army and Navy Journal*, of the Ninth's activities while they were still awaiting orders to advance on the Indians. "They are good riders, are cheerful in the performance of their duty, and are good rifle shots." See ibid., Dec. 27, 1890. According to at least one source, units of the Twenty-fifth Infantry under Colonel J. J. Van Horn were also "stationed around the Pine Ridge and Rosebud Sioux Reservations in response to the Ghost Dance uprising," though their involvement in the events was not nearly as spectacular as that of the Ninth Cavalry. See John H. Nankivell, *Buffalo Soldier Regiment: History of the Twenty-fifth United States Infantry, 1869–1926* (Lincoln: University of Nebraska Press, 2001), pp. xii, 48.

11 Henry, "A Sioux Indian Episode."

12 Kenner, *Buffalo Soldiers and Officers of the Ninth Cavalry*, p. 127; Schubert, ed., *On the Trail of the Buffalo Soldier*, pp. 480, 197; Henry, "A Sioux Indian Episode."

13 *Kansas City Times*, Feb. 22, 1891; Henry, "A Sioux Indian Episode."

14 Kenner, *Buffalo Soldiers and Officers of the Ninth Cavalry*, pp. 124–29; Henry, "A Sioux Indian Episode"; Nelson A. Miles, article for the *North American Review* 152 (Jan. 1891), included in Peter Cozzens, ed., *Eyewitnesses to the Indian Wars, 1865–1890*, 5 vols. (Mechanicsburg, Pa: Stackpole Books, 2001–05), 5:165.

15 Kenner, *Buffalo Soldiers and Officers of the Ninth Cavalry*, p. 129; Henry, "A Sioux Indian Episode." Prather's "Indian Ghost Dance and War" begins,

> *The Red Skins left their Agency, the Soldiers left their Post,*
> *All on the strength of an Indian tale about Messiah's ghost*
> *Got up by savage chieftains to lead their tribes astray;*
> *But Uncle Sam wouldn't have it so, for he ain't built that way.*
> *They swore that this Messiah came to them in visions sleep*
> *And promised to restore their game and Buffalos a heap,*
> *So they must start a big ghost dance, then all would join their band,*
> *And may be so we lead [sic] the way into the great Bad Land.*
>
> *Chorus:*
> *They claimed the shirt Messiah gave, no bullet could go through,*
> *But when the Soldiers fired at them they saw this was not true.*
> *The Medicine man supplied them with their great Messiah's grace,*
> *And he, too, pulled his freight and swore the 7th hard to face.*

For the texts of both poems, see Schubert, *Voices of the Buffalo Soldier*, pp. 170–72.

16 Kenner, *Buffalo Soldiers and Officers of the Ninth Cavalry*, pp. 129–30; Schubert, ed., *On the Trail of the Buffalo Soldier*, p. 105. "The colored troops," Henry later wrote, "make excellent soldiers; in garrison they are clean and self-respecting, and proud of their uniform; in the field patient and cheerful under hardships or deprivations, never growling nor discontented, doing what is required of them without a murmur." Henry was not without condescension, however: he believed that black soldiers needed "proper" (presumably white) officers, because they were, fundamentally, like children. See Henry, "A Sioux Indian Episode."

17 Kenner, *Buffalo Soldiers and Officers of the Ninth Cavalry*, pp. 131–32; Guy V. Henry to Nelson A. Miles, May 13, 1891, in Nelson A. Miles Family Papers, Library of Congress, Washington, D.C.

18 Kenner, *Buffalo Soldiers and Officers of the Ninth Cavalry*, p. 132; *Kansas City Times*, Feb. 22, 1891.

19 Kenner, *Buffalo Soldiers and Officers of the Ninth Cavalry*, pp. 133–36; Guy V. Henry

to Nelson A. Miles, May 13, 1891, in Nelson A. Miles Family Papers, Library of Congress, Washington, D.C.; *Fort Myer Buffalo Soldiers* (Fort Myer, Va.: Equal Opportunity Office, Fort Myer Military Community, n.d.), p. 4.

20 RG 153, Records of the Office of the Judge Advocate General, Army, Court Martial Cases, National Archives, Washington, D.C. (hereafter cited as NARA Court Martials, with the number of the case noted), SS-258, SS-477. See also NARA Court Martials SS-389 and SS-522.

21 Ibid., SS-258, SS-477.

22 Nelson A. Miles to Guy V. Henry, Dec. 30, 1893, in Henry Papers, USAMHI; Frank N. Schubert, *Black Valor: Buffalo Soldiers and the Medal of Honor, 1870–1898* (Wilmington, Del.: Scholarly Resources, 1997), p. 132. The regiment's assignment to Fort Myer ended on Oct. 3, 1894. See *Fort Myer Buffalo Soldiers*, p. 9.

23 Gary B. Nash and Julie Roy Jeffrey, eds., *The American People: Creating a Nation and a Society* (New York: Harper & Row, 1986), p. 584.

24 Jacqueline Jones Royster, ed., *Southern Horrors and Other Writings: The Anti-Lynching Campaign of Ida B. Wells, 1892–1900* (Boston: Bedford/St. Martin's, 1997), pp. 50–51, 52, 60.

25 *A Red Record* is also contained in Royster, ed., *Southern Horrors and Other Writings*. For the 1892–94 statistics, see pp. 10, 86–87, 152–53. See also pp. 36–37.

26 Trumbull White and William Igleheart, *The World's Columbian Exposition, Chicago, 1893* (Boston: Standard Silverware Co., 1893), pp. 11, 41; Dennis B. Downey, *A Season of Renewal: The Columbian Exposition and Victorian America* (Westport, Conn.: Praeger, 2002), p. xi; Nelson A. Miles, *Annual Report, Department of the Missouri, 1891*, in Nelson A. Miles Papers, U.S. Army Military History Institute, Carlisle, Pa. (hereafter cited as Miles Papers, USAMHI). According to White and Igleheart, four cities competed for the privilege of hosting the exposition: New York, Washington, St. Louis, and Chicago, which they refer to as "the giant city of the west" (White and Igleheart, *The World's Columbian Exposition*, pp. 41, 46).

Downey sees in the fair an example of the "culture of renewal" that he associates with the end of the nineteenth century: "In its rituals and rhetoric, the fair reaffirmed the possibilities of renewal and reinvention in a time of profound social and economic reorganization" (Downey, *A Season of Renewal*, p. xviii). I wonder whether it might not be also meaningful to think of the fair of 1893 as an example of American satisfaction with—celebration of—what one might call the "culture of conquest."

27 White and Igleheart, *World's Columbian Exposition*, pp. 12–13, 62, 64. "For centuries," they add, "powerful Lake Michigan had met no obstacle in the attack" on the shoreline. By the time the fair opened, however, the organizers exulted that "where once was rank grass of the marshes is to be seen the most luxuriant of green turf. . . . Where was then a marsh, whose stagnant waters were divided but by hummocks of mud and sand, are now the clear flowing waters of the beautiful system of

lagoons, and, rising out of them, the walls of a city of white palaces, the architec-
tural triumph of modern history" (pp. 62–63). According to Downey, the fair was
also called the "Dream City" and the "Magic City" (Downey, *A Season of Renewal*,
p. 5).

28 Downey, *A Season of Renewal*, p. 32; White and Igleheart, *World's Columbian Exposition*, p. 46.

29 White and Igleheart, *World's Columbian Exposition*, pp. 46–50; Downey, *A Season
of Renewal*, p. 33; *New York Times*, Jan. 23, 1893. It is worth noting that it was in
anticipation of the extended Oct. 1892 dedication of the Columbian Exposition that
Francis J. Bellamy drafted and then published and widely disseminated the original
Pledge of Allegiance. See Robert W. Rydell, *All the World's a Fair: Visions of Empire
at American International Expositions, 1876–1916* (Chicago: University of Chicago
Press, 1993), p. 46. According to one source, Bellamy had planned to put the word
"equality" into the last line of the pledge, but he "knew that the state superinten-
dents of education . . . were against equality for women and African Americans,"
and undoubtedly also Native Americans, so he left the word out. See http://history
.vineyard.net.

30 Donal F. Lindsey, *Indians at Hampton Institute, 1877–1923* (Urbana: University of
Illinois Press, 1995), p. 6; Downey, *A Season of Renewal*, pp. xiv, 2–3, 46; White and
Igleheart, *World's Columbian Exposition*, pp. 50–51; Rydell, *All the World's a Fair*,
p. 40. On Pratt's efforts to ensure a fair representation of the Carlisle students
at the exposition, see Richard Henry Pratt to Thomas W. Palmer, Aug. 8, 1890;
T. J. Morgan to Mrs. Harriet A. Lucas, March 30, 1892; E. C. Culp to Richard
Henry Pratt, July 21, 1892; Nelson A. Miles to Richard Henry Pratt, Oct. 4, 1892;
and R. V. Belt to the Secretary of the Interior, April 7, 1893, all in the Pratt Papers,
Yale University.

　　In his *Personal Recollections*, published in 1896, Miles spoke very favorably of
Pratt and Carlisle: "Out of Captain Pratt's judicious management of this body of
wild savage murderers, has grown the great industrial Indian school at Carlisle,
Pennsylvania. The tribes from which the children have been taken to be educated
have been benefited to an incalculable extent." See *Personal Recollections & Observations of General Nelson A. Miles*, 2 vols. (Lincoln: University of Nebraska Press,
1992), 1:180.

31 White and Igleheart, *World's Columbian Exposition*, pp. 14, 443–55; Downey, *A Season of Renewal*, pp. xii, 64–65.

32 Pratt, *Battlefield and Classroom*, pp. 294–95, 303; Downey, *A Season of Renewal*,
pp. 56, 59; Rydell, *All the World's a Fair*, pp. 55ff.

33 Downey, *A Season of Renewal*, pp. 58–59; White and Igleheart, *World's Columbian
Exposition*, pp. 368–69. See also Franz Boas to Richard Henry Pratt, June 6, 1891,
in the Pratt Papers, Yale University.

34 Elliot M. Rudwick and August Meier, "Black Man in the 'White City': Negroes

and the Columbian Exposition, 1892," *Phylon* (1965): 354–61; Downey, *A Season of Renewal*, p. 27; Rydell, *All the World's A Fair*, pp. 52ff. For a more complete study of black Americans and the Chicago Exposition, see Christopher Robert Reed, *"All the World Is Here": The Black Presence at White City* (Bloomington: University of Indiana Press, 2000).

35   Ida B. Wells et al., *The Reason Why the Colored American Is Not in the World's Columbian Exposition* (Chicago: privately printed, 1893). See also Royster, ed., *Southern Horrors and Other Writings*, p. 37; and Alfreda M. Duster, ed., *Crusade for Justice: The Autobiography of Ida B. Wells* (Chicago: University of Chicago Press, 1970), pp. 115–19.

36   See Reed, *"All the World Is Here,"* pp. 131–39; Rudwick and Meier, "Black Man in the 'White City,'" pp 359–361.

37   Joanne M. Braxton, ed., *The Collected Poetry of Paul Laurence Dunbar* (Charlottesville: University Press of Virginia, 1993), pp. ix–xiii.

38   Rydell, *All the World's a Fair*, p. 40; White and Igleheart, *World's Columbian Exposition*, pp. 561, 572–74, 583; Downey, *A Season of Renewal*, pp. 70–71, 76.

Writes the historian Robert Rydell, the point of this geographically distinct section of the fair was to provide curious visitors with "scientific sanction for the American view of the nonwhite world as barbaric and childlike" as well as with "evolutionary ideas about race" (Rydell, *All the World's a Fair*, p. 40). For valuable and thorough discussions of race theory in late nineteenth-century America see Ivan Hannaford, *Race: The History of an Idea in the West* (Baltimore: Johns Hopkins University Press, 1996); John S. Haller Jr., *Outcasts from Evolution: Scientific Attitudes of Racial Inferiority, 1859–1900* (Carbondale: Southern Illinois University Press, 1995); Thomas F. Gossett, *Race: The History of an Idea in America* (New York: Oxford University Press, 1997); and Audrey Smedley, *Race in North America: Origin and Evolution of a Worldview* (Boulder, Colo.: Westview Press, 1999).

39   Frederick Jackson Turner, *The Frontier in American History* (New York: Holt, Rinehart and Winston, 1962), pp. 1–38. "The time," the historian Ray Allen Billington wrote many years later, "was ripe for just such a heady new interpretation of the American past. At the turn of the century the people of the United States were just sensing their new national destiny"—1893 was, after all, also the year that the Native government of Hawaii was overthrown by combined European and American business interests with support from the U.S. navy. Turner's frontier thesis "appealed to a people suddenly aware that their efforts to build a powerful nation had not been in vain." The America that Turner described, Billlington continued, "was a land in which all, humble and proud alike, had contributed to the national grandeur, where the individual had proven his worth by the conquest of nature, and where continuing progress was ordained by the excellence of time-proven institutions no less than by the perfection of the American character." See ibid., p. x. Unfortunately, neither Turner's nor Billington's "all" included black Americans.

40 Ibid., pp. 6, 14–15. Writes the historian James N. Leiker, "Turner gave race and ethnicity little place in his worldview, regarding with mild curiosity the histories of people of color but making no move to incorporate them into his model." See Leiker, *Racial Borders: Black Soldiers along the Rio Grande* (College Station: Texas A&M University Press, 2002), p. 5.

41 At one point Turner did mention the U.S. army's role in guarding the Union Pacific as it made its way west. See Turner, *The Frontier in American History*, pp. 10, 23.

42 For the full text of this speech, which Douglass first delivered in 1859, see John W. Blassingame and John R. McKivigan, eds., *The Frederick Douglass Papers*, ser. 1, *Speeches, Debates, and Interviews*, vol. 5, *1885–1891* (New Haven: Yale University Press, 1992), pp. 546–66. See also Frederick Douglass to Richard Henry Pratt, April 1, 1893, in Pratt Papers, Yale University. Six years after Douglass visited the school, Pratt received a letter from the great orator's widow, Helen, who was white, praising him for the work he continued to do with Native American children and recalling fondly her 1893 visit to the school with her late husband. "How good a thing Captain Pratt that you were born and have come in time to help save a remnant of these people, our brothers and sisters, to themselves and to the world. . . . I shall always hold in precious memory Mr. Douglass' pilgrimage to Carlisle and the beautiful and generous hospitality we there enjoyed." See Helen Douglass to Richard Henry Pratt, Feb. 22, 1899, ibid.

On the differences Douglass perceived between black and Native Americans, see Douglass's 1865 speech in New York, entitled "Black Freedom Is the Prerequisite of Victory," in Blassingame and McKivigan, eds., *The Frederick Douglass Papers*, ser. 1, vol. 4, pp. 57–58.

43 David W. Blight, *Race and Reunion: The Civil War in American Memory* (Cambridge: Harvard University Press, Belknap Press, 2001), pp. 325, 329. See also *Zion's Herald*, Oct. 9, 1895; *Congregationalist*, Nov. 28, 1895; and *New York Evangelist*, Sept. 19, 1895. The Cotton States Exposition, like the Columbian Exposition, included a "Negro Day," on Oct. 21.

44 L. P. Jackson, "The Origin of Hampton Institute," *Journal of Negro History* 10 (April 1925): 148; Blight, *Race and Reunion*, p. 325; Ruth M. Winton, "Negro Participation in Southern Expositions, 1881–1915," *Journal of Negro Education* 16 (Winter 1947): 34–43. According to Donal Lindsey, for a brief, three-month period, during 1880, Washington was the "leading black" in charge of Hampton's Indian program (Lindsey, *Indians at Hampton Institute*, p. 95).

45 For a thorough discussion of Mims's career with the black militia in Alabama, see Muskat, "Mobile's Black Militia."

46 Christian A. Fleetwood, *The Negro as a Soldier* (Washington, D.C.: Howard University Print, 1895), pp. 2–5.

47 Fleetwood, *The Negro as a Soldier*, pp. 11–14.

48 Ibid., p. 19.

49 For a thorough study of Charles Young's life and military service, see Brian G. Shellum, *Black Cadet in a White Bastion: Charles Young at West Point* (Lincoln: University of Nebraska Press, 2006). According to Shellum, after Young, West Point failed to admit another black student until after World War I (p. 98). On Fleetwood's efforts to be approved for command of a black regiment in the Spanish-American War, see various documents in the Fleetwood Papers, including Christian Fleetwood to William McKinley, June 14, 1898; Christian Fleetwood to John R. Lynch, June 7, 1898. It does appear that Fleetwood was offered the commissioned rank of second lieutenant—Flipper's rank—but he refused it, saying, in his letter to John Lynch, "Being an applicant for the highest position in a regiment, and accepting the lowest is very much like the case of the man who applied for an appointment as a foreign Minister and compromised on a pair of cast off trousers." On black Regulars in the Spanish-American War, see Marvin Fletcher, "The Black Volunteers in the Spanish American War," *Military Affairs* 38 (April 1974): 48–53.

50 On the situation for veterans of the black Regular regiments, see William A. Dobak and Thomas D. Phillips, *The Black Regulars, 1866–1898* (Norman: University of Oklahoma Press, 2001), pp. 267–72. On the situation for USCT veterans, see Donald R. Shaffer, *After the Glory: The Struggles of Black Civil War Veterans* (Lawrence: University Press of Kansas, 2004). See also the July 1924, Oct. 1924, and Dec. 1926 issues of *Winners of the West*, for the quotations from the Tenth Cavalry veterans.

51 Schubert, ed., *On the Trail of the Buffalo Soldier*, p. 148; Pratt, *Battlefield and Classroom*, pp. 7–8. George W. Ford was born free in Virginia in 1847. In 1860, he went to live in New York City with his aunt, and attended school there. In 1867, at the age of nineteen, he enlisted in the Tenth Cavalry as one of its original members. After serving for ten years, in part as a mail courier for the regiment, he was discharged as a quartermaster sergeant. Subsequently, Ford worked in a series of national cemeteries, ultimately, on Grierson's recommendation, receiving an appointment as superintendent of national cemeteries, a post he held for over fifty years and from which he retired in 1930. Ford also enlisted for service in the Spanish-American War and was stationed briefly in Cuba. See Schubert, ed., *On the Trail of the Buffalo Soldier*, pp. 146–48.

52 Blassingame and McKivigan, eds., *The Frederick Douglass Papers*, ser. 1, vol. 5, p. 607.

Index

Page numbers in *italics* refer to illustrations.
Page numbers beginning with 249 refer to notes.

Salt Creek Prairie, 100
Salt Lake City, Utah, 125
Salt Lake Valley, 111
Sample, John, 53, 54, 55, 258
San Antonio, Tex., 58, 100
San Carlos reservation, 108, 112–15
Sand Creek Massacre, 83, 85
Sandy Creek, 91
San Pedro Springs, Tex., 58–59
Satank, 100
Satanta, 100, 101–2, *103*
Saulsbury, Willard, Sr., 39
Savannah, Ga., 37
Schofield, John M., 179, 180, 183, 186, *187*, 188, 222–23, 280
schools:
    black, 31, 138, 139, 157
    desegregation of, 139
    mission, 89, 142, 147, 162, 175
    see also specific institutions
Schubert, Frank N., 54, 55, 225, 252, 254–55, 258, 259, 260, 261, 264, 269, 275, 282–83, 287, 292
Scott, Dred, 182
Scott, Robert, 66–67
scurvy, 71, 114
Sea Islands, 6, 50
Second Cavalry Division, 21
Second Connecticut Heavy Artillery, 49
Second Iowa Cavalry, 48
Seminole Negro Indian Scouts, 117–19, *120*, 269
Senate, U.S.:
    first African American in, 152–53, *152*, 158–59
    Foreign Relations Committee of, 196
    Military Affairs Committee of, 38–39
    Republican control of, 170, 173–74
Sender, Joseph, 191
Settlers, James, 116–17
Seven Pines/Fair Oaks, Battle of, 156
Seventh Cavalry, 43, 49, 88, 89, 132, 214
Seventh Infantry, 58
Seventeenth Infantry, 20, 26, 281

sexually transmitted diseases, 72
Shafter, William R. "Pecos Bill," 26–27, 96, 191–94, 216–17, 253, 265, 281
Shaw, James, Jr., 58, 260
Shaw, Thomas, *118*, 269
Shawneetown, Ill., 45–46
Shenandoah Valley, 11, 49
Sheridan, Philip H., 18–19, 43, 49, 57, 62, 128, 272
    memoirs of, 252
    postwar command of, 85, 87, 88–89, 113
Sherman, Mary, 272
Sherman, William T., 15–19, 23–24, 40, 43, 46, 128, 215, 264, 266, 272, 278
    black troops and, 102–3, 104, 105
    Georgia and Carolinas march of, 49, 162
    memoirs of, 88–89, 252, 264
    remarks on black soldiers by, 168, 170–71, 280
    Texas tour of, 100–103, 104, 105
Shields, J. B., 191
Shiloh, Battle of, 10
Shipp, W. E., 122
Shoshone Indians, 127, 271
Shropshire, Shelvin, 61
Sierra Leone, 3
Sierra Madre Mountains, 112–14
Sierra Mining Company, 196
Signal Service Bureau, 129
"Significance of the Frontier in American History, The" (Turner), 237–38
Simmons, William, 87
Sioux Indians, 76, 78, 80–81, 84, 85, 88
    Army battles with, 43, 80–83, 85, 132–35, 213–23
    Army cooperation with, 213, 217
    confrontation of Custer's Seventh Cavalry with, 43, 132
    Great Uprising of, 80–81, 82, 83
    Great War of, 132–34, 211
    U.S. removal of, 81